THE SECRETS OF DESIGN THINKING MINDSET

More Tools And Techniques To Enhance Your Design Thinking Skill

Dr. Amitkumar Goudar

Chennai • Bangalore

CLEVER FOX PUBLISHING
Chennai, India

Published by CLEVER FOX PUBLISHING 2023
Copyright © Dr. Amitkumar Goudar 2023

All Rights Reserved.
ISBN: 978-93-56482-67-8

This book has been published with all reasonable efforts taken to make the material error-free after the consent of the author. No part of this book shall be used, reproduced in any manner whatsoever without written permission from the author, except in the case of brief quotations embodied in critical articles and reviews.

The Author of this book is solely responsible and liable for its content including but not limited to the views, representations, descriptions, statements, information, opinions and references ["Content"]. The Content of this book shall not constitute or be construed or deemed to reflect the opinion or expression of the Publisher or Editor. Neither the Publisher nor Editor endorse or approve the Content of this book or guarantee the reliability, accuracy or completeness of the Content published herein and do not make any representations or warranties of any kind, express or implied, including but not limited to the implied warranties of merchantability, fitness for a particular purpose. The Publisher and Editor shall not be liable whatsoever for any errors, omissions, whether such errors or omissions result from negligence, accident, or any other cause or claims for loss or damages of any kind, including without limitation, indirect or consequential loss or damage arising out of use, inability to use, or about the reliability, accuracy or sufficiency of the information contained in this book.

PREFACE

Why did I write this book?

> *"If you don't see the book you want on the shelf, write it."*
> — **Beverly Cleary**

Precisely. Liam, Mac, Henry, and many other Design Thinking practitioners, coaches, and students across the Design Thinking community unequivocally faced the same roadblocks.

Design Thinking is a team activity that involves a group of people with different backgrounds, skills, and expertise, including designers, engineers, business analysts, marketing professionals, clients, and others.

Some practitioners, like Liam and Henry, reported that teams during Design Thinking workshops/sessions/activities were falling apart due to misunderstandings, lack of trust, insufficient problem-solving skills, and a shortage of decision-making strategies, among other issues.

Because of these challenges, the teams couldn't complete the entire Design Thinking process to develop innovative solutions or products. Some teams collapsed during the Define phase, some during Design, some during Ideate, and some couldn't even complete the Empathy phase.

None of the current Design Thinking books on the shelf address the shortcomings that professionals and practitioners experience in:

Preface

- Understanding stakeholder behavior/mindset
- Collaborating with team members and cross-functional teams
- Utilizing different methods/tools/techniques for problem-solving
- Employing different methods/tools/techniques for decision-making
- Applying various methods/tools/techniques for time management
- Building trust among team members and stakeholders
- Prioritizing the most promising ideas, solutions, or options
- Creating WOW products/services for your clients, etc.
- Managing and resolving conflicts with your team members and stakeholders

In this book, I have attempted to fill those gaps and have covered them in sufficient detail. Whether you are a student, a professional, an entrepreneur, or simply a curious reader, I believe that the lessons and insights contained within these pages will be of great value to you.

As you turn the pages, you will also gain a deeper understanding of the human-centered approach that underpins design thinking.

HOW TO USE THIS BOOK?

Each of the chapters is mapped and organized as per their Design Thinking relevance; however, a thorough understanding of all the chapters is the secret to successfully carrying out a Design Thinking process end-to-end. The chapters in this book address the concepts along with the tried and tested tools/techniques on

- Problem-solving approaches
- Conflict management and discovering your style of managing or resolving conflicts
- Decision-making tools and techniques
- Building trust within a team and with stakeholders/client

Preface

- Time management
- Stakeholder management
- Prioritizing tasks
- Techniques for creating innovative products

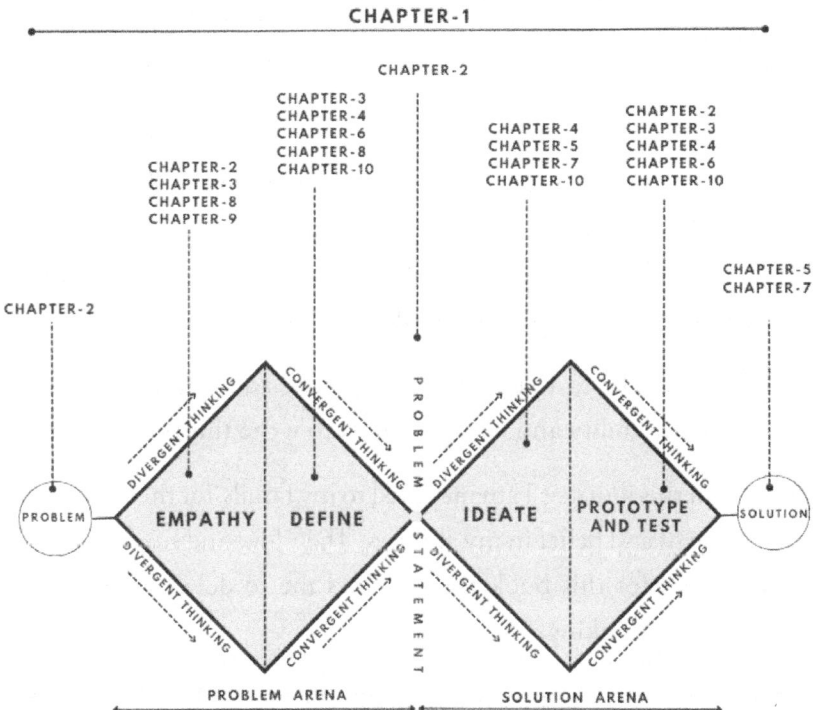

I hope that this book will inspire you includng Liam, Mac, and Henry along with other practitioners, coaches, and students across the Design Thinking community to embrace the power of Design Thinking and to apply its principles and practices in your work and life.

Certainly. Regardless of whether you are a student, a seasoned professional, an entrepreneur, or simply an inquisitive individual, I am confident that the lessons and insights found within these pages will prove highly beneficial to you.

ACKNOWLEDGEMENT

Writing a book is a journey that involves the support and contributions of many individuals along the way. I would like to express my deepest gratitude to all those who have made this endeavor possible and enriched my understanding of the design thinking mindset.

Firstly, I would like to thank the omnipotent and omniscient God for granting me the ability and circumstances to write this book.

At the core of this journey, I am indebted to my family for their unwavering encouragement and belief in my abilities. Their love and support provided the foundation for this book and inspired me to delve deeper into the world of design thinking.

I extend my heartfelt appreciation to my mentors, **Dr. (Prof.) Nishant Sharma** (IIT-B) and **Gowri Balasubramanyam** (Global Head of Learning and Organizational Development, SLK Group), as well as my esteemed colleagues in the field of design thinking and behavioral sciences. Your wisdom and guidance have been invaluable in shaping my understanding of this innovative approach.

I wish to acknowledge the valuable assistance and generosity of **Vijay Rao** (CEO, Apierso Inc, an NTT Data Company), **Venkat Mudupu** (COO, Apisero Inc, an NTT Data Company)**,** and **Charles D'Souza** (EVP & CLO, Apisero Inc, an NTT Data Company) for their steadfast support and contributions.

I would also like to express my gratitude to the numerous professionals, entrepreneurs, and individuals who generously shared their experiences and insights with me during the research phase. Your real-world stories added depth and authenticity to the principles presented in this book.

To my editor and the publishing team, thank you for believing in the potential of this project and for your diligent efforts in bringing it to fruition. Your expertise and dedication have been instrumental in making this book a reality.

Finally, to all the readers, I am grateful for your interest in exploring **The Secrets of Design Thinking Mindset**. It is my sincere hope that this book will inspire and empower you to embrace a design thinking mindset in your personal and professional pursuits.

Thank you all for being a part of this wonderful journey.

– **Amit**

CONTENTS

1. WHY DESIGN THINKING IN BUSINESS IS IMPORTANT? 1
    WHY DID THE INITIAL AUTOMATED TELLER MACHINE (A.T.M.)
    KEYPAD DESIGN FAIL? 2
    WHAT IS DESIGN THINKING? 3
    WHY IS DESIGN THINKING IN BUSINESS IMPORTANT? 4
        Focus on the customer 4
        Innovation 4
        Efficiency 4
        Collaboration 4
        Competitive advantage 4
        Iterative process 4
        Risk mitigation 4
    WHAT IS THE CONSTRUCT OF DESIGN THINKING? 5
    DIVERGENT THINKING 6
    CONVERGENT THINKING 7
    PUTTING DIVERGENT-CONVERGENT TOGETHER 8
    WHAT IS EMPATHY? 9
        Empathy Interview 11
    HOW TO CREATE AN EMPATHY INTERVIEW FOR A SMARTWATCH? 12
        1. Identify your target audience 12
        2. Find participants 12
        3. Getting ready for the interview 12
        4. Conduct the interview 12
        5. Gather the data 13
        6. Analyze the data 13
        7. Summarise the results 13

Contents

WHAT IS DEFINE? 14
CONSTRUCT AFFINITY DIAGRAM 15
HOW TO CONSTRUCT AFFINITY DIAGRAM FOR A SMARTWATCH? .. 16
THE DEFINE PHASE EQUATION 17
EMPATHY MAPPING 18
HOW TO BUILD AN EMPATHY MAP? 18
HOW TO CREATE PERSONAS? 21
HOW MIGHT WE? 23
HOW TO APPLY HMW? 24
WHAT IS IDEATE? 25
WHAT IS A PROTOTYPE? 29
WHAT IS TESTING? 30
THE SECRETS OF DESIGN THINKING MINDSET – A BLUEPRINT 32

2. DO YOU SOLVE PROBLEMS OR SYMPTOMS? 33

HAVE YOU BEEN IN AMEER'S SITUATION? 34
WHAT IS A PROBLEM? 34
HOLDING THE WRONG END OF THE STICK? 36
BARKING UP THE WRONG TREE? 37
THE 8-DIMENSIONS OF PROBLEM-SOLVING 38
   D0 - Awarness of the Problem 39
   D1 - Form a Team 39
   D2 - Define the Problem 40
   D3 - Implement a Quick Fix to Contain the Problem 44
      1. Process Flowchart 45
      2. Decision Flowchart 46
      3. Rummler-Brache Diagram 48
   D4 - Root Cause Analysis (RCA) 50
      1. The 5 Whys 51
         How to Apply the 5 Why? 51
      2. The Ishikawa Diagram 53
         How to Apply the Fishbone Technique? 56
      3. Fault Tree Analysis 64
         How to Apply the FTA? 67
   D5 - Develop and Verify the Corrective Actions 69
   D6 - Implement Permanent Corrective Action 70

Contents

    D7 - Prevent Recurrence 70
    D8 - Congratulate the Team 71

3. WHAT…? NOW WHAT…? SO WHAT…? 72

    HAVE YOU BEEN IN TRACY'S SITUATION? 73
    IT IS NOT MY PROBLEM! 73
    WHAT IS CONFLICT MANAGEMENT AND RESOLUTION? 74
    HIGH FIVE WITH YOUR STAKEHOLDERS! 74
    WANT TO RESOLVE YOUR CONFLICTS IN STYLE? 75
        Competing [C-1] 76
            When to Use this Style? 76
        Collaborating [C-2] 77
            When to Use this Style? 78
        Compromising [C-3] 78
            When to Use this Style? 79
        Avoiding [A-1] 79
            When to Use this Style? 80
        Accommodating [A-2] 81
            When to Use this Style? 81
    WHAT IS YOUR STYLE OF CONFLICT MANAGEMENT ? 82
        A Self-Assessment 82
    HAVE YOU PROFILED YOUR STAKEHOLDER? 86
    MENDELOW'S STAKEHOLDER MATRIX 87
        How to Apply Mendelow's SM 88
    DECISION-RESPONSIBILITY MATRICES FOR YOUR PROJECT 92
        ARMI Matrix 92
            Approver 93
            Resource 93
            Member 93
            Interested Party 93
        RACI Matrix 93
            Responsible 94
            Accountable 94
            Consulted 94
            Informed 95
    YOUR CONFLICT MANAGEMENT STYLE 97
        A Self-Assessment 97

Contents

4. STILL USING GUT FEELING FOR MAKING DECISIONS? 100
- HAVE YOU BEEN IN DANNY OR RON'S SITUATION? 101
- WHAT IS A DECISION? 101
- PAIRED DECISION MAKING 102
  - How to Apply Paired Decision Making (PDM)? 105
- PUGH MATRIX ANALYSIS 109
  - How to Apply Pugh Matrix? 109
- PROBABILISTIC DECISION-MAKING TREE 114
  - How to Calculate the Terminal Values? 118
  - How to Calculate Rollback Values? 119
- **WHAT IS YOUR DECISION-MAKING STYLE? 121**
  - A Self-Assessment 121
- VROOM-YETTON-JAGO DECISION-MAKING MODEL 122
  - 1. Quality of the Decision 122
  - 2. Collaboration and Team Work 122
  - 3. Time Constraints 123
  - The Five Decision-Making Styles of V-Y-J Model 123
- SIMPLE DECISION MATRIX (SDM) 127
  - How to Apply SDM? 128
- WEIGHTED DECISION MATRIX (WDM) 131
  - How to Apply WDM? 132
- WHAT IF YOU HAVE INFINITE CHOICES? 134
- N/3 VOTING 134
  - How to Apply N/3 Voting? 135
- EASE-BENEFIT MATRIX 138
- PLUS-MINUS-INTERESTING (PMI) 139
  - How to Apply PMI? 140
- PICK CHART 141
- KJ ANALYSIS 144
  - How to Apply KJ Method? 144

5. HOW TO CREATE WOW PRODUCTS FOR YOUR CLIENT? 148
- HAVE YOU BEEN IN KEVIN'S SITUATION? 149
- FIND THAT X-FACTOR TO ADD TO YOUR PRODUCT 149
- THE KANO REACTION MODEL 150
  - Who is Kano? 150

Contents

What is the Kano Model? 150
X-Axis Spectrum 151
Y-Axis Spectrum 152
ANATOMY OF THE KANO MODEL 153
   1. Must-be (Basic or Must-have) Features 154
   2. Performance Features 156
   3. Attractive or Excitement Features 158
   4. Indifferent (Neutral) Features 161
   5. Reverse Features 162
PUTTING IT TOGETHER 164
   How to Apply Kano Model to your Products? 164
   Kano's Response Evaluation Grid 166
   Discrete Response Analysis 166

6. HOW TO PRIORITIZE YOUR PRIORITIES? 169

HAVE YOU BEEN IN SOPHIA'S SITUATION? 170
WHAT IS COOKING IN YOUR PROJECT?....R I C E? 170
WHAT IS R I C E? 171
   The R I C E Equation 171
   REACH 171
   IMPACT 172
   CONFIDENCE 173
   EFFORT 174
PUTTING R I C E TOGETHER 176
VITAL FEW AND TRIVIAL MANY TECHNIQUE 177
   Who is Pareto? 177
   How to Apply Pareto's 80:20 Rule? 178
WEIGHTED PARETO ANALYSIS 183
LET'S BREAK THE ICE 188
   How to Apply the I C E Frameworks? 188
   IMPACT 189
   CONFIDENCE 189
   EASE 190
   Putting the ICE Together 190
WHICH IS THE CAPITAL OF RUSSIA? 191
   How to Apply MoSCoW for Products/Services? 192

Contents

7. FALLING SHORT OF PRODUCT IDEAS AND INNOVATION? 200
    HAVE YOU BEEN IN LOGAN'S SITUATION? 201
    INNOVATIONS AHEAD OF THE PACK..201
    SCAMPER...202
        How to Ideate Using SCAMPER? 203
        Substitute 203
        Combine 205
        Adapt 206
        Modify (Magnify, Minify) 207
        Put to Another Use... 208
        Eliminate 209
        Reverse (Rearrange, Reorder) 210

8. HOW TO BUILD AND REPAIR TRUST WITHIN THE TEAM? 214
    HAVE YOU BEEN IN NOEL'S SITUATION? 215
    WHAT IS TRUST EQUILIBRIUM?..215
    HOW TO BUILD AND REPAIR TRUST?...216
    WHAT IS CREDIBILITY? 217
    WHAT IS RELIABILITY? 218
    WHAT IS INTIMACY? 219
    WHAT IS SELF-ORIENTATION?..220
    KNOW THYSELF THROUGH JO-HARI'S WINDOW 221
    JOHARI WINDOW CONSTRUCT...222
        1. Arena or Open Area... 223
        2. The Blind Spot or Blind Self 223
        3. The Latent or Hidden Self or Façade 224
        4. Unknown or Unknown Self.. 225
    HOW TO INCREASE THE SURFACE AREA OF THE ARENA?.............226
    MORE WINDOW ANALYSIS 227
    DISCOVER YOUR WINDOWS 229
        List of Adjectives and Descriptors 230
    FIND OUT YOUR BLIND SPOT 232
        A Self-Assessment 232
    CHARTING YOUR SCORES...239
    WHY DO YOUR TEAMS HAVE CONFLICTS? 240
        What is Forming? 241

Contents

    What is Storming? 242
    What is Norming? 243
    What is Performing? 245
    What is Adjourning? 245

9. K.Y.C. – DO YOU KNOW YOUR CLIENT ENOUGH? 247

    HAVE YOU BEEN IN JOHN'S SITUATION? 248
    LET US DISC-USS IT! 248
    DO YOU KNOW YOUR DISC PERSONALITY TYPE? 249
        A Self-Assessment 249
    WHAT IS DISC? 255
    HOW CAN DISC HELP YOU ON A DAILY BASIS? 255
    WHAT IS THE DISC CONSTRUCT? 256
        The D-Style 257
            How To Identify a High-Dominance Person in Your Project? 257
        The I-Style 258
            How To Identify a High-Influence Person in Your Project? 258
        The S-Style 259
            How To Identify a High-Steadiness Person in Your Project? 259
        The C-Style 260
            How To Identify a High-Compliance Person in Your Project? 260
    JOHN AND MATTHEW'S CASE 261
    AVOID PUTTING THE CAT AMONG THE PIGEONS 265
    WHAT IS THE ENERGY LINE? 272
    DECODING YOUR PERSONALITY STYLE 274
    DISC INTENSITY LOW-HIGH RANGES 276
    KYC: FOR YOUR STAKEHOLDERS, TEAM MEMBERS 277
        Stakeholder Assessment 277
    HOW DO YOU DEAL WITH A HIGH-D STAKEHOLDER? 284
    HOW DO YOU DEAL WITH A HIGH-I STAKEHOLDER? 285
    HOW DO YOU DEAL WITH A HIGH-S STAKEHOLDER? 285
    HOW DO YOU DEAL WITH A HIGH-C STAKEHOLDER? 286

10. IMPORTANT, OR NOT SO IMPORTANT? 287

    HAVE YOU BEEN IN ERIC'S SITUATION? 288
    FORGET ABOUT FORGETTING YOUR TASKS 288

WHAT IS A WORK LIST? 289
STOP PUTTING THE CART BEFORE THE HORSE 291
EISENHOWER MATRIX 291
    Who Is Eisenhower? 291
    What is Eisenhower Matrix? 291
    How to Apply Eisenhower Matrix? 292
    DO Quadrant 293
    DECIDE Quadrant 293
    DELEGATE Quadrant 293
    DELETE Quadrant 294

INDEX **295**

"Whether you are a CEO or an engineer or a musician or an artist, you must include Design Thinking in all processes, not just certain processes or projects"

– **Anonymous**

1

WHY DESIGN THINKING IN BUSINESS IS IMPORTANT?

WHY DID THE INITIAL AUTOMATED TELLER MACHINE (A.T.M.) KEYPAD DESIGN FAIL?

H.T.M. Pvt. Ltd. company was asked to design an A.T.M. keypad by a leading nationalized bank.

The company designed and delivered the (as shown here) keypad for the cash dispensing machine.

After installing this keypad at pilot locations within the city limits, the keypad was rejected and sent for redesign.

Why? What is wrong with the keypad design?

After much deliberation, the following keypad was redesigned and installed.

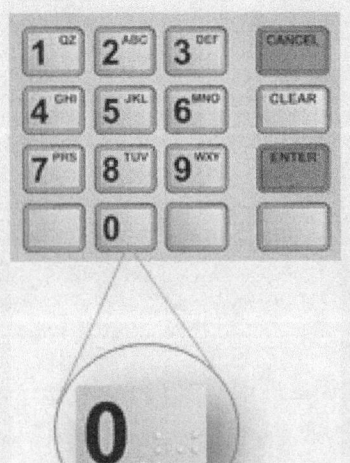

What is the difference between the two keypad designs?

The first design failed because the blind users of A.T.M. were unable to operate the machine to withdraw cash.

In the latter, braille was incorporated into the design to accommodate the usage of A.T.M. for the blind (persona).

Explore this chapter and book to know some tools and techniques to overcome redesigns/recalls/withdrawal of a product or service.

WHAT IS DESIGN THINKING?

Design thinking is a mindset and an approach to **problem-solving** that puts the requirements of the **customer first**. It depends on **empathetically** watching how your customers interact with their environment/software/tools/products and using a hands-on, iterative process to develop **creative and innovative solutions**.

Design thinking encompasses the following two core beliefs:

1. It can **solve wicked (ill-defined) problems** from all facets – IT services, products, sales, education, manufacturing, health care, etc.
2. It can be **used and applied by anyone** – school children, engineers, doctors, lawyers, laymen, leaders, politicians, etc.

John E. Arnold, a professor of engineering at MIT and later at Stanford, was one of the first individuals to write on **Design thinking**. Arnold advocated a science of innovation to enhance engineering and business innovations. Arnold is a pioneer who, in the 1950s, established the principles on which modern design and innovation are based.

Design thinking began as a method for developing cutting-edge new goods and technologies. However, this practice is now extensively employed in both the public and commercial sectors as well as for both professional and non-profit endeavors globally.

Design thinking can only be successful if it is **iterative**, as opposed to **conventional problem-solving**, which is a **linear process** of recognizing a **problem** and then **brainstorming solutions**. It serves more as a technique for evolving your thinking, perspectives, viewpoints, and responding to customer demands than as a strategy to arrive at a single solution.

WHY IS DESIGN THINKING IN BUSINESS IMPORTANT?

Focus on the customer

Design thinking puts the client at the forefront of the problem-solving process, resulting in solutions that more closely satisfy their wants and requirements.

Innovation

Design thinking promotes the development of fresh ideas and viewpoints, which can result in the creation of novel goods and services.

Efficiency

The design thinking method aids in locating and getting rid of inefficiencies, which results in simplified procedures and cost savings.

Collaboration

Design thinking encourages cross-functional teamwork and collaboration, which produces more creative and practical solutions.

Competitive advantage

Businesses that apply design thinking are frequently able to set themselves apart from rivals by providing more client-centered, creative, and effective solutions.

Iterative process

The design thinking method is iterative, which implies that improvements are made to solutions in response to input from consumers and stakeholders.

Risk mitigation

Design thinking helps to reduce the risk of creating goods or services that fall short of client expectations by concentrating on their requirements and needs.

Overall, design thinking is a useful technique for businesses that want to develop products and solutions that not only satisfy the requirements and wants of their consumers but also succeed in the market.

WHAT IS THE CONSTRUCT OF DESIGN THINKING?

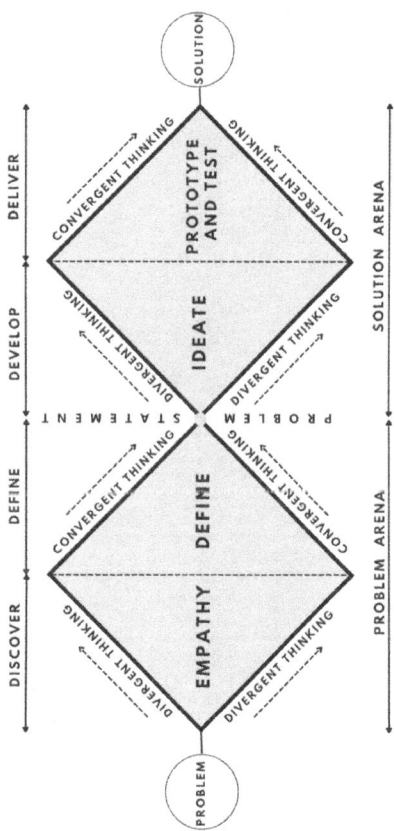

The **design thinking** process can be understood with a **double-diamond thinking** framework as shown in the figure.

The **double-diamond** structure is used to comprehend your consumers' needs and challenges, then explore innovative solutions that will satisfy and delight them.

The **double-diamond** approach uses two styles of thinking viz., **divergent thinking** and **convergent thinking**

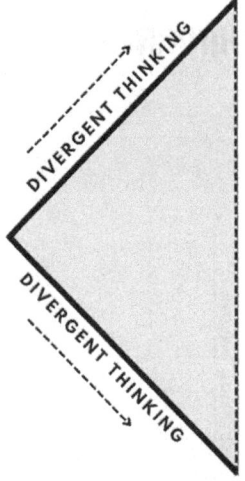

- Helps Identify Options
- It is Creative
- Generates a Range of Alternate Solutions

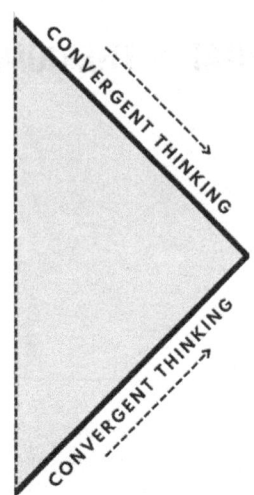

- Data Driven
- Logical
- Based on Facts
- Finalizing 1 correct solution

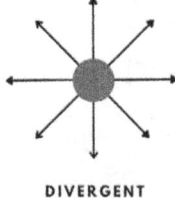

DIVERGENT

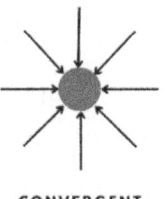

CONVERGENT

DIVERGENT THINKING

To investigate a wide range of potential solutions, **divergent thinking** includes coming up with original ideas. It entails widening your horizons and experimenting with diverse solutions to a problem.

In addition, **divergent thinking** is **spontaneous**, **unstructured**, and **non-linear**, and it results in a lot of fresh and distinctive thoughts. In a short period, it involves a large number of potential solutions or ideas.

Let's say, you would like to buy a car. You are knowingly or unknowingly applying **divergent thinking** which is generating the options/choices/alternatives regarding whether you want to buy a hatchback, sedan, SUV, MUV, etc.

Again in each of these categories, which brand and model. This exercise of **divergent thinking** generates a lot of options and alternatives from which you can choose your car or the feasible solution.

CONVERGENT THINKING

Convergent thinking is a way of thinking where the goal is to identify **one**, **proven** or **feasible solution** to a problem. It is focused on determining the best response, or frequently the right approach, to a problem. **Convergent thinking** stresses facts, data, and logic.

Continuing the same **car example** from above, once you have populated the options that you have to buy from, next you need to start putting the constraints – budget, color, number of seaters, BHP, etc. – to narrow down the options to that one car so that you can go ahead and buy it

If you don't taper down your options to one then you will never be able to buy a car. So, **convergent thinking** facilitates you to choose the best solution among the possible choices under the given set of constraints.

The Secrets of Design Thinking Mindset

> **YOUR TURN!** For the current project that you are working on, apply the divergent-convergent thinking process and generate ideas/options/alternatives.
>
> ○ _____
> ○ _____
> ○ _____
> ○ _____
>
> ○ _____

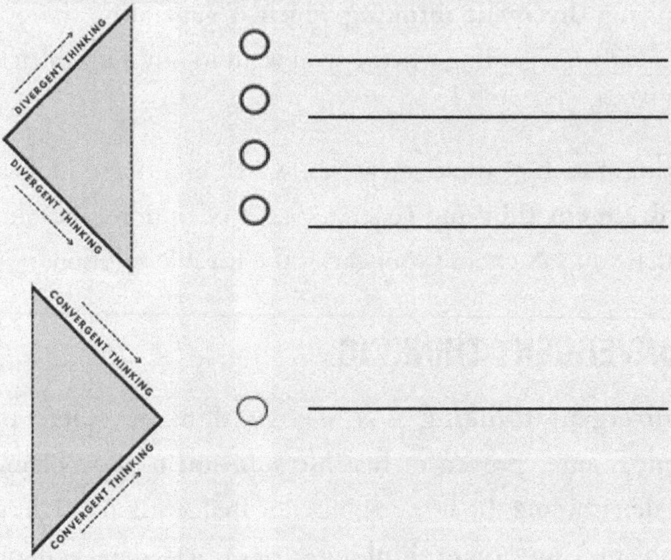

PUTTING DIVERGENT-CONVERGENT TOGETHER

Once we juxtapose two sets of **divergent-convergent** processes, it forms a **double-diamond** structure.

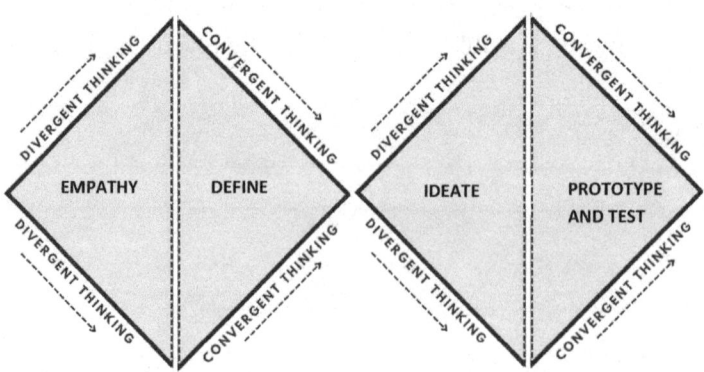

Design thinking has **five phases** – **Empathy, Define, Ideate, Prototype,** and **Test.**
- 1st Divergent Thinking Phase – **Empathy**
- 1st Convergent Thinking Phase – **Define**
- 2nd Divergent Thinking Phase – **Ideate**
- 2nd Convergent Thinking Phase – **Prototype and Test**

WHAT IS EMPATHY?

Many confuse the word **empathy** with **sympathy** or **pity**. One of the visuals from *Harvard Business Review (HBR)* clearly distinguishes all 4 altruistic traits – **pity, sympathy, empathy,** and **compassion.**

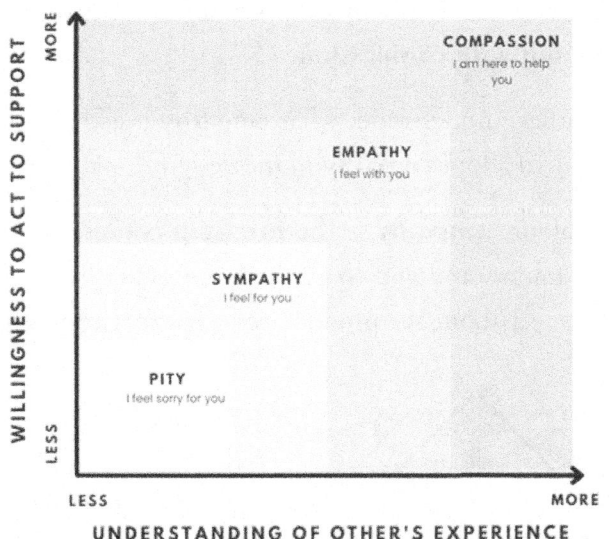

Pity can be located in the bottom left. When we feel **pity**, we are less likely to take action and have **less empathy** for other people. Simply put, we feel bad for them.

We develop **sympathy** as we move up and to the right on the chart. Our eagerness to provide assistance and our knowledge of the other have both somewhat increased. We sympathize with the other person.

We now reach the next stage, which is **empathy**. When we are empathetic, we are deeply and viscerally aware of the other person's experience. We share their emotions. We literally adopt the other person's sentiments and make them our own with a willingness to support and help them. **Finally,** the highest form of understanding other's/client's experiences/pains coupled with the highest form of willingness to support and help them can be understood as **compassion.**

Usually, compassion is not business-oriented, it does not expect anything in return for goods/money.

The deeds of Mother Teresa were with compassion where she did not expect anything in return for her services.

Discuss with your team why the Design Thinking process starts with empathy and not with compassion.

Now that you have understood, what **empathy** exactly means, you will next know how to adopt **empathy** in the design thinking framework.

In design thinking, **empathy** is the **first step** because it is a skill that allows you to understand and share the same feelings that your clients/team members feel about the product, service, experience, etc.

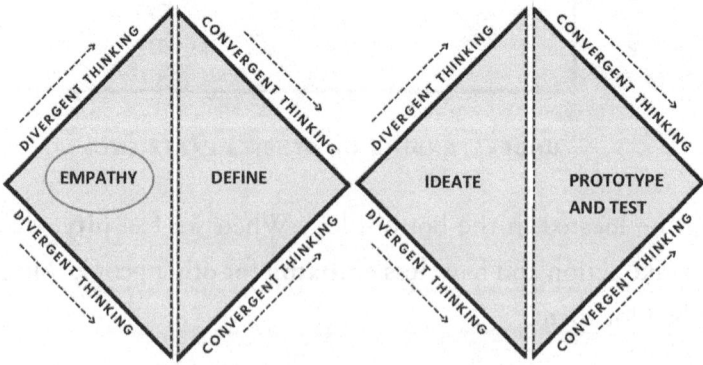

Through **empathy**, you will be able to not only put yourselves in the shoes of your client/team members but also walk a mile in those shoes to know the shoe bites and pain experienced by the user/client/customer/team members about their problem, circumstance, and situation.

During **empathy**, you will try to gain insights into what they need, what they want, how they behave, feel, and think, and why they demonstrate such behaviors, feelings, and thoughts when interacting with the product/service in real-world settings.

Conducting interviews, experimental discovery, questionnaires, surveys, etc. are used to understand the user experience during the empathy phase.

Empathy Interview

1. Create a **questionnaire/list** of questions before the interview.
2. Use the **five elements approach** for capturing the initial problem statement which will be further refined in the convergent phase.

The Five Elements Approach

1. I am...
   [Who is this person/customer/client? Anything that identifies your customer and gives you a clue of who this person is or what problem they are facing.]
2. I am trying to ...
   [This is where you capture your customer's/client's/team's action. What is it that they are trying to do or achieve?]
3. but ...
   [Here, you will capture what is stopping your customer/client to achieve their goal or purpose through the product or service.]
4. because ...
   [Here, the causes of impediments and issues are captured.]
5. which makes me feel ...
   [As a result of the above, how is your customer feeling – frustrated, delighted, sad, etc.]

3. Use the **5-WTH (Fw-Th) technique** (covered in Chapter-2) to capture more information.
4. The data collected in this phase could be qualitative and/or quantitative.
5. You can also perform a **Gemba walk** to understand the issue.
6. The responses have to be collected in terms of stories and anecdotes.

HOW TO CREATE AN EMPATHY INTERVIEW FOR A SMARTWATCH?

1. Identify your target audience

Choose the individuals/cohorts you want to interview to learn more about their perspectives, requirements, and reactions to wearing a smartwatch.

2. Find participants

Look for willing participants who meet the requirements of your target audience and are receptive to taking part in the interview. Take into account elements like age, gender, employment, and smartwatch usage trends.

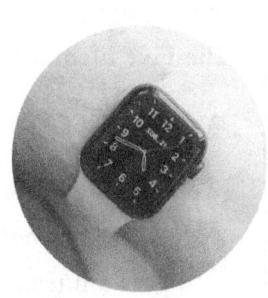

3. Getting ready for the interview

Create a series of open-ended questions with the goal of better comprehending the emotions, challenges, and experiences your participants have with wearing a wristwatch.

4. Conduct the interview

Begin by making an introduction and outlining the reason for the meeting. After then, ask open-ended questions and pay close attention to the answers.

The following are some examples of interview questions for a smartwatch empathy test:
- What types of activities do you perform with your smartwatch?
- Can you give an example of a recent time when you struggled to use your smartwatch?
- In what ways does your smartwatch simplify your life?
- Could you describe an instance when you were annoyed with your smartwatch?
- What significance do you place on your smartwatch?

Encourage the subject of the interview to provide as much detail as they can; refrain from interjecting or taking the initiative.

5. Gather the data

Record the interview by taking notes and, if the subject agrees, by capturing it on audio or video.

6. Analyze the data

Look over the notes and recordings to find important trends, insights, and topics regarding the use of smartwatches. Look for shared feelings, emotions, difficulties, challenges, and experiences among the respondents.

7. Summarise the results

Create an **empathy map** (explained in the Define phase), a **persona** (explained in the Define phase), or other design thinking tools using the information you learned from the empathy interviews to better understand the needs and experiences of your target audience as they relate to using smartwatches.

In general, doing empathy interviews for a smartwatch may help you develop a better comprehension of the requirements, preferences, and feelings of your target audience towards utilizing a smartwatch.

The Secrets of Design Thinking Mindset

WHAT IS DEFINE?

In this phase, you will **define** an appropriate and practical problem statement that the design thinker will concentrate on solving in the second diamond phase.

The data collected (structured, unstructured, qualitative, or quantitative) during the **empathy phase** is gathered and processed on collaborative tools like Miro, Mural or sticky notes, etc.

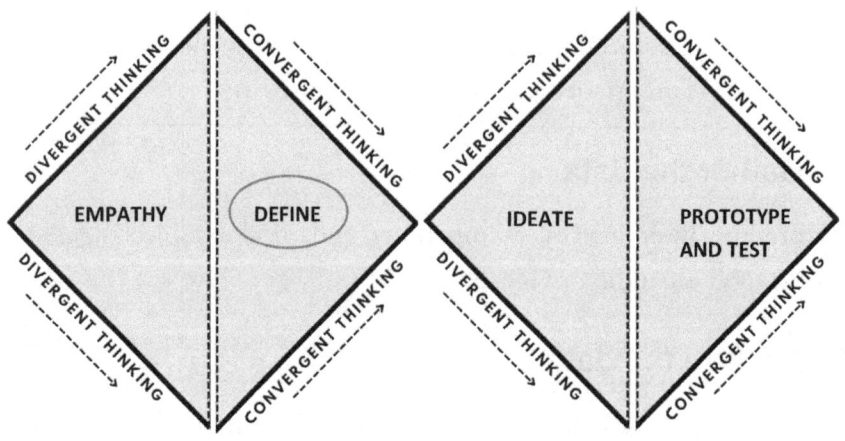

	Response from Respondent-1	Response from Respondent-2	Response from Respondent-N	Insight-1	Insight-2
Question-1					
Question-2					
Question-3					
Question-N					
Observation-1					
Observation-2					
Observation-N					

Organize all the responses from all the respondents to the questions from the questionnaire and observations. Finally, draw insights from those responses and record them.

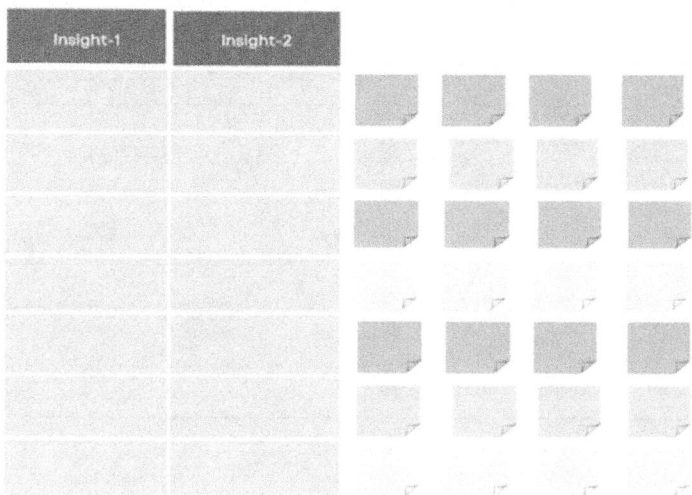

CONSTRUCT AFFINITY DIAGRAM

A huge quantity of unstructured data, ideas, and information that was generated during the empathy phase is organized and understood using the design thinking technique known as an **affinity diagram**. It is a graphical technique for classifying and arranging, grouping, and clustering the ideas, feedback, and pain points made during the empathy phase.

You can observe how in the **convergent phase**, which is the **define phase,** different responses gathered from the empathy phase are tapered down or narrowed to a single apex point which is the **prioritized action.**

The Secrets of Design Thinking Mindset

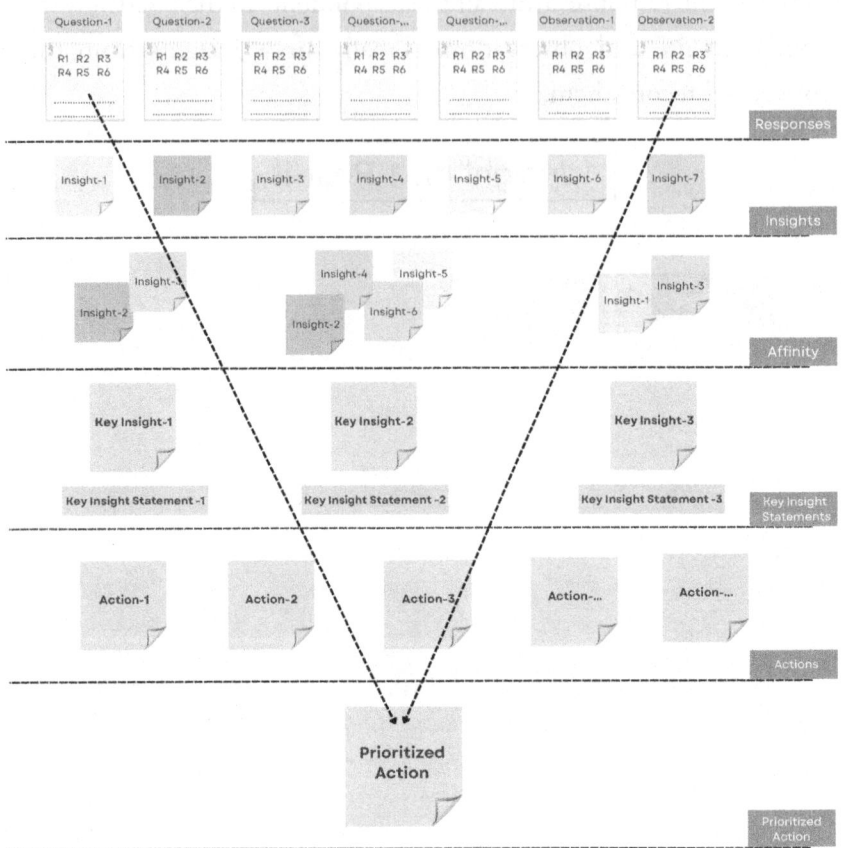

HOW TO CONSTRUCT AFFINITY DIAGRAM FOR A SMARTWATCH?

1. **Gather information/data** – Compile information on user needs, preferences, and problems with using smartwatches. Surveys, interviews, and observation may be included in this.
2. **List down ideas** – Put each idea on a card or sticky note. Each concept should be based on a specific user need, requirement, desire, or problem.

3. **Form clusters** – Put related thoughts together by arranging them next to one another on a board or wall. Put labels on each category and describe it.
4. **Label the clusters** – Give each group/cluster a name that is evocative of the shared concept or subject among the sticky notes in that group.
5. **Detect patterns** – Analyse the differences and similarities between the groups in search of patterns. Analyze the information to find any trends, patterns, or recurring themes.
6. **Optimise the groups/clusters** – Refine by merging or dividing them as necessary. If required, move certain sticky notes to different groupings.
7. **Prioritise ideas** – Rank each group's ideas in order of significance to users. To convey importance, use colored dots or other visual clues.
8. **Classification** – Based on patterns that develop, create categories/classifications. Related groups should be included in each category.

Organise research results into a set of design concepts or rules that will direct the creation of your smartwatch. Throughout the design phase, utilize your affinity diagram as a guide to make sure your design is in line with user demands and preferences.

THE DEFINE PHASE EQUATION

The following is the summarized equation of the first diamond which is the first convergent-divergent phase of design thinking.

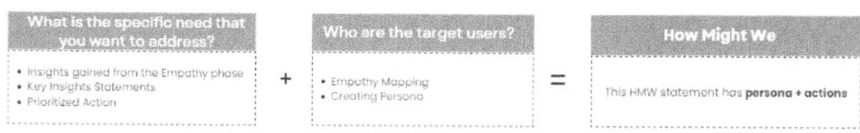

EMPATHY MAPPING

It is a helpful tool that enables you to comprehend your users/clients/team members more thoroughly. To create **empathy** for **end users, stakeholders**, marketing and sales, product development, or creative teams, you might participate in a straightforward workshop exercise called **empathy mapping**.

An **empathy mapping** exercise is an excellent way for teams working on the design and engineering of goods, services, or user experiences to "get inside the brains" of people.

HOW TO BUILD AN EMPATHY MAP?

1. Take a print of the map (below) on an A-1 or A-2 sheet or draw it on a large whiteboard.
2. Allocate 45 to 60 minutes (or more) for the session depending on the issue being solved.
3. **Identify the customer or user group you want to focus on** – Start by identifying the customer or user group you want to understand better. This could be based on demographics, behavior, or other criteria.

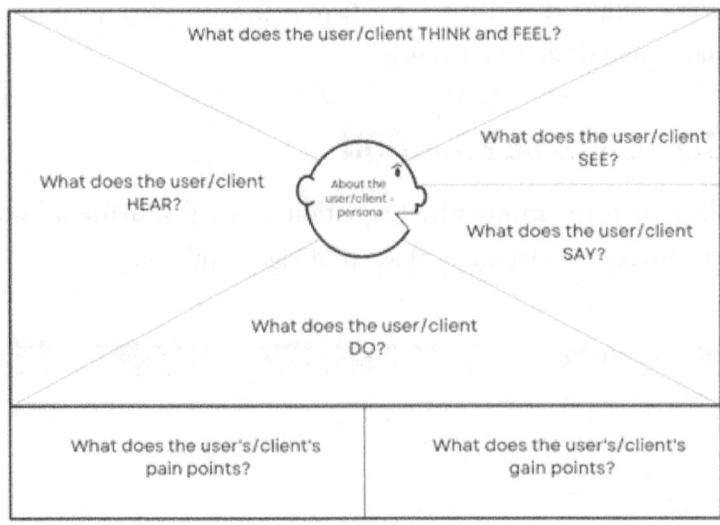

4. **Define the context** – Identify the context in which the customer or user will use the product or service. This could include the environment, the situation, and the task at hand.
5. **Gather information** – Gather information about the customer or user group by conducting research, talking to them, and observing their behavior. This could include customer surveys, interviews, focus groups, and user testing.
6. **Invite the key players** – Form a diverse team (that has but is not limited to) such as the product manager, developers, marketers, and other designers, of course.
7. On the empathy map that is shown do the following:
    a. **Thinking and feeling:** What are the customer or user's thoughts and feelings about the product or service? What are their goals, aspirations, and fears?
    b. **Seeing and hearing:** What do they see and hear when using the product or service? What are their experiences and perceptions?
    c. **Saying and doing:** What do they say and do when using the product or service? What are their actions and behaviors?
    d. **Pain points and gains:** What are the customer or user's pain points, challenges, and frustrations? What are their gains, needs, and desires?
8. **Fill in the empathy map** – Use the information you gathered in step 3 to fill in each quadrant of the empathy map. Try to be as specific and detailed as possible, and use quotes or anecdotes to illustrate your points.
9. **Analyze the empathy map** – Use the empathy map to identify patterns, insights, and opportunities for improvement. Look for areas where the customer or user's needs are not being met, and brainstorm ways to address these issues.
10. **Iterate and refine** – Use the empathy map as a starting point to create new ideas, concepts, and solutions. Test your ideas with the customer or user group and refine them based on their feedback.

The Secrets of Design Thinking Mindset

By following these steps, you can build an empathy map that helps you understand and empathize with your customers or users, and create products and services that meet their needs and expectations.

Once the exercise is completed, the empathy map will get populated similar to the shown visual.

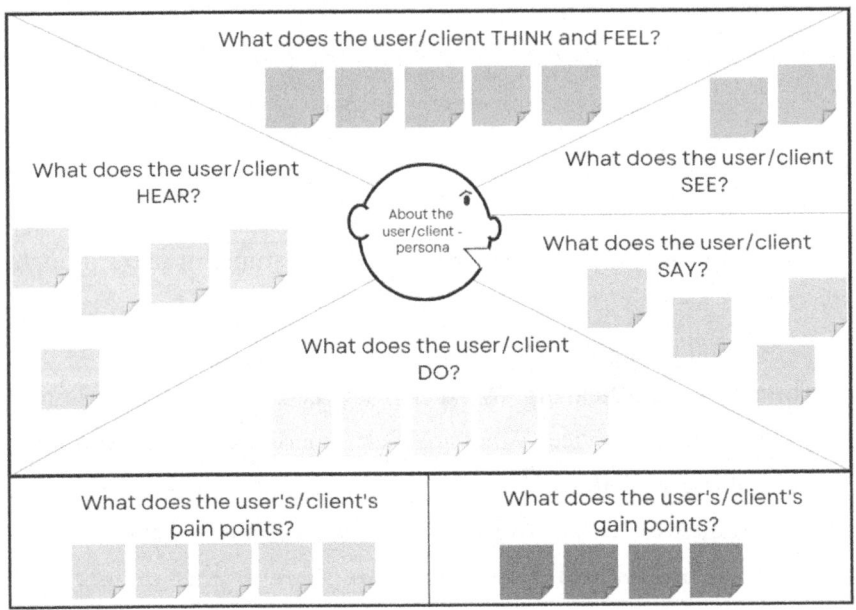

CREATING PERSONAS

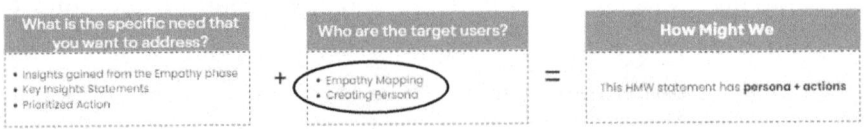

Personas serve as representations of target users' (clients, customers, team members) want, requirements, and objectives. Consider a **persona** as your usual or ideal client/consumer. Whom can you picture utilizing your app/product/service?

Why Design Thinking in Business Is Important?

Creating **personas** aids in avoiding generalizing about all your users and assuming that they all have similar requirements and objectives.

Additionally, it helps you avoid adopting the mindset that you will use an app/product/service in the same way as your clients/team members.

Think of **personas** more as a profile or **job descriptions** for a job role. A job description of a software engineer will not fit into a job role of an HRBP.

Imagine you would like to design a bicycle. Whom will you design it for?

HOW TO CREATE PERSONAS?

1. **Gather information** – To learn more about your target audience, conduct research. Surveys, interviews, focus groups, and user observations in their natural surroundings are some examples of this. Learn as much as you can about their actions, requirements, and preferences.
2. **Find the similarities** – Analyse the information you've acquired for patterns. Find trends and patterns that can aid you in understanding the wants, requirements, and actions of your target market.

3. **Describe your persona** – Make up a fictitious persona to represent your target audience based on the traits you've determined they share. Your persona should have a name, a photo, and a thorough description that includes details about their age, occupation, hobbies, and behavior.
4. **Describe their motives and ambitions** – Outline the motivations and aims of your persona. What do they want to accomplish? What motivates them to act? This will enable you to comprehend the fundamental causes of their behavior.
5. **Identify their pain points** – Understand the difficulties your persona has in pursuing their objectives. This will assist you in identifying potential markets for your goods or services.
6. **Describe their approach** – Draw out the path taken by your persona, from the moment they first learn about your goods or services to the moment they make their ultimate purchase. Determine the touchpoints they come across and the feelings they have at each level.
7. **Incorporate the persona into the design** – Integrate your persona into the layout of your product or service. Take into account how your persona will use your product or service and how you might modify your design to suit their requirements.
8. **Test your persona** – Have people test your persona to determine how accurate it is and to find out where it needs work. Based on customer input, modify your persona and change your design.

These methods will help you develop a persona that will help you comprehend your target market and produce goods and services that will satisfy their requirements and needs.

HOW MIGHT WE?

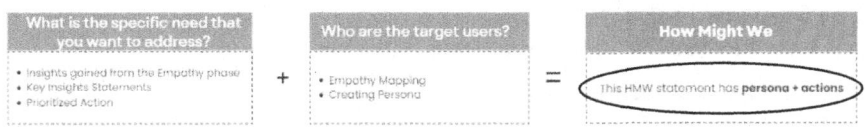

How Might We (or **HMW**) is a common abbreviation for the framework. An issue can be reframed using the **How Might We** framework. You're not only attempting to think about the problem from a positive angle, but you're also widening your thinking and, as a result, your options for potential new solutions.

By using the **How Might We** framework to reframe your problem statement, you may truly transform impediments into possible solutions.

Although you might not get it correct the very first time, remember that it takes practice. It's an essential tool for improving one's ability to produce innovative responses to problems.

This kind of problem-reframing technique opens up a plethora of potential solutions.

How: Encourages the team members to feel that the solution is available but that we should investigate as we do not yet know the best solution to the problem.

Might: Since you're not making any promises, it provides the uncertainty you and your team need. It's entirely OK if your suggested remedy doesn't work.

We: The "**I**" is not present; only "**We**" which accentuates it is a collaborative work with the team and stakeholders.

HOW TO APPLY HMW?

1. Examine the problem or the problem statement at hand first. Put **HMW** before your remark to rephrase it.
2. Your main focus should be on looking for new possibilities. Try to think of several **HMW insights** and examine the questions you could have and see if you can think of a range of possible solutions.
3. If unable to, return to the previous step and add wider-ranging questions. Consider creating some questions that you can brainstorm and validate with your stakeholders.
4. A good problem statement is neither too general nor too specific. Your questions should provide enough leeway or flexibility for your stakeholders to come up with workable responses or solutions.

- Avoid suggesting a solution in the **HMW**.

Insight	*Employees often do not* update *their WSR timely*
Poor HMW	*How Might We tell employees to* update *their WSR timely?*
Better HMW	*How Might We* support our employees and educate them to update *their WSR confidently?*

- **HMW** should be outcome-based.

Insight	*Employees keep calling the HR and Finance team for tax information*
Poor HMW	*How Might We* stop employees from calling *HR and Finance team?*

| Better HMW | *How Might We make our* employees feel confident with all the artifacts and information *available to them on-the-fly?* |

- **HMW** Questions should be framed in a positive tone.

Insight	*Employees are finding it difficult to submit their investment proofs for tax filing*
Poor HMW	*How Might We make the investment submission* less difficult*?*
Better HMW	*How Might We make the investment submission* quick and easy*?*

WHAT IS IDEATE?

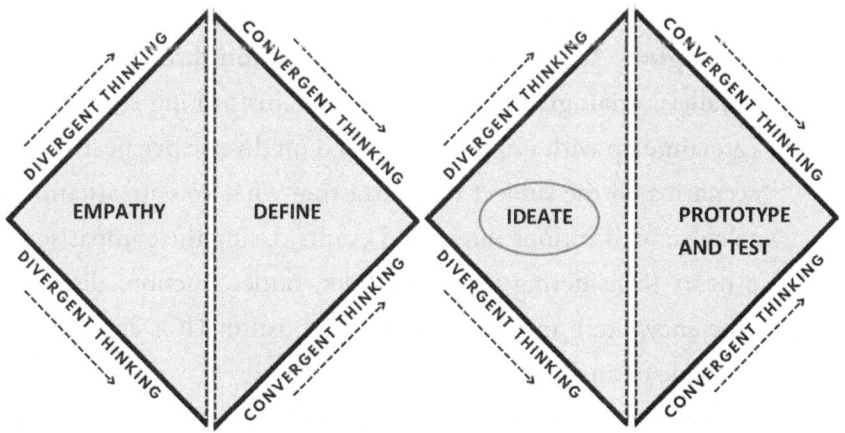

In the previous define phase, you created a problem statement with an **HMW phrase**.

Ideate is again a **divergent process** where you will start finding possible solutions or feasible options to the previously defined problem.

Following are some of the the methods for **ideation process** and you can use any of them or a combination of each to yield the results or outcomes you are looking for.

- **Brainstorm**: **Brainstorming** is the process of openly discussing ideas with the group and using the resulting synergy. When using the **brainstorming process**, participants build on one another's ideas to develop a final concept. This functions best in an atmosphere of trust where people feel comfortable speaking openly without fear of judgment.
- **Braindump:** This is extremely similar to brainstorming, except that in a **braindump**, individuals write on post-it notes separately before sharing them with the team, as opposed to speaking freely with the group.
- **Brainwalking: Brainwalking** makes use of motion to encourage creativity. Participants go about the room to various ideation stations rather than passing papers around in a circle, where they then expand on the ideas of other participants.
- **Analogies:** As they advance comprehension through the use of parallels, **analogies** may be a good brainstorming strategy. You can come up with unique ideas based on diverse perspectives and scenarios on the subject by contrasting what you are attempting to solve with various things and events. Using the comparison of a heart (considering its valves, inlet, outlet, suction, discharge, efficiency, etc,) and an internal combustion (IC) engine as an example of analogy.
- **Crowdstorm:** Approaching the audience to generate ideas and assess the ideas or solutions you have generated is known as **crowdstorming**. **Crowdstorming** provides you with a solid foundation on which to base your ideas by utilizing polls, reviews, and social media. Even while it occasionally falls short of advancing the finest possible concept, this may be quite insightful.

- **Cheatstorm: Cheatstorming** is a fantastic technique to learn what your competitors are doing in the space. Instead of coming up with ideas from scratch like most of the other ways described, **cheatstorming** makes use of what others are already doing. **Cheatstorming** is a form of cognitive sustainability or recycling of prior knowledge.
- **Bodystorm:** Participants in this approach take on the role of the user. A greater product or service may result from the team's ability to imagine themselves as the user in the problem-solving scenario. Being physically active rather than just theorizing about the issues might be quite effective.
- **Gamestorming: Gamestorming** is a form of brainstorming that leverages the use of games. Designers can increase customer engagement with a product or service by incorporating gameplay features into non-gaming contexts, a process known as **gamification** or **gamestorming**.

  Designers may increase user engagement with an existing system by including sufficiently entertaining elements like leaderboards and badges.
- **SCAMPER:** A quick, simple, and direct method of creative brainstorming is **SCAMPER**. It Utilizes each of the seven prompts **S-C-A-M-P-E-R** and facilitates directional thinking so that you ask right and relevant questions about the current product/service/solution to form a broader horizon of options/alternatives.

  The abbreviation **SCAMPER**, which stands for "**S**ubstitute, **C**ombine, **A**dapt, **M**odify, **P**ut to other use, **E**liminate, and **R**everse," stands for these seven directives. This activity-based thinking approach encourages ideation.

  SCAMPER is covered extensively in chapter-7

The Secrets of Design Thinking Mindset

- **Mindmapping:** A **mind map** is a visual representation of thoughts and concepts. It is a visual thinking tool that aids in information structure, enhancing your capacity for analysis, comprehension, synthesizing, memory, and idea generation.

   Information is organized far more precisely to how your brain actually functions in a **mind map** than it is in standard note-taking or a linear text. It activates your brain in a much, much fuller level and supports all of its cognitive processes since it is an activity that combines analytical thinking with creative expression.

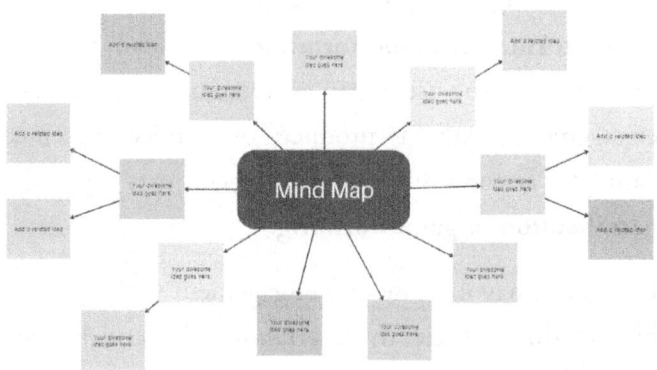

- **Sketchstorming:** In a unique method of brainstorming called **sketchstorming**, sketches are used to create ideas. Each team member sketches a solution to the current challenge and shares it with the other team members as they practice **sketchstorming**. Next, the group decides which suggestion is the best. Before delving into the specifics, **sketchstorming** not only enables a product team to swiftly identify a large number of potential solutions but also to gain a deeper grasp of the issue area.

   Sketchstorming is particularly helpful in the early phases of the product design process when product teams must investigate the issue space, talk about numerous concepts, and decide on the design direction.

WHAT IS A PROTOTYPE?

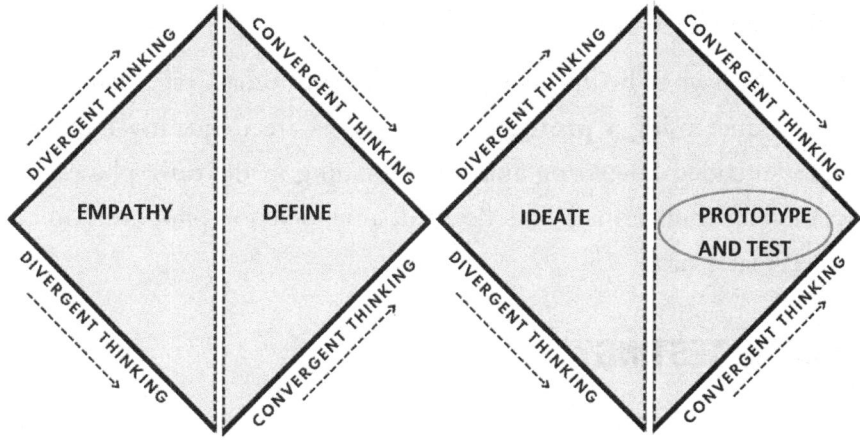

The final testing phase frequently uses **prototyping**, which is a crucial stage in the **design thinking** process. Every product has potential customers and is created in some manner to address their needs.

You build an **almost-working model** or **mock-up** of the product, known as a **prototype**, and test it with potential customers and stakeholders to see whether it truly answers the issues of its consumers.

As a result, **prototyping** enables you to check the viability of the existing design and maybe look into what potential customers may think and feel about the product.

It permits appropriate testing and investigating design ideas before an excessive amount of resources are employed.

You may build **basic, scaled-down prototypes** of your product through **prototyping**, and then use them to **monitor, record**, and **evaluate** user performance levels or users' general behavior and responses to the overall design. Then, you may make the necessary improvements or potential changes in the right trajectory.

Simple sketches, storyboards, crude paper prototypes, and even **role-playing prototypes** that represent a service offering are all examples of **prototypes**.

They don't have to be finished goods. In fact, you may test a component of a product using a **prototype**. **Prototypes** are frequently rapid and crude, intended for testing and understanding in the early phases, and occasionally full-formed and detailed, intended for pilot tests in the project's later stages.

WHAT IS TESTING?

To evaluate your product/service design's performance and discover areas that require improvement, testing entails obtaining input from actual or intended consumers.

The Test and Prototype phases typically follow one another, with prototypes being modified (or replaced) in response to user feedback before being tested once more until the final stage when the product or service is ready for launch.

The **test stage** is crucial to:
- Keep the **user at the center** of decision-making by determining whether the product/service design meets their needs rather than being driven by assumptions.
- Identify usability and accessibility issues early so that the user experience can be optimized before implementation, thereby saving time and money.
- Make unanticipated discoveries that were not made during the **Empathize stage** and this might invalidate or reframe the issue or the proposed solution.

Why Design Thinking in Business Is Important?

ABC Pvt. Ltd. company is planning to launch a mobile phone exclusively for those who are above 60 years of age.

1. Can you use the design thinking process and suggest a solution?
2. Study the chapters in this book and then attempt to design the phone again.

You will be amazed to see the difference in both the solutions.

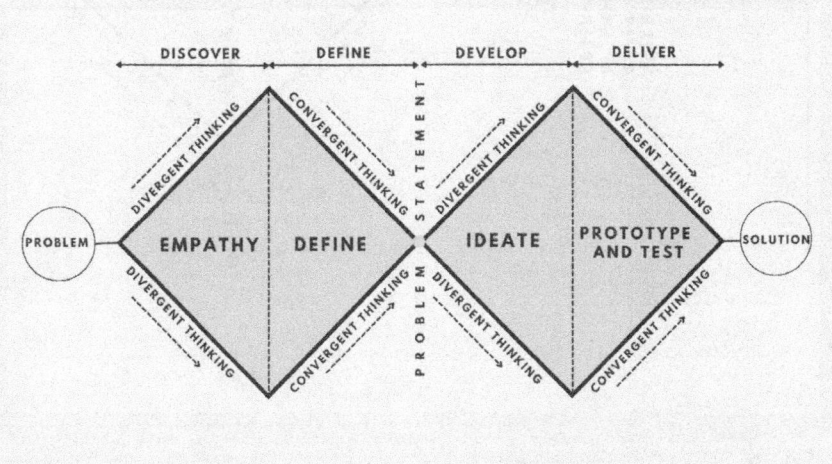

THE SECRETS OF DESIGN THINKING MINDSET – A BLUEPRINT

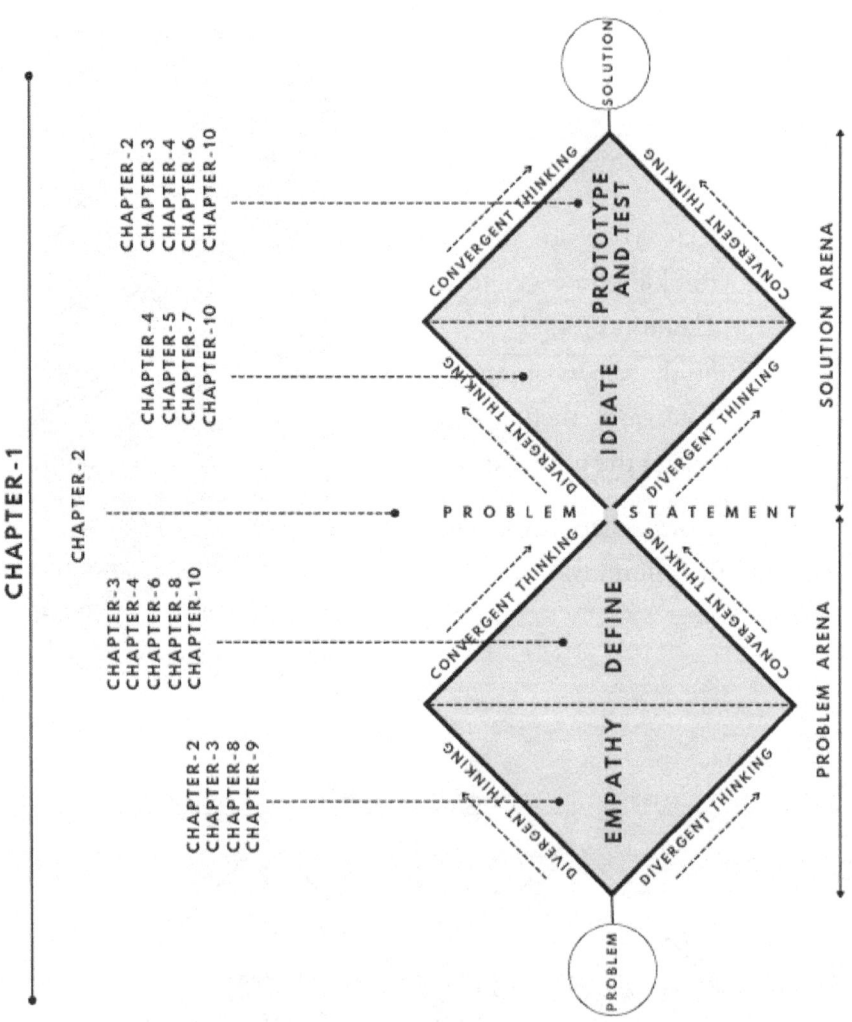

"The formulation of the problem is often more essential than its solution, which may be merely a matter of mathematical or experimental skill"

– **Albert Einstein**

2

DO YOU SOLVE PROBLEMS OR SYMPTOMS?

HAVE YOU BEEN IN AMEER'S SITUATION?

Ameer who has been working on a project has been experiencing challenging times. Four times in a row, in his new role, his diagnosis of the issues is not yielding positive results.

Whenever there is an escalation on an issue by the client, Ameer is very quick in giving solutions to those issues or problems. So, what is wrong with offering quick solutions?

For all the issues for which he had given quick solutions, the problem reappeared after a certain timeframe.

It was discovered by the upper management that Ameer, in the process of getting rid of the issues/problems ASAP, is coming up with solutions to the problem which are the so-called band-aid solutions.

In other words, Ameer was not solving the real problem, but the symptoms of those.

Have you been in a situation where the problem that you think you have solved keeps resurfacing repeatedly?

In this chapter, you will discover some tools and techniques to help you identify the problem and solve it effectively.

WHAT IS A PROBLEM?

What do you understand from the picture in the next page?

Do You Solve Problems or Symptoms?

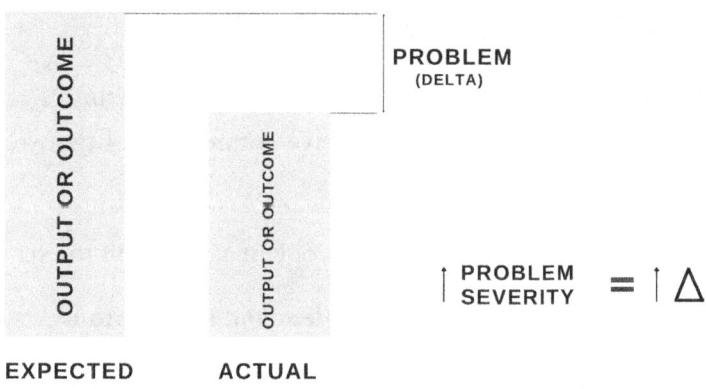

Now, can you correlate? Yes, the difference between the expected output/outcome and the actual one is called a **problem**.

So, the intensity of the problem is directly proportional to the difference between the expected and actual output or the outcome which is the gap, or the delta.

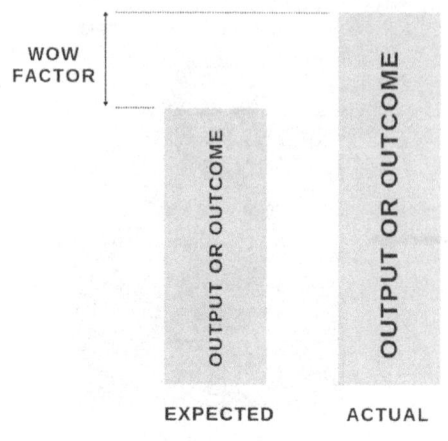

On the other hand, what if the expected and actual are reversed?

It creates a **WOW factor** and your customer will be pleased with the service or the product you offer.

Study the **Kano Reaction model** in this book (Chapter-5) to know more about how to create WOW moments with exciting features in your service or product.

HOLDING THE WRONG END OF THE STICK?

If the problem or the issue or an undesired event is recurring or repeating at frequent time intervals, then you have gotten hold of the wrong end of the stick.

In such cases, you are not solving the problem at hand but the symptoms.

What is the difference between a **problem** and its **symptoms**?

The distinction between treating a condition's symptoms and curing it in medicine is straightforward.

God forbid! If you have a fracture in your arm, for instance, it hurts or pains a lot! You can get rid of this pain by taking painkillers. It will soothe you and mask the real pain, but only for a stipulated time, say, for two hours.

What happens after those two hours? Yes, the pain resurfaces. Again, you take the painkillers, this time at a higher dosage. It will again mask your pain may be for four hours this time.

What happens after those four hours? You will start feeling the pain again.

Why?

Because you have not addressed the fracture but the symptom of that fracture – the pain.

BARKING UP THE WRONG TREE?

Most of the time, we fail to distinguish between the problem and its symptoms.

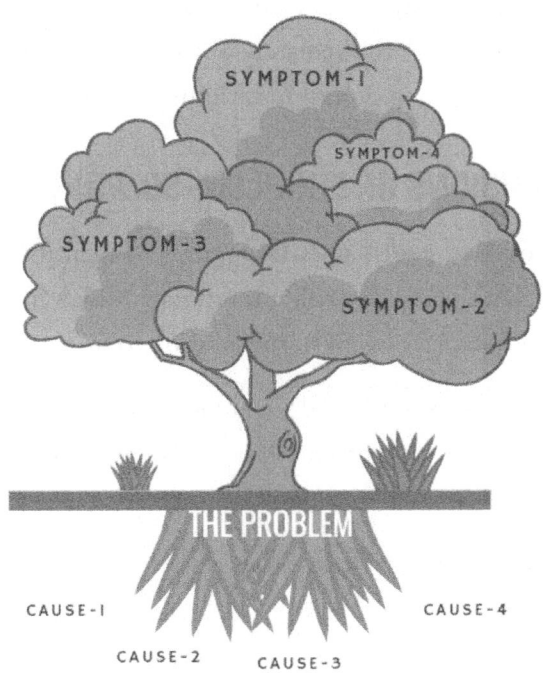

What you see, feel or experience through your five senses, ninety-nine percent of the time, is the **symptom**. To get to the real problem, we need to go a little deeper or dig a little deeper.

Can you find where **the problem** is located in the tree picture?

Yes, it's below the surface.

It is very human to react to the issues/problems that go wrong and immediately try to fix them. As this immediate fix gives immediate results (like the pain disappearing), all humans are tempted to take this route. It is not your fault. That is how the brain works – the threat response.

And also, finding the real problem will take time as you have to analyze, and diagnose the current issue, but worth the time spent on it rather than being on painkillers until the next worse thing happens.

But what should you do if a problem in the project, team, or family occurs? Do you treat the symptoms right away or do you pause to think if a deeper issue genuinely needs your attention? If you only take care of the symptoms, or what is immediately obvious, the problem will almost certainly come up again and need to be addressed again.

THE 8-DIMENSIONS OF PROBLEM-SOLVING

The **8-D** approach of **problem-solving** aims to identify the underlying cause of a problem, come up with a temporary, quick fix to contain the problem, and put in place a long-term solution to stop reoccurring issues.

The **8-D** approach is a great initial step to identify and solve the problems when it's obvious that your product/service is flawed or isn't meeting the needs of your consumers.

Here is the flow diagram of the 8-D process.

Keep reading!

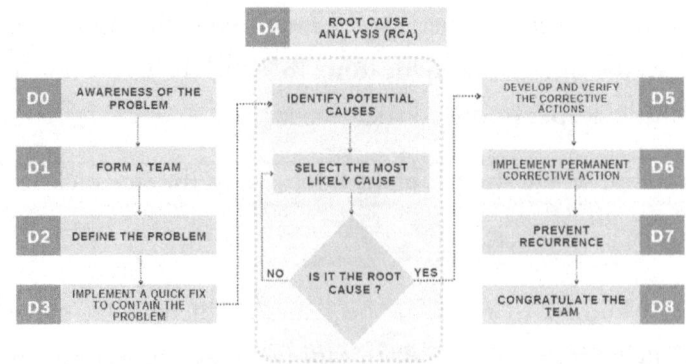

- **D0 - Awarness of the Problem**

You should have complete cognizance of the problem before heading to forming a CFT (Cross Functional Team).

If possible, you can do a **Gemba walk** and thoroughly understand the following:

1. Who is being impacted?
2. How significant or serious is the impact?
3. Is it an emergency?
4. When was the problem observed?
5. Where has the problem occurred?
6. Is there a trend?

- **D1 - Form a Team**

A **Cross-Functional Team (CFT)** team of 3 to 5 from different departments or disciplines or functions representing the product, process, and data must be formed.

Any problem or issue is always multidisciplinary and one person may not have adequate information about the issue at hand.

Here the team can apply the **inductive** techniques or **deductive** techniques to collect, analyze and brainstorm the issue at hand.

There must always be a **champion** to moderate the session and communicate with all the stakeholders.

▪ D2 - Define the Problem

With the team in place and having collected the primary data, now the problem has to be defined.

A wrong problem statement will lead to a wrong result or solution which would waste your time, money, and resources.

Let's do an exercise:

I strongly recommend you write a problem statement as per your current understanding of it – about the issue that you or your client is facing.

You will write the same problem statement again after learning the technique and you will appreciate the difference in your understanding of the problem definition.

Write Your Problem Statement Here:

_____

_____

_____

_____

One of the techniques to write an effective problem statement is **5WTH**.

Do You Solve Problems or Symptoms?

	QUESTIONS	YOUR ANSWERS
WHO	Who is impacted? Who is the customer?	**NAME** Alpha Beta Pvt. Ltd.
WHAT	What is the impact of the problem?	**MAGNITUDE IN NUMBERS** The company reported a 23% reduction in the sale with an estimated cost of $ 26000 (USD)
WHERE	Where has the problem occurred?	**LOCATION** The problem is from the service provider's end
WHEN	When did the problem occur?	**TIME/DATE** The decline in numbers was first noticed 4 months ago
WHY	Why is it a problem?	**PAIN POINTS** The repeated decline in their monthly sales
HOW	How is the problem observed?	**SYMPTOMS** lesser QoQ and QTD revenue
HOW MANY	How Much/How Many times?	**FREQUENCY/QUANTITY** Every month on an average of $8500 (USD) was the loss

Let us take an example and frame a robust problem statement.

Putting all the **5WTH** answer pieces together.

> *For the past 4 months, Alpha Beta Pvt. Ltd. has reported a 23% reduction in their sale which is estimated at $26000 (USD) against the target.*
>
> *This issue has been found to have originated from XYZ Pvt. Ltd. (service provider's end).*
>
> *This issue has been reappearing month-on-month for the past 4 months with an average monthly loss of $8500 (USD).*

The Secrets of Design Thinking Mindset

 Fill up this template with an issue or problem that you or your client/team is facing.

QUESTIONS	YOUR ANSWERS
WHO — Who is impacted? Who is the customer?	**NAME**
WHAT — What is the impact of the problem?	**MAGNITUDE IN NUMBERS**
WHERE — Where has the problem occurred?	**LOCATION**
WHEN — When did the problem occur?	**TIME/DATE**
WHY — Why is it a problem?	**PAIN POINTS**
HOW — How is the problem observed?	**SYMPTOMS**
HOW MANY — How Much/How Many times?	**FREQUENCY/QUANTITY**

Compile Your Problem Statement Here:

_____

_____

_____

_____

Do you observe the difference in the problem statement that you had written earlier and now?

Of course, to write a problem statement based on the **5WTH** technique, you will have to research a bit more to gather the facts to answer those questions which will take some time, but worth it.

As you know, the devil is in the details or detailing. The more detailed and quantitative your problem statement is, the easier to find the root cause and the solution.

Alternatively, you can use the following template to quickly report or understand the issue.

You are reporting the problem statement to your manager or the management on behalf of the user or customer.

> _____ (person/entity/customer), who is our _____ (relationship with the person/customer), is trying to _____ (action verb), but he/she/they is/are facing _____ (impediment, barrier) because _____ (cause), since/for _____ (period/timeframe) which is making them feel _____ (emotional reaction). This has led to a _____ impact/loss (business impact in numbers or percentage as applicable).

This is how your problem statement gets evolved.

*Krishnan, who is our **premier customer**, is trying to **login into a portal**, but he is facing **issues with the website being hanged** because **of internet connectivity** for **the last two days** which is making him feel **frustrated**. This has led to a **delay in the online submission of the document**.*

One more.

ABC Pvt. Ltd.**, who **has signed up with us for digital marketing services**, is trying **to get 50% more buyers for their products from the e-commerce websites**, but they are facing **challenges in the number of visitors to their product page** since **the beginning of this year**, which is making them feel **unhappy that we have not delivered on our promises**. This has led to **a 20% reduction in product sales and a 34% drop in revenue collection.

- ## D3 - Implement a Quick Fix to Contain the Problem

After defining the problem, next, you need to implement a temporary fix or solution to contain or curb the problem at hand so that it does not aggravate and cause more damage.

Usually, in the conventional so-called problem-solving method, individuals or teams jump to this D3 phase without doing D0, D1, and D2 due diligence whenever they face the problem and stop the process at D3. Because at D3, you will see immediate green shoots, which is instant relief from the problem, and hence the team thinks they have solved the problem – but, on the other side, there is an accident waiting to happen, which eventually they will confront after a specified time frame.

Back to Earth, in this phase, we find an **Interim Corrective Action (ICA)**, sometimes referred to as **First Aid treatment**, which is adopted temporarily until a **Permanent Corrective Action (PCA)** is taken and eventually replace with **ICA**.

To contain the problem, you need to identify the whole pipeline – the start of the process till the end. The reason a quick fix or an interim solution has to be adopted is we can't always halt the process and wait until the **Permanent Corrective Action** is identified and deployed. A band-aid has to be applied until the problem is solved. That is why it is also referred to as a **first-aid treatment.**

This is the phase, where you have to study the process document and flow charts to identify the slip.

You will learn about the widely used three types of flowcharts viz.,

1. Process flowchart
2. Decision flowchart
3. Rummler-Brache chart (Swimlane chart)

You can study the relevant charts which can give you a thorough understanding of the flow to identify the gaps and suggest a quick fix.

Let's see them one by one:

1. Process Flowchart

A **process flowchart** is a diagram that outlines the **sequential steps** and the decision-making stages that must be taken for the process to proceed. Every step in the chart is denoted by a shape. To depict the flow and direction of the process, arrows and lines are used.

☐ Start or end of the process

☐ Steps or processing function

▱ Input or output

◇ Decision-making and branching

→ ↓ ← ↑ Flow lines

There are more symbols, but we will stick to the above, the most ubiquitous symbols.

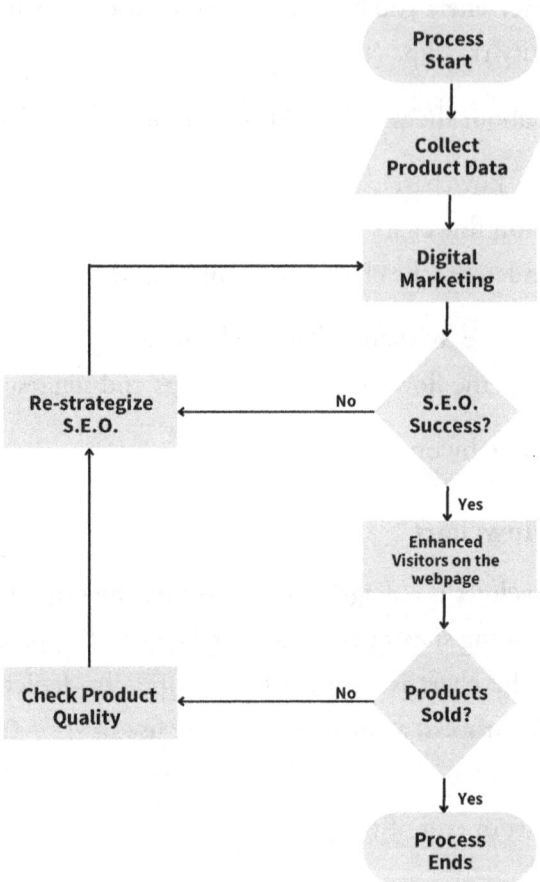

The above is a simple flowchart of the sale of a product. Can you interpret the process? Discuss it with your team.

2. Decision Flowchart

A **decision flowchart** can be of immense assistance to you in weighing the effects of a certain decision you wish to make.

Let's say you are at the fork end of the road and unable to make a decision from the array of choices. A decision flowchart in this situation aids you in putting it out visually and helps in the **decision-making** process.

Do You Solve Problems or Symptoms?

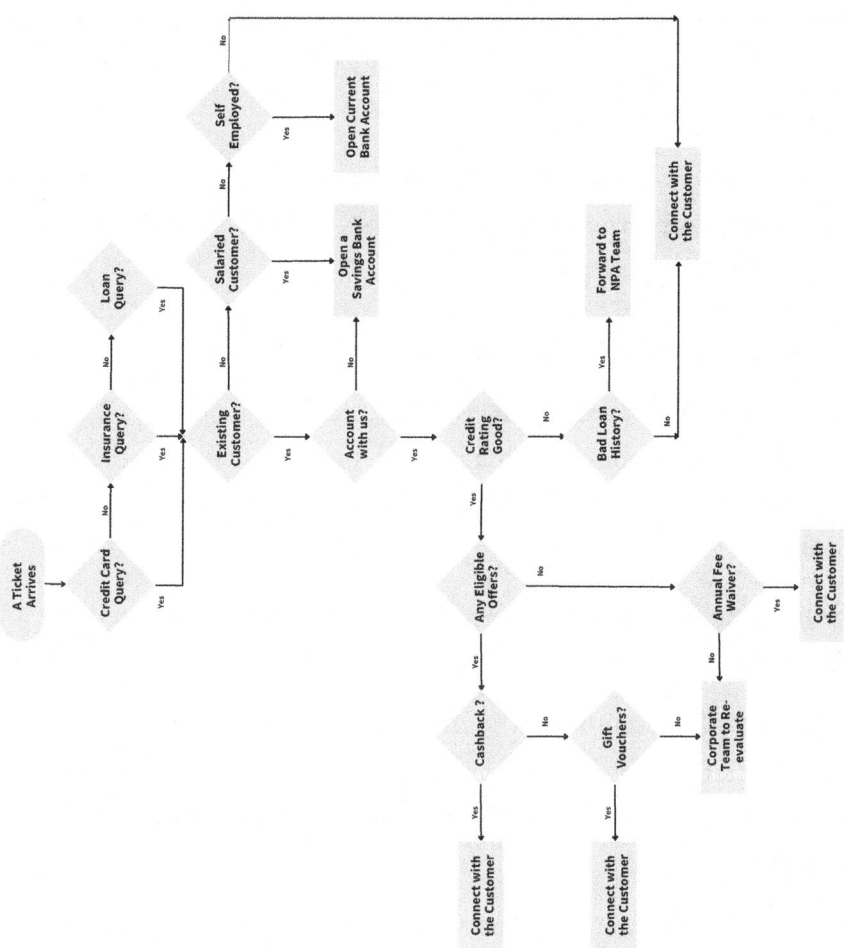

A **decision flowchart** always contains decision shapes like the one you saw in the process chart, even if decision symbols may occasionally be used in a conventional flowchart.

In the **decision flowchart**, at every level, you will see the decision symbol.

You can make out the difference between a **decision flowchart** and a **conventional process flowchart**.

Take a look at the **decision flowchart** for a ticket that fairly represents a commercial banking system that is prepared for a banking intern to make a primary decision.

Can you interpret the process? Can you fix the flaw in the **ticketing decision flowchart** so that the bank does not end up giving any of its products to a defaulter?

3. Rummler-Brache Diagram

A **Rummler-Brache diagram** is a sort of flowchart, where it not only depicts a process from beginning to end, but it also classifies these phases to indicate which departments or individuals are in charge of each set of activities.

Swimlane diagrams were described in detail by **Geary Rummler** and **Alan Brache** in their 1990 book *Improved Processes*.

In honor of the authors who created the initial model, this type of flowchart is often referred to as a **cross-functional diagram** (with swimlanes being dubbed **functional bands**) or a **Rummler-Brache diagram**.

These lanes, which are rows, maintain visual separation between various tasks.

A **swimlane** chart clarifies roles better than a typical flowchart. Knowing which department is in charge of what when trying to enhance procedures may expedite the process of addressing inefficiencies and removing delays.

Swimlanes aid in pinpointing not just the bottlenecks in a process but also the functional area in charge of each one during any process/improvement endeavor.

In a world where departments frequently don't understand what the other departments do, a swimlane diagram helps define the duties and assists the departments to work together.

Do You Solve Problems or Symptoms?

The following swimlane refers to an online order placed by the client. Can you identify a flawed notification in the swimlane chart?

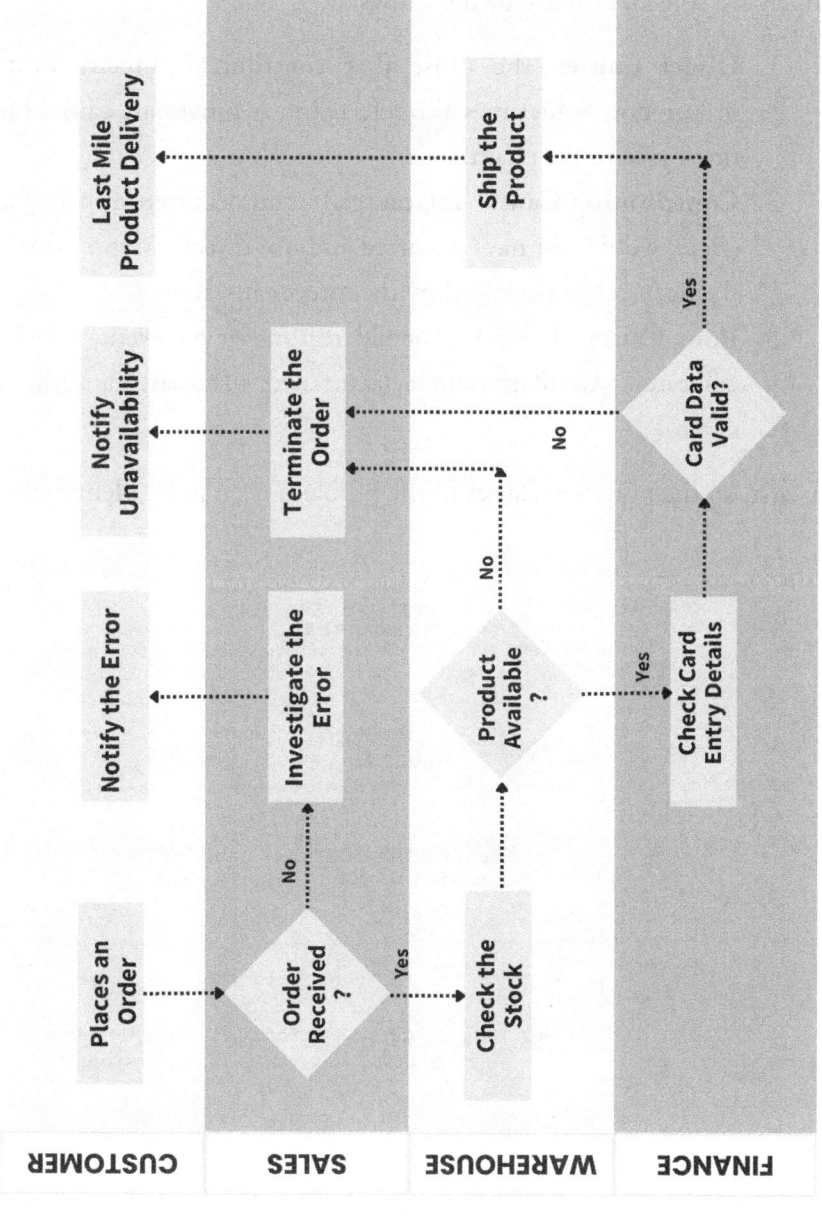

▪ D4 - Root Cause Analysis (RCA)

After having **defined the problem** and made a thorough study of the process, the next is to do the **Root Cause Analysis (RCA)**.

Largely we consider the following causes:

1. **Direct Cause:** The cause that contributed directly to the occurrence. Sometimes also referred to as proximate causes (The first cause in the chain).
2. **Contributing Cause:** The cause(s) of an occurrence that, if left alone, would not have occurred and not directly responsible for the occurrence (followed by the direct causes).
3. **Root Cause:** The fundamental reason for an event, which if corrected, would prevent a recurrence. (The last cause in the chain).

So, first, all the potential causes of the problem need to be identified.

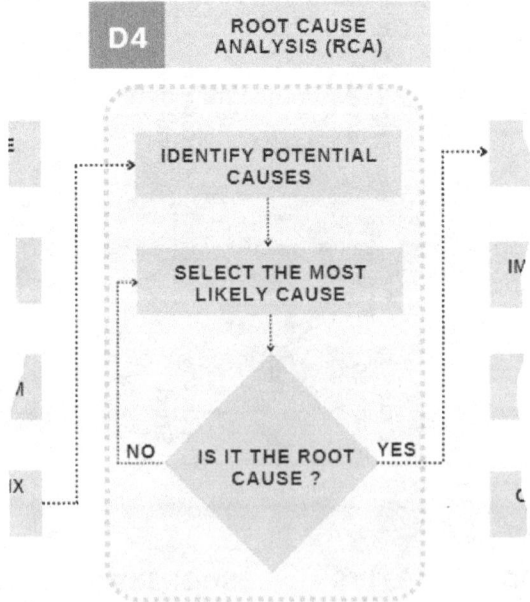

The following are the three methods we will discuss for finding the potential causes:

1. The 5 Whys
2. The Ishikawa Diagram
3. Fault Tree Analysis (FTA)

1. The 5 Whys

A **problem-solving** strategy known as the **Five Whys (5-whys)** focuses on the basic causes and implications of particular problems.

The Japanese inventor and industrialist, **Sakichi Toyoda**, is credited with devising the **Five Whys technique**. In the Toyota Motor Corporation, this technique spread quickly and is still often applied today.

The primary goal is to determine the root cause of a problem or fault by continuously asking "**Why?**" According to anecdotal evidence, the answer to the question "**Why?**" can usually be discovered after five repetitions of the **WHY** statement, which is why the number five is included in this phrase.

The number five is only a generalization. After two or three instances of asking "**Why**", the fundamental reason is occasionally already discovered; other times, more than five times of asking "Why" are necessary.

The core concept is to break down an issue by continually questioning it (often five times) about the **WHY** until it can no longer be further broken down, bringing it to the lowest common denominator, which hopefully leads to the root reasons truly sought.

How to Apply the 5 Why?
Step-1

Form a **Cross Functional Team (CFT)** with members from several departments. Each representative must be knowledgeable about the investigation procedure.

Having a cross-functional team will allow you to hear various perspectives.

This will assist you in gathering sufficient data to make a wise conclusion. Be aware that the team must work together to complete this mission, which cannot be done alone.

Problem

Why?	Proximate Cause
Why?	Contributing Cause
Why?	Contributing Cause
Why?	Contributing Cause
Why?	The Root Cause

Root Cause

Step-2

Start with a specific problem that you have already defined in the **D2 phase**. What exactly are you struggling with? This might assist the team in concentrating on the same issue.

Ask, *why the issue occurred?* and then note the response beneath the exact issue you identified in step one.

Ask **"why"** to each of the subsequent responses you record, until you identify the problem's underlying cause.

Once more, it could require more or less than five whys. Make sure your team agrees on the final root cause and each of the questions being addressed.

Do You Solve Problems or Symptoms?

A five is just a generalization. Sometimes the essential root cause is already known after two or three times of asking "Why," while other times, more than five times of asking "Why" are required.

The e-bike was recalled from the market	Problem
Why?	Because there were a series of incidences of bikes catching fire
Why?	Because the battery was overheated
Why?	Because the thermal runaway phenomenon
Why?	Because the voltage and temperature crossed the critical values
Why?	Poor quality electrodes used by the battery manufacturer
Root Cause	

In this example of **recalling the e-bikes** from the market by the manufacturing company.

You will notice how a series of asking **Why** questions have led to identifying a root cause.

You observe that the poor quality of electrodes used in the battery were the root casue of the recall.

Step-3

Once the root cause has been identified, you need to proceed to find the **corrective actions (D5)**.

2. The Ishikawa Diagram

Ishikawa diagram (also called **fishbone diagrams** or **herringbone diagrams**, or **cause-and-effect diagrams**) essentially aids in understanding the **cause and effect** link. It is a very useful tool because it provides a visual picture of what causes issues or phenomena.

Who is Ishikawa?

Dr. Kaoru Ishikawa, a Professor at the University of Tokyo's engineering school, well known for his quality management techniques, is the pioneer of the **Ishikawa Diagram (fishbone diagram)** and made a significant contribution to the Japanese concept of quality management. Understanding the significance or justification of the **Ishikawa Diagram (fishbone diagram)** is essential in identifying the potential causes of a problem.

It is referred to as a fishbone because of the form it takes after being created. Its composition mimics the bones or spines of fish.

The rightmost section, the fish's head, has the problem written there. Its spine, which features arrows that resemble bones leading to the **primary causes**, runs on the left. The **secondary causes** are established under those primary causes.

In a typical diagram, causes are often classified, with the following categories being the most prevalent::

1. **8 Ms** (typically for manufacturing plants)
   Men/people, Machines, Methods, Materials, Measurement, Mother Nature, Management/Money, Maintenance
2. **8 Ps** (typically for marketing)
   Product, Price, Promotion, Place, People, Process/Procedure, Packaging, Physical evidence
3. **5 Ss** (typically for the service industry)
   Surroundings, Suppliers, Standardized Documentation, Systems, Skills
4. **7 Ss** (model by McKinsey)
   Strategy, Structure, Systems, Shared Values, Skills, Style, Staff

Do You Solve Problems or Symptoms?

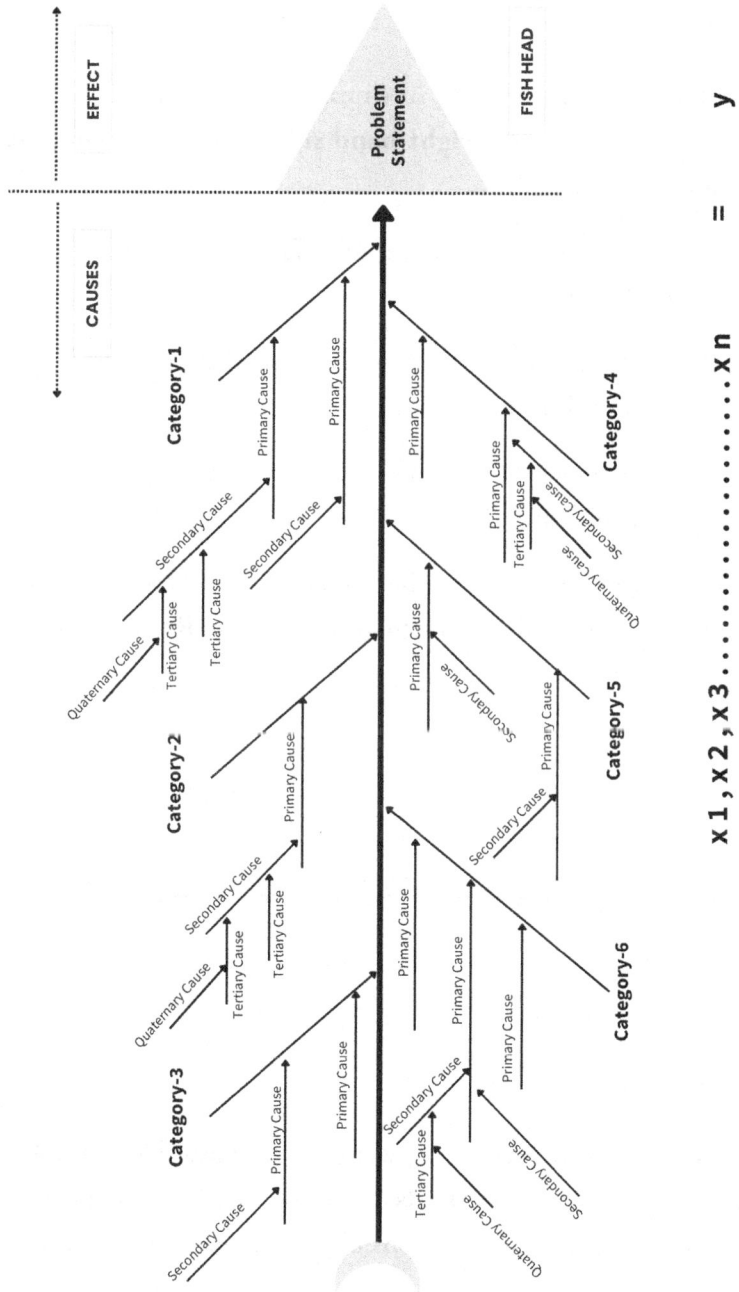

The Secrets of Design Thinking Mindset

How to Apply the Fishbone Technique?

Step-1

The **problem statement** or the **business problem** that has been defined needs to be written on the **right-hand side** which is the **effect section** (fish head).

Let's take an example of **Incomplete Tickets** for a non-production service in an IT company.

The **problem statement** is written on the **effect side** of the fishbone which is also called the **fish head**.

This problem statement is the same one that you learned in the **D2 phase – Define the Problem**.

In this example, after all the due diligence, the team has found that incomplete tickets are the problem at hand whose **Root Cause Analysis (RCA)** has to be done.

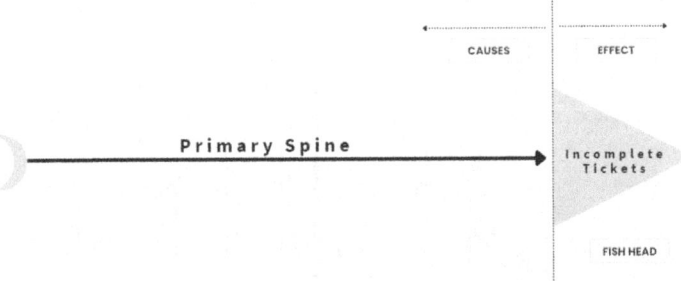

Step-2

A **cross-functional team** (both upward and downward responsible teams) has decided that **Men, Methods, Systems, Skills, Management**, and **Suppliers** are the categories responsible for the incomplete tickets.

These finalized categories are depicted on the **secondary spines** of the fishbone.

Do You Solve Problems or Symptoms?

Mathematically, the incomplete tickets problem (y) is the **function** of Men, Methods, Systems, Skills, Management, and Suppliers (x's).

$$f(x) = y$$

$$f(men, method, system, skill, management, supplier) = y$$

```
                              CAUSES          EFFECT

       Systems      Method      Men
          \           \          \
           \Sec.Spine  \Sec.Spine \Sec.Spine
            \           \          \
    ─────────────────────────────────────→  Incomplete
            /           /          /         Tickets
           /Sec.Spine  /Sec.Spine /Sec.Spine
          /           /          /           FISH HEAD
       Skills     Management   Supplier
```

$$x_1, x_2, x_3 \ldots\ldots x_n = y$$

Note: if the head of the fish is on the left-hand side then we can write **y = f(x)**. Mathematically, it doesn't make any difference as long as **x's** are **independent variables** and **y** is a **dependent variable**; however, to align (with the diagram) the head with **y** and the spines with **f(x)**, **f(x) = y** has been used.

Step-3

Once, the main categories have been finalized, next, the team will **brainstorm** on the **primary responsible causes** for each of these categories.

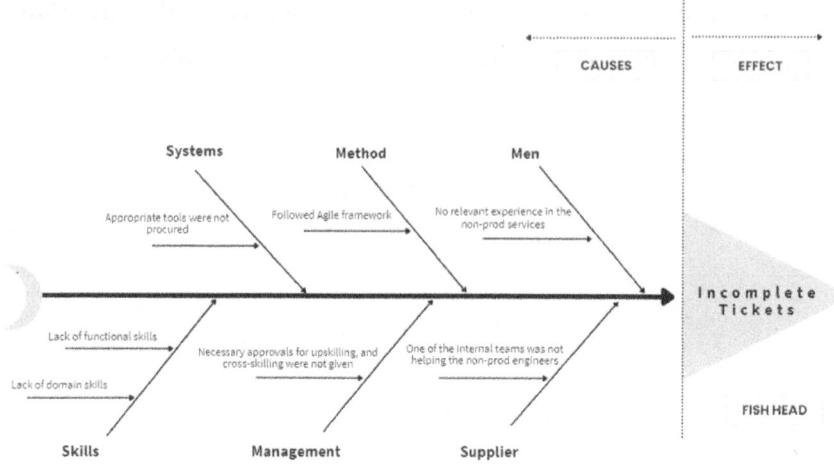

The team has discovered the **primary causes** and depicted them on the **secondary spines** of the fish body on the left side.

Step-4

The next step is to find the **secondary causes** for each of the **primary causes**.

Determine the higher levels of cause details, then continue classifying them into related causes or groups. Asking a series of **Why questions** will help you achieve this.

Here a **Why** or the **5-Why technique** will be adopted. Keep asking the series of **Why** to each of these **primary causes** to get to the **secondary causes**.

Example: We'll use a series of **why** questions to fill in the detailed levels for the **primary causes** listed under each of the main categories.

Q: Why there is no relevant experience in non-prod services?
A: The talents were moved from the different internal teams.
      Q: Why were they moved from the different internal teams?
      A: There were excess team members in their teams.
      A: The hiring was frozen.

Do You Solve Problems or Symptoms?

Q: Why followed the Agile framework?
A: A team member had completed an online agile course.
A: The entire org was following, so we also followed.
    Q: Why did you follow the org?
    A: We would be left as an odd one out in the org.

Q: Why the appropriate tools were not procured?
A: Lack of money.
A: Nobody is aware of the tools.

Q: Why there was a lack of domain knowledge?
A: No training was given to the team.
    Q: Why was no training given?
    A: There is no training team.
        Q: Why there is no training team?
        A: The company is new. Only 2 HR personnel.
A: No domain expert to train
    Q: Why no domain experts?
    A: They have not been hired.

Q: Why were necessary upskilling/cross-skilling approvals not given?
A: No representation of the team at the management level.

Now, represent those staggered Q&As on the fishbone.

Likewise, you need to populate the other spines of the fishbone.

A fully formed fishbone is constructed for enhancing your understanding.

The Secrets of Design Thinking Mindset

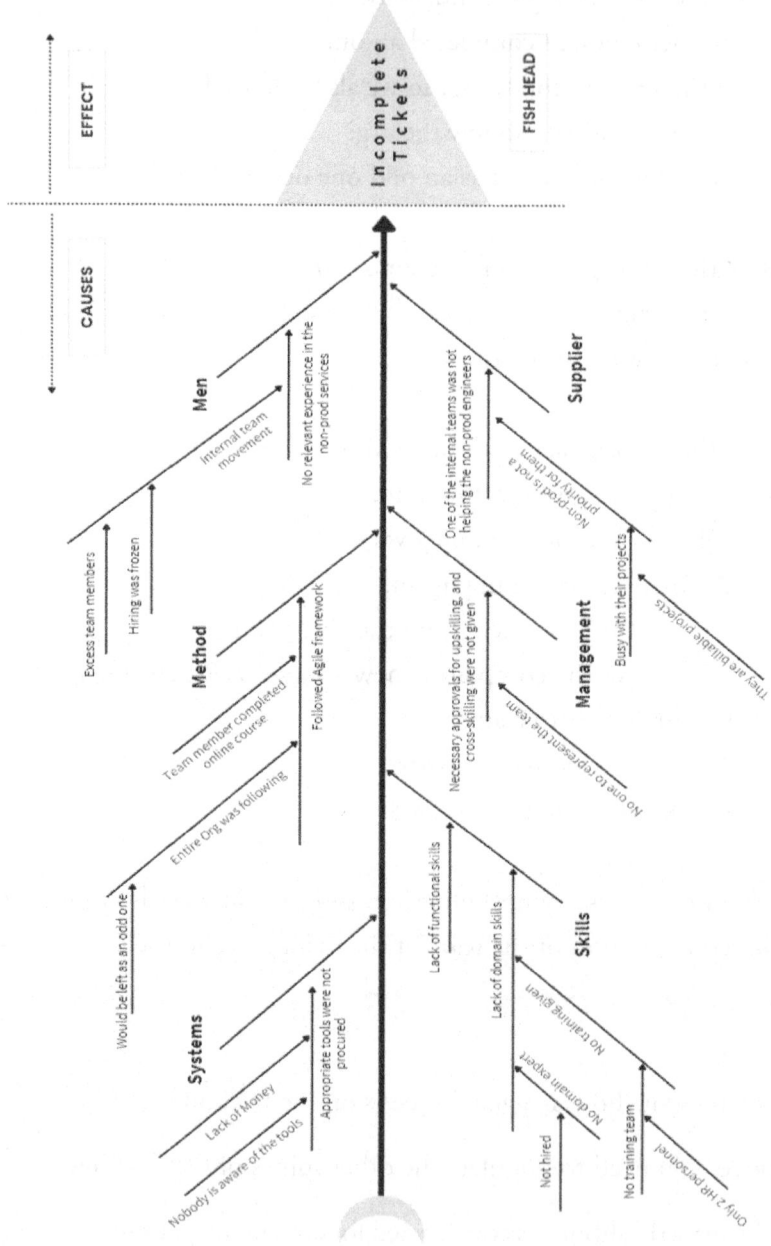

As you can see the fishbone now has matured with all the potential reasons for the problem.

Primary causes lead to **secondary causes**, which further lead to **tertiary causes**, which, further lead to **quaternary** causes, which can further lead to **quinary causes**, and so on – senary, septenary, octonary, nonary, and denary, until the dead end for the cause is reached.

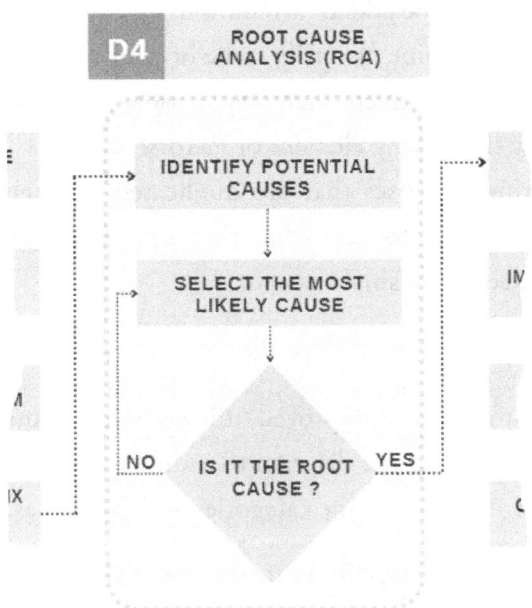

It must be kept in mind that $f(x1, x2,.....xn) = y$; which means all the sub-causes you have listed at each level must affect the problem which is mentioned on the fish head.

Step-5

At this stage, it is wise to step back and re-look at the causes and prune the branches, if any, of the $f(x)$ causes are irrelevant to y – **the problem**.

You can ask the following questions to resize the fishbone:

- Was the **problem statement** overly vague, and is my diagram far too complicated? If yes, can it be made simpler by changing the statement or by dividing the diagram into different diagrams that deal with relevant issues?
- Are there any categories left that still make logical sense? Should any sub-cause be added or removed?
- Can you combine or clarify some of your main causes?
- Have you examined each key reason thoroughly enough to identify the driving element or factors?
- Are primary causes that are duplicated throughout categories largely unique to each one they appear in, or can they be combined into a single category?

Step-6

After the diagram has been improved, it is necessary to quantify them by the **weighting values** to the diagram to indicate the degree of influence or likely impact that each of the categories and causes has.

The objective of this stage is to make the diagram more usable by emphasizing the most significant discoveries, identifying different finding types, or adding information to the diagram to make it more useful.

One straightforward way to do this might be to bold or use a red color font for the description of the one key reason under each category that is thought to have the biggest effect on that category.

You can **prioritize** these sub-reasons with **High-Medium-Low impact** levels and at a **category level**, you can distribute the weights as percentages summing to 100%.

For example:

- Men (10%)
- Method (15%)
- Systems (30%)

Do You Solve Problems or Symptoms?

- Skills (20%)
- Management (5%)
- Supplier (20%)

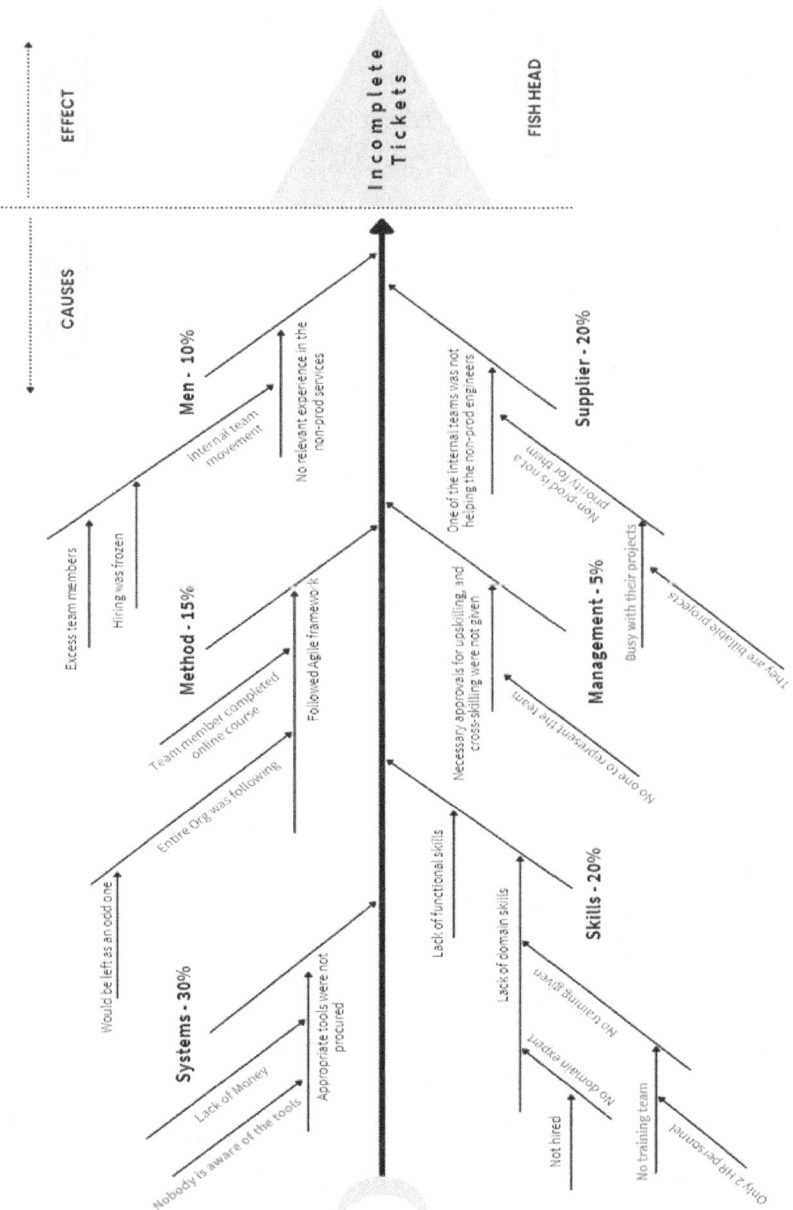

Step-7

The next step is to scan the entire diagram for the significant underlying causes that will be the subject of the subsequent phases. These could be the factors that cross numerous categories, receive the greatest weighted impact ratings, or are deemed the most critical by the evaluation committee, and these root causes that you can effectively address in the time, scope, or money you have available. Then, to achieve your desired goals, you must determine which "root" factor is the most crucial and act on it first.

3. Fault Tree Analysis

The **Fault Tree Analysis** uses **Boolean algebra** to identify a **problem's root cause**. It is a logical, deductive, visual method to find the root cause.

Using a graphical representation known as the **Fault Tree**, it starts with a clearly stated problem and works backward to uncover what elements contributed to the problem. It follows a **top-down methodology**, beginning with the problem and analyzing the contributing components. By analyzing key events to determine the reasons for breakdowns, shutdowns, malfunction, etc., **Fault Tree Analysis** employs **logical symbols** to pinpoint faults at the lower levels of a system. A **Fault Tree** diagram uses **events** and **logic gates** to show the failure chain. To identify the cause of failure, it links events tested on true/false claims together.

STANDARD SYMBOLS IN FTA

- Event Symbols

The components at the lowest level in a **Fault Tree** diagram are **events**. They represent the occasions that precede higher-level gates and finally the top-level gate. Events frequently have an associated probability of occurring. The probabilities of all the intermediate levels and the top-level gates may be calculated as event probabilities propagate up the diagram.

Do You Solve Problems or Symptoms?

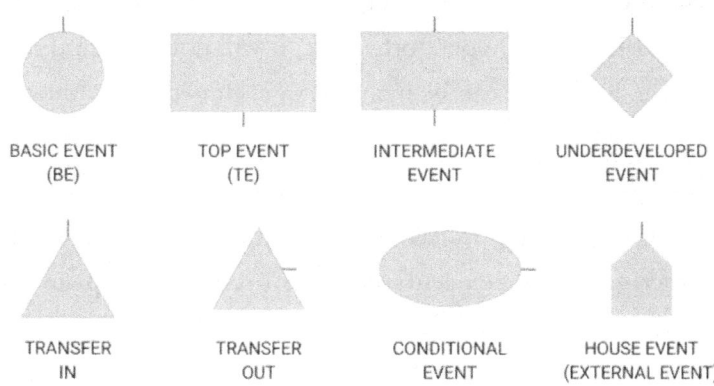

Basic Events (BE): In most cases, the top event is caused by these events. At the base of the Fault Tree, is where they are always located.

Top Event (TE): These kinds of occurrences are at the root of the Fault Tree and call for a system failure investigation. Because it is the beginning of the failure, it has a single input but no related outputs.

Intermediate Events (IE): These occurrences are typically brought on by one or more other events. It features an input as well as an output. Its failure might be brought on by another incident, which most likely leads to other failures lower down the Fault Tree.

Underdeveloped Events (UE): These events are classified as subtrees because they lack sufficient information.

Transfer Events (TE): These events are used when a Fault Tree is too lengthy to fit on paper. A symbol hides larger portions of the tree, which extend in a different tree. Transfer-out and transfer-in events are two different categories. Transfer-in events have input at the top of the triangle, whereas transfer-out events have a triangle with output to the right.

Conditional Events (CE): These events take place as prerequisites for an inhibit gate, a particular class of gate.

House Event (HE): These events are used to turn events on and off. If the event is set to 1, it will happen; otherwise, it will not happen if it is set to 0. Parts of the Fault Tree can be included or excluded using house events.

▪ GATE SYMBOLS

The different ways that a process or system might fail are represented by **gates**. Sometimes, a single occurrence might result in a **top-level failure** (or a disastrous failure). A top-level failure event can occasionally result from the interaction of several separate events. Below is a description of the many gates in **FTA**.

▪ TRUTH TABLE

Inputs		Outputs		
A	B	AND	OR	XOR
0	0	0	0	0
0	1	0	1	1
1	0	0	1	1
1	1	1	1	0

AND Gate: All the input events to the gate must occur for the events to take place.

OR Gate: This kind of gate can have one or more inputs, and if one or more input events take place, the output will also happen.

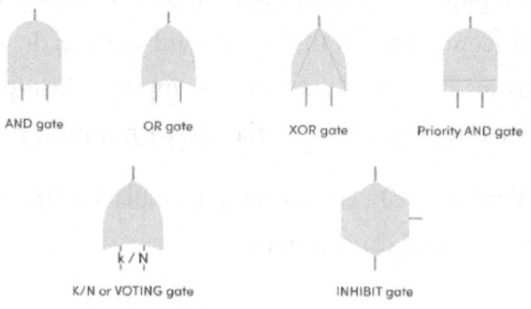

XOR Gate: This gate is a little less typical. Only when one input element appears does an output take place.

Priority AND Gate: This gate opens if the input events all take place in the same set sequence.

k/N Gate: It is also often known as the voting gate, and resembles the OR gate aesthetically. There will be one output event, k, and many input events, N. When the number of input events takes place, the output event does as well. The precise number of inputs must be met to invoke this gate.

How to Apply the FTA?
Step-1

A team with a diversified range of perspectives, viewpoints, knowledge, and skills need to be assembled to perform the FTA. A good FTA conclusion may be ensured through professional-led **brainstorming sessions** and discussions as well as unconventional ideas from participants from the **upstream and downstream process**.

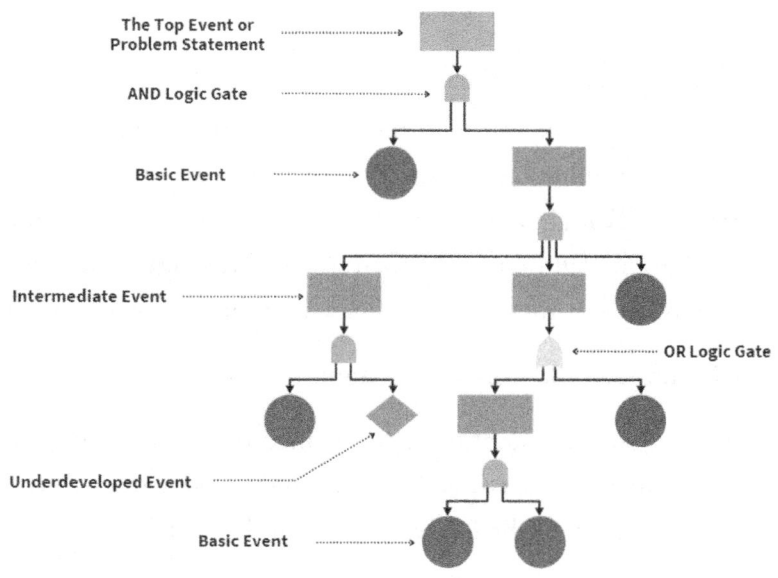

Step-2

Define your system or process which includes the scope of analysis and a definition of what constitutes a failure or a problem – this exercise of defining the problem is already done in the **D2 phase**. Your system or process may have one component or event fail or one function which stops working while the rest of the system continues to work.

The primary goal here is to detect possible failures to construct the **Fault Tree** diagrams. The entire FTA procedure considers the top event and deconstructs the events at all levels and tries to determine how that specific event may have happened.

Step-3

In this step, define or identify the **top-level fault** which can be further discretized using **Boolean**.

Once the possible failures or problems are identified along with their interdependencies, the **Fault Tree** can be drawn. In this step, the endeavor is to visually present the functionality of the system or the problem at hand and its process using **Boolean logic symbols**.

Step-4

In this step, what events might result in the top-level problem? Sort the reasons for the failure according to whether they can happen on their own using their **OR logic gate** symbol, or whether several events must take place before the failure may happen using **AND logic gate** symbol and likewise using the other logic gates based on the event's dependability.

Here is one example from a car manufacturing assembly line.

From these, you can identify the high, medium, and low-impact causes and accordingly choose corrective action and implement it. You will learn this in **D5** and **D6** of the **8-D approach** in the next section.

Do You Solve Problems or Symptoms?

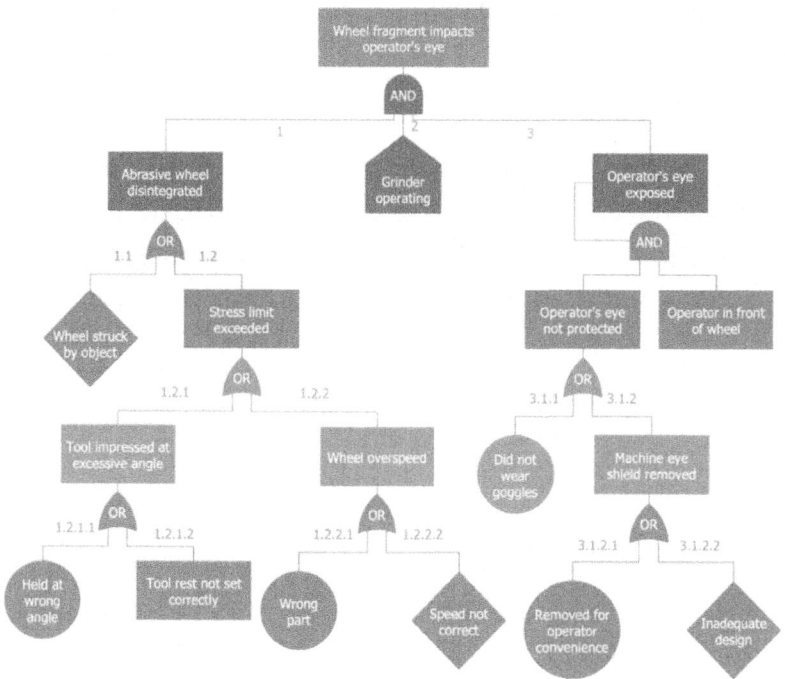

- **D5 - Develop and Verify the Corrective Actions**

Once you are certain that you have identified the underlying **root cause** of the problem from the techniques suggested in the **D4 phase**, it is time to develop a long-lasting remedy. The action taken in this phase will replace your current first aid solution that you came up with in the **D3 phase** to contain the problem.

Note that your problem has been given an interim fix till now – revisit the **D3 phase** for a quick fix.

In this phase, the **corrective action** that you take, apply it on a smaller scale pilot batch, and record or observe if the root cause that you have finalized has subsided the problem under question.

If you observe the problem has been taken care of, then do a **full-scale implementation**. If not, revisit the problem statement or the RCA phase and repeat the exercise.

From the **Performance-Time** chart, **D5** aims to make sure that from **point C** on the graph, you bounce back to **point D** which forms the **J curve** which is also a **recovery curve**. If this **hockey stick recovery** is not observed then you may have to revisit your problem statement and RCA.

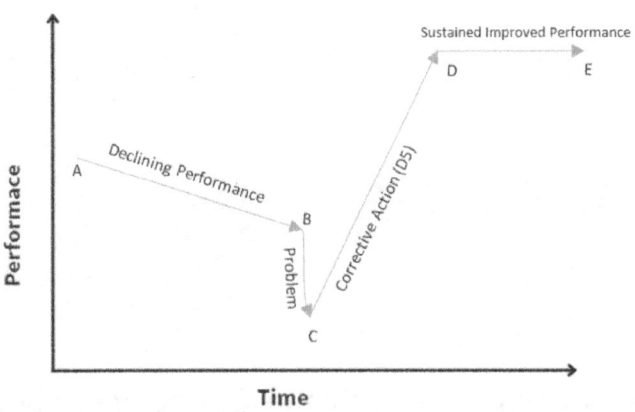

- ### D6 - Implement Permanent Corrective Action

Now, that you see a recovery in the process, you need to implement it across the board and communicate the same to the stakeholders, train the relevant team members, and conduct knowledge-sharing sessions to implement the corrective action as **Permanent Corrective Action (PCA)**.

- ### D7 - Prevent Recurrence

Now, accordingly, your process documents, standard operating procedure, and policies should be updated.

▪ D8 - Congratulate the Team

This is the last step in the 8-D process where you recognize the cross-functional team's performance either by applauding them in the town halls or all-hands or a personal note or incentivizing them.

1. For your current project, can you identify the phase you are in?
   a) A-B?
   b) B-C?
   c) C-D?
   d) D-E?

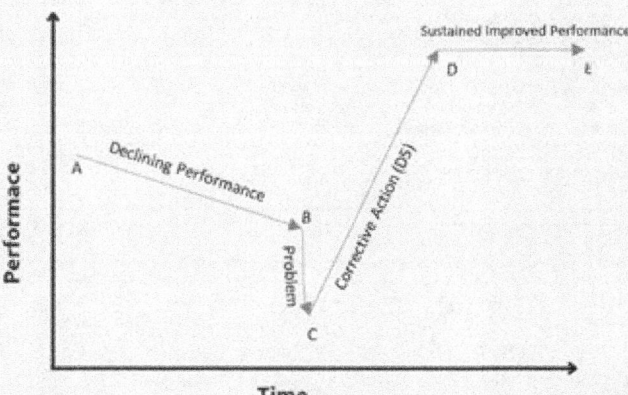

2. After applying the corrective action, does your project experience a J-curve (hockey stick) recovery?
3. Are the process, checks, and balances you have for your project able to reduce the A-B phase? Discuss with your team the implications of the length and slope of the A-B curve.

"Conflict can and should be handled constructively; when it is, relationships benefit. Conflict avoidance is "not" the hallmark of a good relationship. On the contrary, it is a symptom of serious problems and poor communication."

– **Harriet B. Braiker**

3

WHAT…? NOW WHAT…? SO WHAT…?

What…? Now What…? So What…?

> ## HAVE YOU BEEN IN TRACY'S SITUATION?
>
> Of late, Tracy has been promoted to a new role and designation. After taking over the new role, she has been losing her cool and blows her top for petty issues at work and also at home.
>
> With the new senior HR manager role in a private firm, she, now, is responsible for a team of ten HR professionals from recruitment, talent acquisition, compensation and benefit along with the onboarding team reporting to her.
>
> She also interacts with business units in her new role. As the responsibilities are high, her stakeholders feel she is not collaborating well.
>
> Furthermore, she has been perceived as a very aggressive person, which has sometimes led to escalations to the CHRO. There is a lot of unrest and chaos in the team and with every passing day it is becoming difficult for her to work with her team.
>
> Have you been in a similar situation either within your team, with your stakeholders, or with your clients where you have issues with collaborations and/or conflicts?
>
> In this chapter, you will discover some tools and techniques to help you deal with different stakeholders and handle different types of conflict.

IT IS NOT MY PROBLEM!

One of your stakeholders from your project is always exerting himself to prove his point. In some instances, when his idea or the solution does not yield the expected results, he tries to over-power you with his positional muscle.

You are often compromising your brilliant ideas and concepts around your project as he coerces his way through.

The entire team is unhappy about this project environment and they are feeling demotivated as their voice is not heard.

They, including you, are unable to figure out what needs to be done, and with every passing day, the productivity of the team is diminishing.

If you are finding yourself in a similar situation, then in this chapter, you will learn some techniques for **conflict management** and **stakeholder management**.

WHAT IS CONFLICT MANAGEMENT AND RESOLUTION?

Although conflict occurs frequently, effective conflict resolution and management need experience. It's critical to know if a conflict will be constructive and lead to relationship growth.

If the conflict is not immediately handled, it might lead to problems in the relationship.

Conflict can be resolved or managed by either conflict management, conflict resolution or a mix of the two. While conflict resolution will attempt to avoid or mitigate the conflict, conflict management enables the stakeholders to cooperate even in the presence of conflict.

HIGH FIVE WITH YOUR STAKEHOLDERS!

Dr. Kenneth Thomas and **Dr. Ralph Kilmann**, researchers, created a model for dealing with conflicts. This conflict management model is called as **Thomas-Kilmann** model.

According to the **Thomas-Kilmann** model, the following are the important points:

1. There are five methods for resolving disputes: **Competing, Avoiding, Accommodating, Collaborating,** and **Compromising.**

2. Every strategy has pros and cons. Select the best option for the relevant circumstances.
3. **Assertiveness and cooperativeness** are the two elements on which the **Thomas-Kilmann** model is built.

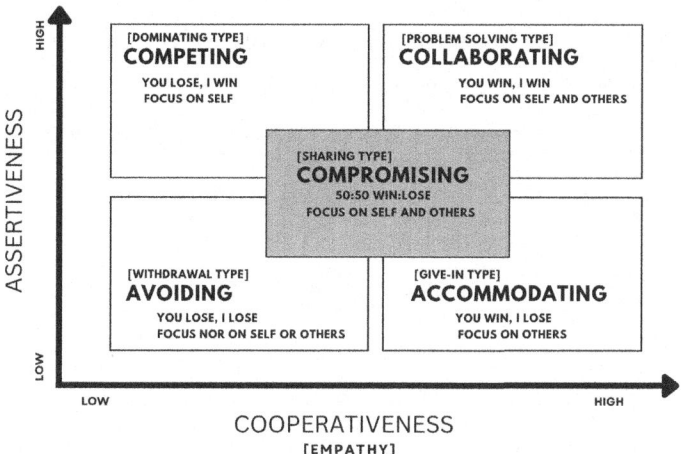

WANT TO RESOLVE YOUR CONFLICTS IN STYLE?

Thomas-Kilmann's model, as you see in the chart, has **five styles** of **conflict management C-1**, **C-2**, **C-3**, **A-1**, and **A-2** (for competing, collaborating, compromising, avoiding, and accommodating, respectively).

Different styles for handling conflict are represented by these five strategies.

Each of them has particular advantages and disadvantages. The appropriate course of action will vary depending on the particular situation you are in. All five styles are appropriate for specific situations and each represents a set of useful social skills.

Let us study each of these strategies in detail and try to discover which is your dominant style of handling conflicts with your team or stakeholders.

▪ Competing [C-1]

The first style of conflict in the T-K model is **competing**, which is **high assertiveness** and **low cooperativeness** (empathy) as shown on the chart's upper left tile.

Competing is the primary method of resolving conflicts. Because my "win" comes at the price of your stakeholder's "loss", this situation is a win-lose or **zero-sum**. Cooperativeness is not accepted, but assertiveness is.

Not all competitions are detrimental. When we compete, we are more likely to succeed and progress. Healthy competition has to be present within the team.

But there are certain problems with this style of conflict. **First**, competition frequently results in unfavorable feelings like animosity, hostility, rage, and frustration. **Second**, because you don't listen to what other people have to say, it doesn't help you develop strong connections.

In the end, you can miss out on opportunities since your counterpart (either your team member or stakeholder) no longer wants to collaborate with you.

It indicates concentrating only on one's own issues at the expense of those of others. It is a power-oriented mode where one leverages the power of his/her position to a positive outcome for him/her.

The most important factor in competing is defensive – it solely means standing up for your convictions and coercing yourself to win against all odds.

When to Use this Style?

The competing style works the best during:

- When you know you are correct and your decisions are right, with matters crucial to the wellbeing of the organization or your team.

- Situations that call for swift decision-making, such as crises or some emergencies.
- When it comes to pressing matters, it is sometimes necessary to take controversial measures, such as implementing unpopular measures and regulations, and cutting costs, to name a few.
- To defend oneself from those who would exploit you.

Collaborating [C-2]

The second style of conflict in the T-K model is **collaborating**, which is **high assertiveness** and **high cooperativeness** (empathy) as shown on the chart's upper right tile. With this mode of conflict, you can expect a lot of better and positive results from your stakeholders.

The objective here is to solve the problem at hand and seek an optimal solution. This necessitates using imagination to create a **win-win** or maximal positive-sum result for both you and the stakeholders.

When you work collaboratively, you reasonably address problems. You try to strike a balance between your own authority and that of another. You also look for areas of agreement and cooperation to accomplish a common objective.

If both sides are dedicated to coming to a mutual agreement, it is the best option. To come to an understanding with each other is the objective here.

But keep in mind that cooperation isn't always simple. It necessitates the exchange of private thoughts and emotions. It also requires two people who respect and believe in one another.

To develop a flawless solution that completely solves the group problem, collaboration involves a voluntary effort to cooperate with your stakeholders.

To identify the crucial demands of the stakeholders or your team members involved, collaboration entails digging deeply into a problem. Working

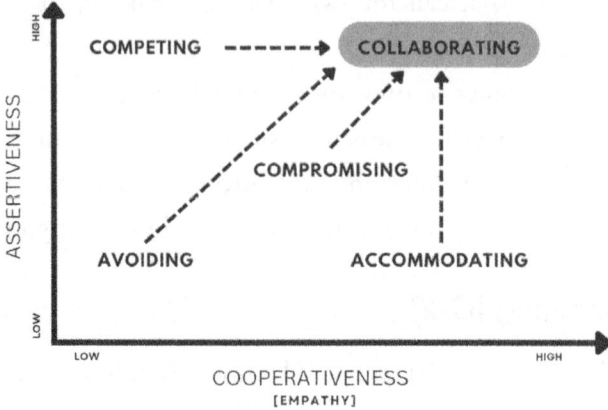

together can take the shape of an effort to comprehend the "why" behind a disagreement between two or more individuals.

Collaboration entails making an effort to seek out original solutions to interpersonal problems and growing from the perspectives of others.

When to Use this Style?

The collaborating style works the best during:

- When you and your team member or stakeholder's issues are too crucial to be ignored, to develop an integrated and total solution.
- If your team members' or stakeholders' point of view or ideas makes sense, make them also a part of the decision that has been reached in agreement, to win commitment.
- When learning is your main objective, such as when you are trying to grasp other people's opinions or verifying your own hunches.

▪ Compromising [C-3]

The third style of conflict in the T-K model is **compromising**, which is **medium assertiveness** and **medium cooperativeness** (empathy) as shown on the chart's central tile.

Fairness is the objective in this mode of conflict. Assertiveness and cooperation are partially but not entirely fulfilled as a result; the effect is positive but restricted.

You choose the middle ground between opposing ideas when you compromise. This involves embracing some terms and ignoring a few other terms. Additionally, flexibility is crucial because you're attempting to resolve a conflict.

With this strategy, both sides typically feel as though they have benefited from the disagreement, creating a **partial lose-lose or partial win-win situation**.

When to Use this Style?

The compromising style works the best during:

- When you are seeking temporary solutions for difficult problems.
- When you and your stakeholder with equal authority are fervently dedicated to opposing objectives; for example, during the employee's exit after his/her negative performance in PIP.
- When you are seeking to solve problems quickly under time constraints.

▪ Avoiding [A-1]

The fourth style of conflict in the T-K model is **avoiding**, which is at the bottom left tile of the chart with **low assertiveness** and **low empathy**.

When your team member or the stakeholder knows they don't have any control over you because of various reasons, they will employ this conflict resolution technique.

They choose to ignore or completely avoid the disagreement to prevent conflict. They also decide to completely disregard the problem.

It's common to perceive avoiding as passive and weak. However, if you wish to avoid a fight, then you can adopt this style because neither assertiveness nor cooperativeness is achieved, this is a **lose-lose situation**.

If you don't want to deal with your team member's concerns or the issues of others, you are adopting avoid style of conflict.

Avoiding might occasionally be interpreted as a diplomatic ploy to sidestep or ignore the problem. It could also entail delaying the matter until a suitable moment or just removing oneself from a risky or uncomfortable circumstance.

When to Use this Style?

The avoiding style works the best during:

- When the problem looks unrelated to or indicative of a more fundamental one.
- When your stakeholder/team member can settle the dispute more successfully.
- When the benefits of delaying decision-making surpass the benefits of acquiring additional information.
- When the risks of engaging in a dispute surpass the advantages of its resolution, this gives your stakeholder a chance to calm down, i.e., to bring tensions down to a manageable level and let them restore their composure.
- When you believe there is little hope of resolving your issues; for instance, when you have little influence or are upset about something that would be exceedingly difficult to alter.

▪ Accommodating [A-2]

The fifth style of conflict in the T-K model is **accommodating**, which is at the bottom right tile of the chart, with **low assertiveness** and **high empathy**.

This strategy is based on making accommodations or peace. For instance, rather than debating the issue of your stakeholder's requests or demands, you agree to comply or give in to their request.

When you don't have the power to resolve a problem, this method works well. However, use caution since by giving in, you run the risk of letting go of control of your own agenda.

How then can you determine whether giving in is worthwhile? Be careful to consider both sides before making a choice.

Sustaining harmony in the relationship is the objective of this style of conflict. This is a win-lose scenario. One person's gain is a loss for the opposite person.

Although cooperation is achieved, assertiveness is abandoned.

When to Use this Style?

The accommodating style works the best during:

- When it is more crucial to maintain peace and prevent any bad blood among the stakeholders.
- Enabling subordinates to try and learn from their own errors which will help them improve as managers.
- When you are losing and outmatched in a discussion or knowledge sharing, i.e., when continuing to compete will only hurt your cause.
- When meeting your stakeholders' demands and demonstrating your logic is more essential to your stakeholder than meeting your own.

WHAT IS YOUR STYLE OF CONFLICT MANAGEMENT ?
A Self-Assessment

Think about instances where your desires/decisions/actions conflict with another person/team member/stakeholder. How do you typically respond to circumstances like these?

There are various pairs of statements that describe potential behavioral reactions on the following pages. Please mark the "A" or "B" statement for each combination that best describes your conduct.

Please choose the response that you would most likely use, even though neither the "A" nor the "B" statement is frequently or particularly representative of your conduct.

1. A   There are instances when I delegate the task of problem-solving to others.
   B   I attempt to emphasize the points on which we both agree rather than trying to negotiate the points on which we disagree.
2. A   I look for potential compromises.
   B   I make an effort to address all of their and my problems.
3. A   I often pursue my objectives with persistence.
   B   I might make an effort to fix the other's sentiments and keep our friendship intact.
4. A   I look for a middle-ground answer.
   B   I occasionally give up my own desires to fulfill those of others.
5. A   I continuously ask others for assistance in coming up with a solution.

B   I attempt to take the necessary steps to prevent unnecessary conflicts.

6. A   I make an effort to not make things uncomfortable for myself.

   B   I Strive to win the argument.

7. A   I try to put off the decision until I have given it considerable thought.

   B   I trade some of my points for others.

8. A   I often pursue my objectives firmly.

   B   I make an effort to address any worries and difficulties right away.

9. A   I believe that not all disparities are cause for concern.

   B   I do my best to get my way.

10. A I am firm in pursuing my goals.

    B I try to find a compromise solution.

11. A I make an effort to address any worries and difficulties right away.

    B I might make an effort to restore the other's sentiments and keep our friendship intact.

12. A I occasionally refrain from taking stances that might spark debate

    B If he gives me some of his positions, I'll give him some of mine in return.

13. A I suggest finding a medium ground.

    B I exert pressure to make my point

14. A I tell him my opinions and ask what his are.

	B	I make an effort to convince him of my position's merits and rationale.
15.	A	I might make an effort to restore the other's sentiments and keep our connection intact.
	B	I attempt to take the required steps to keep things calm.
16.	A	I make an effort to avoid offending anyone.
	B	I make an effort to persuade the other individual of the validity of my argument.
17.	A	I often pursue my objectives firmly.
	B	If he gives me some of his positions, I'll give him some of mine in return.
18.	A	I might let him keep his opinions if it makes the other person happy.
	B	If he gives me some of his positions, I'll give him some of mine in return.
19.	A	I make an effort to address any worries and difficulties right away.
	B	I make an effort to put off the decision until I have had some time to consider it.
20.	A	I make an immediate effort to resolve our issues.
	B	I make an effort to balance everyone's profits and losses.
21	A	I make an effort to be respectful of the other party's views while entering discussions.
	B	I always prefer to address the issue head-on.
22.	A	I look for a middle ground between his and my position.
	B	I assert my intentions.

23. A   I think about fulfilling all of our wishes frequently.

      B   There are instances when I delegate the task of problem-solving to others.

24. A   If the other person seems to value his stance highly, I will do my best to accommodate him.

      B   I try to get him to settle for a compromise.

25. A   I make an attempt to convince him of my position's benefits and reasoning.

      B   I make an effort to be respectful of the other party's views while entering dialogues.

26. A   I offer a compromise.

      B   I almost always want to grant all of our requests.

27. A   I occasionally refrain from taking views that might provoke debate.

      B   I might allow him to continue holding his ideas if it makes the other person happy.

28. A   I often pursue my aims with determination.

      B   Whenever I need help coming up with a solution, I generally ask the other.

29. A   I suggest finding a midway ground.

      B   I believe that not all disparities are cause for concern.

30. A   I make an effort to avoid offending anyone.

      B   I always discuss the issue with the other person so we can find a solution.

Note: You will find the keys to this assessment towards the end of this chapter.

The highest score on the score sheet is your dominant style of conflict.

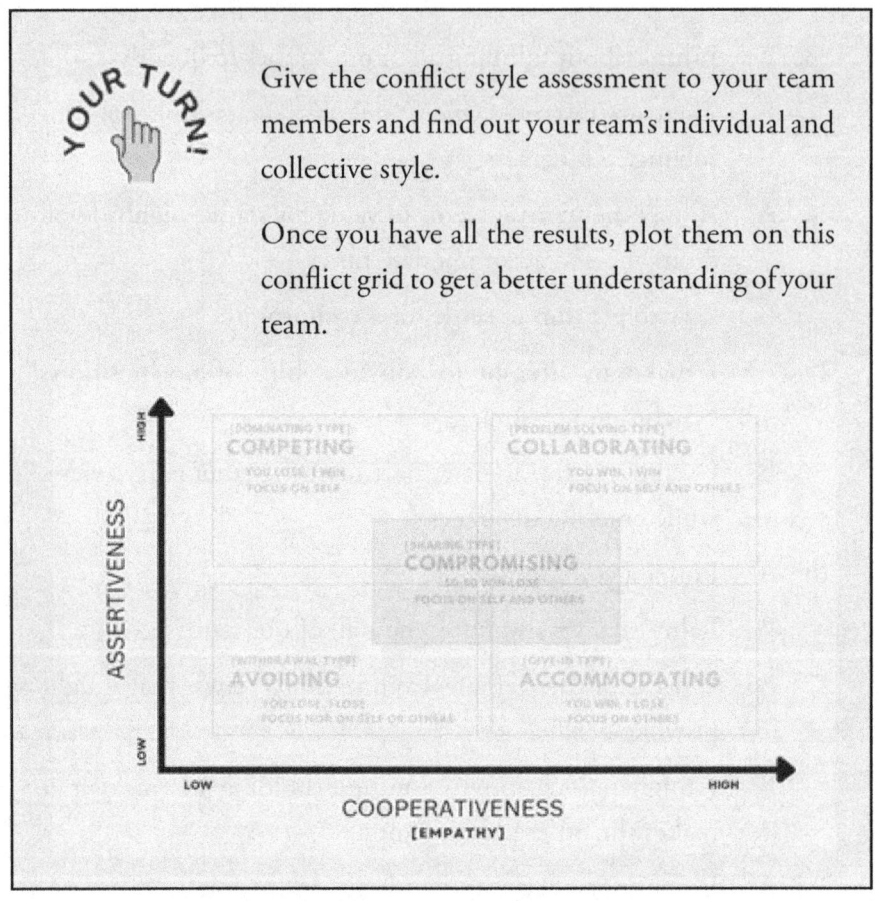

HAVE YOU PROFILED YOUR STAKEHOLDER?

An individual or a group with an interest in the project or assignment is referred to as a **stakeholder**. Each stakeholder has a part of the responsibility for the accomplishment or failure of the project or assignment.

Investors, employees, clients, and suppliers make up the majority of the stakeholders in a typical business. Stakeholders can be internal or external to the organization. The public at large might occasionally be considered a stakeholder.

The stakeholder notion can also be extended to encompass communities and governments.

To avoid any kind of conflict, misunderstanding, or abrasion in the relationship, you must know who is your stakeholder and their role in the assignment.

If you have been struggling to profile your stakeholder, then this section will help you understand some techniques of stakeholder analysis and management.

MENDELOW'S STAKEHOLDER MATRIX

The **Mendelow Stakeholder Matrix** which is sometimes referred to as the **Stakeholder Analysis Matrix** and the **Power-Interest Matrix** is a simple and direct structure for organizing your stakeholders.

Successful people apply the discipline of **stakeholder management**, which is crucial for gaining support from others. It is the process used to find the important individuals who need to be persuaded. The support necessary for your success is then built via stakeholder planning.

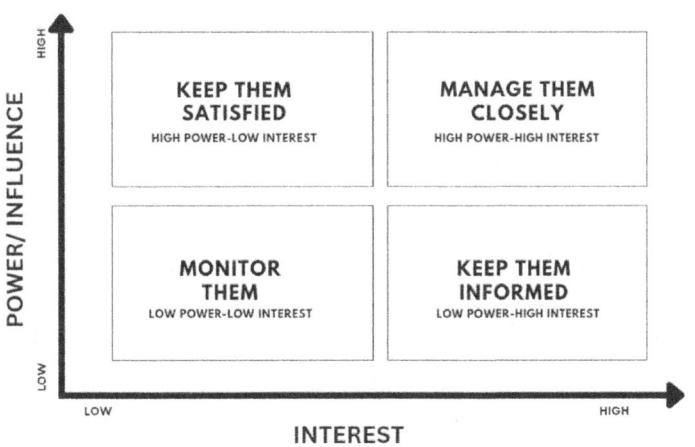

Using a **stakeholder-based strategy** has the following advantages:

The most influential stakeholders may help you develop your initiatives early on and their advice can raise the caliber of your project.

Gaining the endorsement of influential stakeholders can allow you to secure additional funding/support/endorsement, increasing the likelihood that your activities will be successful.

You can make sure that your stakeholders completely understand what you are doing and the advantages of your project by talking with them early and regularly. As a result, they will be able to actively assist you when necessary.

Here you will learn the **step-by-step** procedure for doing the **stakeholder analysis**.

How to Apply Mendelow's SM
Step-1

Brainstorm who your stakeholders (including from your upstream and downstream activities) are along with your team and make a list.

List of Stakeholders

Name	Role
_____	_____
_____	_____
_____	_____
_____	_____
_____	_____
_____	_____

Consider everyone who will be impacted by your project or assignment, who can influence it, or who has a stake in whether it succeeds or fails.

Although **stakeholders** might be both **individuals** and **organizations**, keep in mind that you must communicate with people in the end. In a stakeholder organization, be sure to pinpoint the appropriate individual stakeholders.

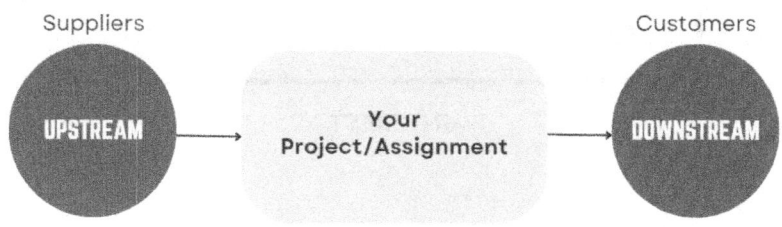

Step-2

You've compiled the list of the individuals (internal or external) and groups (internal or external) that your project will impact. Some of them could be capable of blocking your project or expediting it. Others might not care, while some could be interested in what you are doing.

To categorize and prioritize the stakeholders, the **Power-Interest grid** might be useful. As a result, stakeholders are more easily identified based on their influence and commitment to the project. You may assess which stakeholders have a lot of or little influence on your project, as well as who has a lot or little interest in it, by plotting them on a **Power-Interest grid**.

High power and high interest groups need to be kept happy and informed respectively. Be careful to pay attention when a stakeholder has both.

Let us learn each of these quadrants in detail.

The Secrets of Design Thinking Mindset

- **HIGH INTEREST AND HIGH POWER**

Key Players | Manage Them Closely | Regularly Engage

These stakeholders are quite powerful and very interested in your project or assignment. Upper management, directors, significant investors, or partners might be included. They will demand that communication and their participation in decision-making be given top emphasis.

- **LOW INTEREST AND HIGH POWER**

Keep Them Satisfied | Actively Consult

These stakeholders are quite powerful yet have little desire. These might be legislative bodies, regulatory or governmental agencies, banks, insurance firms, or law enforcement.

- **HIGH INTEREST AND LOW POWER**

Keep Them Informed

This category of stakeholders, which includes employees, vendors, communities, organizations, and business partners, has little power but strong interest. They should frequently be updated since they are interested and keen on your project. You will receive a lot of feedback from them.

- **LOW INTEREST AND LOW POWER**
Monitor Them | Low Priority

The fourth group is for stakeholders who have little influence and little motivation. This might include vendors, community associations, and the general public, depending on the project. These teams need little time and effort, but they should at least be monitored for any status change.

PRO TIP:

You should periodically keep checking the status of these stakeholders.

As time passes by, a Low Power-High Interest stakeholder, may come into power by promotion or election and the entire dynamics of your project will change.

Step-3

Once the profiling of your stakeholder is done, and you are able to categorize them in **Mendelow's grid**, next you should plan for stakeholder management regarding their roles and responsibilities.

This we will study in the next section.

For your current project or assignment, do the following:

1. Brainstorm all the internal and external stakeholders with your team
2. Categorize them based on their power or influence and their interest in your project or assignment

The Secrets of Design Thinking Mindset

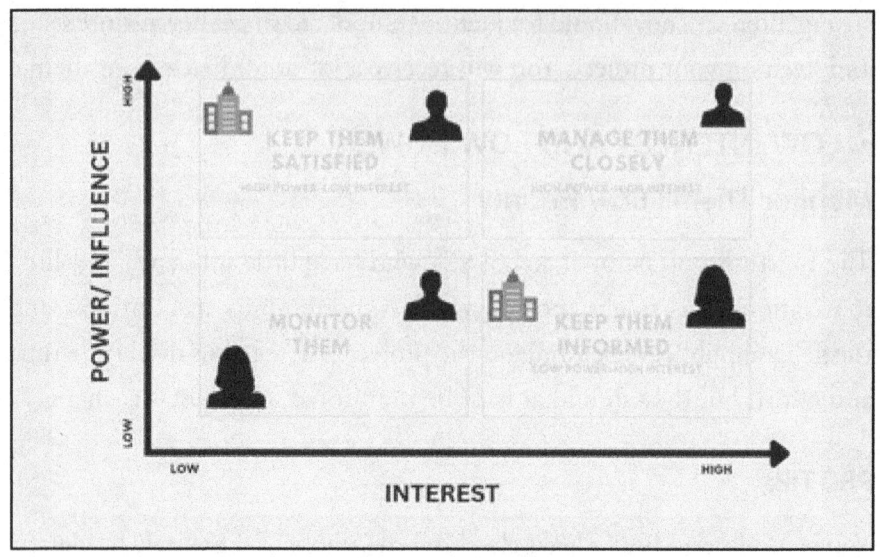

DECISION-RESPONSIBILITY MATRICES FOR YOUR PROJECT

Now, that you have profiled your stakeholders, next you will learn how to assign roles and responsibilities based on the relevance of their contribution or influence on the project or assignment.

- **ARMI Matrix**

The degree of support from project stakeholders may be evaluated using the project management tool, **ARMI**.

ARMI is an acronym for **Approver**, **Resource**, **Member**, and **Interested party**. These are the four levels of assistance that may be given to different stakeholders.

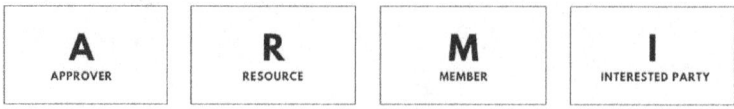

- **Approver**

A person or a business leader who must approve something, such as a sponsor or a corporate executive.

- **Resource**

A resource is a specialist or an SME whose expertise is required for a specific amount of time.

- **Member**

Your full-time team members.

- **Interested Party**

A person who you need to ensure is apprised of the project's status.

A sample **ARMI grid** for some phases in an **SDLC cycle** is shown in the below table. Each stakeholder's position within the project team is clarified by **ARMI**.

Names	Role	Requirement Gathering	Design	Coding & Testing	Deploy	Maintenance
HARRY	DIRECTOR	A & R	R & M	A & R	I	I
MONA	QUAILITY	A	A & R	A & R	I	R & M
JOSHUA	CSM	A & R	I	A & R	I	A
BOB	TEAM LEAD	A & R	A	R & M	R & M	R
MARY	SME	A & R	A	A	R	A
TINA	INTERN	M	M	M	M	M

ARMI aids in removing any confusion about these people's duties and responsibilities.

- **RACI Matrix**

An easy-to-use tool for defining project roles and responsibilities is the **RACI matrix**, which offers a detailed breakdown of who is **Responsible**, **Accountable**, **Consulted**, and **Informed** at every stage.

The **RACI matrix** is a responsibility assignment chart that lists every action, milestone, and important choice that must be made to complete a project. It also specifies which roles are responsible for each action item, which staff members are accountable, and, when necessary, who needs to be consulted or informed. The four roles that stakeholders may take on in each project are represented by the acronym **RACI**.

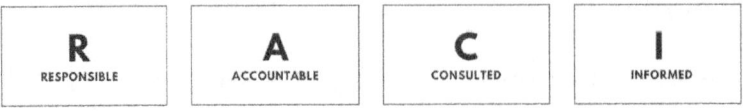

- Responsible

There must be at least one **responsible** team member for each job who completes the necessary tasks.

Usually, the person or people in charge of the job or deliverable are also in charge of creating the product or finishing the work. Usually, the **responsible parties** are working-level project team members, such as the project manager, business analyst, developers, or, for example, those who produce marketing collateral and technical documentation. These people take action.

However, the RACI matrix may assign more than one **responsible party**.

- Accountable

This team member is in charge of assigning tasks and approving deliverables before they are labeled as finished. On the RACI chart, the **accountable** team member is occasionally also the responsible team member. However, not always the project manager is the person who is responsible for each job.

- Consulted

This team member who will evaluate output and offer recommendations that place it in the context of the entire project or just within the organization's expectations.

People who have been **consulted** should have their opinions and suggestions sought out. Subject Matter Experts (SMEs), legal and information security, compliance, and/or from other departments in the business that may be affected might be the parties that are **consulted**. This may practically be the entire company if you are working on new product development.

Prior to beginning a work or deliverable, individuals or groups should be **consulted** to understand the needs, limitations, and risks. They should also be **consulted** after completion to confirm that all relevant factors have been taken into account.

- **Informed**

Although they don't have the same amount of responsibility as those listed above, these team members nevertheless need to be aware of what is occurring with task execution. Instead of going into specifics, you might just give them an overall update on how things are doing.

You should always keep **informed** people in the loop. These people are not required to be consulted or included in the decision-making process. Add this group/individual to your cc list to be **informed** about issues, choices, and developments. Invite this group as an optional participant to start meetings and project demonstrations as well.

Here is an example of a condensed RACI model for a sample SDLC project.

Names	Role	Requirement Gathering	Design	Coding & Testing	Deploy	Maintenance
HARRY	DIRECTOR	R & C	R	A & R	I	I
MONA	QUAILITY	I	A & R	I	C	C
JOSHUA	CSM	R	I	R & C	A	A
BOB	TEAM LEAD	R	C	R & C	R	R
MARY	SME	A	C	C	R	R & C
TINA	INTERN	R & C	R	R	R	R

RIGHT INFORMATION TO THE RIGHT PEOPLE

You can efficiently communicate the right information to the right stakeholders at the right time with the help of a communication plan. The strategy will specify the messages you need to share, who you're targeting with them, and which channel or medium to communicate.

Communication plans are useful not just during disasters but also when introducing new projects or items.

An official determination of the messages you wish to convey to your target audience and the clarification of the aim of a product launch or new initiative may be made with the aid of communication plans.

You must take into account a few fundamental questions when creating a communication plan:

1. Why do you wish to interact with this stakeholder? (What is the purpose?)
2. To whom do you want to communicate this? (Who are you writing for?)
3. What are you attempting to communicate? (What do you want to say?)
4. How would you like to communicate it? (What means of communication will you employ?)
5. What steps should you take to use those modes, and whom should you contact? (How will your message be propagated?)

Following is one of the sample templates which you can use for your communication planning.

INFORMATION	AUDIENCE	MEDIUM	FREQUENCY	TIME	SOURCE
Project Status	Management	E-Mail/Video Call	Weekly	Friday	Richa
WHAT?	TO WHOM?	HOW?	HOW MANY TIMES?	WHEN?	WHO?

What...? Now What...? So What...?

Hope with this information, you will be able to plan your communication strategy.

1. For your project or assignment, plot the RACI and ARMI model of the decision-responsibility matrix
2. Explore these additional decision-responsibility matrices
   a. RASIC
   b. PARIS
   c. CAIRO
   d. DACI
   e. RAPID

   Discuss with your team which of these models is the most suitable for your assignments.
3. Prepare a communication plan for your current project or task using the template.

YOUR CONFLICT MANAGEMENT STYLE
A Self-Assessment

Here are the keys to the assessment you had taken earlier in this chapter.

Circle the letters below that match the letter you circled on each assessment question, and then add up how many of those items are in each column.

The style with the highest total will be your dominant conflict management style.

Accordingly, give the assessment to your team members to know what is the team's conflict management style.

The Secrets of Design Thinking Mindset

Use the T-K grid and put the name of your team members on the corresponding tile to have a visual reference on the team's collective style of conflict management.

Q	Competing	Collaborating	Compromising	Avoiding	Accommodating
1	x	x	x	A	B
2	x	B	A	x	x
3	A	x	x	x	B
4	x	x	A	x	B
5	x	A	x	B	x
6	B	x	x	A	x
7	x	x	B	A	x
8	A	B	x	x	x
9	B	x	x	A	x
10	A	x	B	x	x
11	x	A	x	x	B
12	x	x	B	A	x
13	B	x	A	x	x
14	B	A	x	x	x
15	x	x	x	B	A
16	B	x	x	x	A
17	A	x	x	B	x
18	x	x	B	x	A
19	x	A	x	B	x

What…? Now What…? So What…?

	Competing	Collaborating	Compromising	Avoiding	Accommodating
20	x	A	B	x	x
21	x	B	x	x	A
22	B	x	A	x	x
23	x	A	x	B	x
24	x	x	B	x	A
25	A	x	x	x	B
26	x	B	A	x	x
27	x	x	x	A	B
28	A	B	x	x	x
29	x	x	A	B	x
30	x	B	x	x	A
TOTAL	___	___	___	___	___

My Name: _____

My Highest Score: _____

My Dominant Style: _____

"Give us the tools and we will finish the job"
— **Winston Churchill**

4

STILL USING GUT FEELING FOR MAKING DECISIONS?

> ## HAVE YOU BEEN IN DANNY OR RON'S SITUATION?
>
> Danny and Ron are from the same graduate school and got placed in the same company as software developers. But now, within two years, Ron is promoted to a senior software developer role while Danny didn't get promoted.
>
> Why?
>
> In their initial years on the project, Danny was taking decisions based on his 6th sense or his gut feeling which sometimes were successful and sometimes miserable failures. When the client asked Danny how he arrived at a particular decision, he never was able to give a convincing answer or justify his decision as they were just based on intuition, perception, or gut feeling.
>
> On the contrary, Ron while working with his clients was taking scientific approaches and evaluating the decisions objectively. In his management discussion, Ron was able to reason on what basis he has been taking the decision and why his decisions were yielding a 90% and more success rate.
>
> Ron was made a part of the think-tank panel where he excelled in helping the team on narrowing down from the trivial many possibilities or choices or ideas to a vital few and then further clearly take a decision.
>
> Please read through this chapter to know the techniques Ron was using for making the decisions.

WHAT IS A DECISION?

A choice of action made to accomplish organizational or administrative objectives or goals can be referred to as a **decision**.

To find a solution for a particular issue or problem, **decision-making** is choosing a plan of action from among two or more viable options.

The following are the forms of decisions taken at different levels in an organization:

1. **Strategic decisions** are usually done by the top management which is at an organizational level with a long-term view (5 years or more).
2. **Tactical decisions** are broadly done by the managers to achieve those strategies on a short-term basis (usually 1 year).
3. **Operational decisions** are taken by all the employees of the organization daily to accomplish the daily/weekly/monthly tasks or actions.

Decision-making is inevitable and ubiquitous and hence it becomes imperative that you know some tools and techniques to help you make decisions. In this chapter, you will learn some of the most powerful tools for making decisions.

PAIRED DECISION MAKING

It is a process for assessing the possibilities/options/choices by evaluating them with one another i.e., with respect to their relative importance. It is a practical and simple method for evaluating and ranking choices when the assessment or the performance criteria are inherently subjective. When choices are radically distinct from one another, when objectives are not sufficiently clear, or when there is a lack of objective evidence on which to make our decision, this is practically beneficial.

It is also called **paired comparison analysis or pairwise comparison method**. It can also help you in prioritizing the choices or options.

A square matrix or a grid is used in **paired decision-making analysis** and is constructed as shown.

Still Using Gut Feeling for Making Decisions?

	Option A	**Option B**	**Option C**	**Option D**
Option A	Option A Vs Option A	Option A Vs Option B	Option A Vs Option C	Option A Vs Option D
Option B	Option B Vs Option A	Option B Vs Option B	Option B Vs Option C	Option B Vs Option D
Option C	Option C Vs Option A	Option C Vs Option B	Option C Vs Option C	Option C Vs Option D
Option D	Option D Vs Option A	Option D Vs Option B	Option D Vs Option C	Option D Vs Option D

You can observe that some cells or grids are duplicate comparisons and some are not possible.

The following are the duplicate comparisons:

1. Option A Vs Option B and Option B Vs Option A
2. Option A Vs Option C and Option C Vs Option A
3. Option A Vs Option D and Option D Vs Option A

The following comparisons along the principal diagonal are not possible:

1. Option A Vs Option A
2. Option B Vs Option B
3. Option C Vs Option C
4. Option D Vs Option D

The Secrets of Design Thinking Mindset

Blocking these ten cells from the square matrix.

	Option A	Option B	Option C	Option D
Option A		Option A Vs Option B	Option A Vs Option C	Option A Vs Option D
Option B			Option B Vs Option C	Option B Vs Option D
Option C				Option C Vs Option D
Option D				

Basically, in all the **paired comparison methods**, we consider only the **upper triangle** of the matrix.

In this case, you have only 6 valid and unique relative comparisons.

1. Option A Vs Option B
2. Option A Vs Option C
3. Option A Vs Option D
4. Option B Vs Option C
5. Option B Vs Option D
6. Option C Vs Option D

You can use the following formula to arrive at the total for the valid and unique relative cells:

$$\text{Total Cells for Comparision} = \frac{N(N-1)}{2}$$

N is the number of options.

In this example, it is 4 – A, B, C, and D.

$$\text{Total Cells for Comparision} = \frac{4(4-1)}{2} = \frac{4(3)}{2} = \frac{12}{2} = 6$$

Likewise, say, if you have 8 options (N=8): A, B, C, D, E, F, G, H. How many valid and unique relative cells are for comparison?

The answer is 28.

How to Apply Paired Decision Making (PDM)?

Step-1

Assemble a Cross Functional Team (CFT) and identify the alternatives or choices that you would like to assess.

List down the choices you plan to evaluate. Label each of these choices with a letter or word or name.

Suppose your HR is hiring a developer for one position and 5 candidates are shortlisted – say, Arnold, Emily, James, Clifton, and Ruth.

Step-2

Arrange them in rows and columns to form a square matrix.

Can you use the formula and figure out how many valid and unique relative cells will we have?

Here it is.

$$\text{Total Cells for Comparision} = \frac{N(N-1)}{2}$$

$$\text{Total Cells for Comparision} = \frac{5(5-1)}{2}$$

$$= \frac{5(4)}{2}$$

$$= \frac{20}{2}$$

$$= 10$$

	Arnold (A)	Emily (B)	James (C)	Clifton (D)	Ruth (E)
Arnold (A)		Arnold Vs Emily	Arnold Vs James	Arnold Vs Clifton	Arnold Vs Ruth
Emily (B)			Emily Vs James	Emily Vs Clifton	Emily Vs Ruth
James (C)				James Vs Clifton	James Vs Ruth
Clifton (D)					Clifton Vs Ruth
Clifton (D)					

Step-3

Choose a scale of your choice: either 1, 2, 3, or 1, 2, 3, 4, 5, and define them.

1, 2, 3 (1 = Never, 2 = Sometimes, 3 = Always)

1, 2, 3 (1 = Low, 2 = Medium, 3 = High)

Still Using Gut Feeling for Making Decisions?

1, 2, 3, 4, 5 (1 = Least Important to 5 = Very Important)

We will choose a scale of 3, where

>   1 - is low performance in the overall interview process
>   2 - is medium performance in the overall interview process
>   3 - is high performance in the overall interview process

Step-4

Here we assign either 1 or 2 or 3 to each cell based on the relative comparison.

1. Arnold Vs Emily – Arnold, 2
   This means between Arnold and Emily, Arnold's performance in the interview was medium.
2. Arnold Vs James – James, 3
   This means between Arnold and James, James' performance in the interview was high.
3. Arnold Vs Clifton   Clifton, 3
4. Arnold Vs Ruth – Ruth, 2
5. Emily Vs James – Emily, 1
6. Emily Vs Clifton – Clifton, 3
7. Emily Vs Ruth – Emily, 2
8. James Vs Clifton – Clifton, 3
9. James Vs Ruth – James, 3
10. Clifton Vs Ruth – Clifton, 3

Step-5

Substitute all the 10 values in the matrix.

>   Add all the values and convert them to percentages.
>
>   Arnold = 2 = 2/(Total Points) = 2/(2+6+12+3+2) = 8%
>
>   James = 3 + 3 = 6 = 6/(2+6+12+3+2) = 24%

The Secrets of Design Thinking Mindset

> Clifton = 3 + 3 + 3 + 3 = 12 = 12/(2+6+12+3+2) = 48%

Emily = 1 + 2 = 3 = 3/(2+6+12+3+2) = 12%

Ruth = 2 = 2/(2+6+12+3+2) = 8%

Please make note that the sum of all the percentages should add up to 100% : 8% + 24% + 48% + 12% + 8%.

	Arnold (A)	Emily (B)	James (C)	Clifton (D)	Ruth (E)
Arnold (A)		Arnold, 2	James, 3	Clifton, 3	Ruth, 2
Emily (B)			Emily, 1	Clifton, 3	Emily, 2
James (C)				Clifton, 3	James, 3
Clifton (D)					Clifton, 3
Clifton (D)					

From the percentages, we infer Clifton is the best choice among the shortlisted candidates. HR can go ahead and roll out an offer to among.

If for some reason, Clifton declines the offer, you know whom to hire from that list.

PUGH MATRIX ANALYSIS

The **Pugh Matrix**, which bears the name of its originator **Stuart Pugh**, is a tool for comparing competing ideas to a core idea while making decisions. Stuart Pugh was a professor and head of the design division at the University of Strathclyde in Glasgow.

This analysis is based on a set of specified, criteria that compare different alternatives or options or choices.

It is also known as **Decision Matrix, Selection Matrix, Problem Matrix, Criteria-based Matrix, Multi-Attribute Utility Theory, Pugh Controlled Convergence (PuCC)** or **Opportunity Analysis**. It is sometimes used for **prioritization**.

How to Apply Pugh Matrix?
Step-1

Assemble a Cross Functional Team (CFT) and identify the alternatives or choices that you would like to assess.

List down the choices you plan to evaluate. Label each of these choices with a letter or word or name.

Also, identify the **performance parameters** that you would like to compare for each of the alternatives or choices.

Identify a **reference** or a **datum**, which might be a product or a service, or an individual to which/whom you want to compare your choices or alternatives to.

For example, you can use ratings of worse (-1), the same as the datum or reference (0), or better (+1) to compare each alternative to the baseline for each criterion on a three-point scale.

Likewise, on a five-point scale, a much finer rating scale of 2, 1, 0, -1, -2, worse (-2), same as the datum or reference (0), or better (+2) or a seven-point scale of 3, 2, 1, 0, -1, -2, -3, can be utilized.

Let's see the same hiring example with the **Pugh analysis**.

To construct the **Pugh matrix** you need the following details:

1. List of choices or alternatives (along the horizontal)
   In this example, all the shortlisted candidates for the interview – Arnold, Emily, James, Clifton, and Ruth
2. Criteria to compare (along the vertical)
   The candidates are being hired on their competencies in technical, domain, functional, process, and behavioral aspects.
3. A datum or reference
   In our case, we have to choose an ideal candidate against whom we can do the comparison.
   Let's say that Morgan is an exceptional employee in the company and the HR wants to hire a candidate like Morgan from the shortlisted ones who has a close resemblance in all the competencies.
4. Scores for comparison

   Let us choose a 5-pointer scale – 2, 1, 0, -1, -2,

   2 – best skillset compared to the datum (Morgan)

   1 – better skillset compared to the datum (Morgan)

   0 – the same skillset compared to the datum (Morgan)

   -1 – bad skillset compared to the datum (Morgan)

   -2 – worst skillset compared to the datum (Morgan

5. Weights for each criterion

   The weight spectrum can be either from 1 to 3 or 1 to 5, or 1 to 10.

Still Using Gut Feeling for Making Decisions?

Where 10 means the most important feature, skill, etc., and 1 means the least important feature or skill.

Likewise, 1 to 3 and 1 to 5.

We will choose a 1 to 5 weight spectrum, where 1 means least important skill and 5 means most important skill for the role that is being hired for.

	Weight	Morgan	Arnold	Emily	James	Clifton	Ruth
Technical	4	0	D A T U M				
Domain	3	0					
Functional	5	0	D A T U M				
Process	2	0					
Behavioral	5	0					

The noteworthy column here is the **datum column** which serves as a reference for comparing Morgan's skill sets with the shortlisted candidates. The **datum** or **reference** column will always be **zero**. In this example, it is an individual (Morgan). In other cases, it could be an ideal product, concept, service, etc.

And the weight column with weights is how critical or important these skills are to the role being hired for.

Step-2

Populate the rest of the cells with the scores 2 to -2.

	Weight	Morgan	Arnold	Emily	James	Clifton	Ruth
Technical	4	0	0				
Domain	3	0	-2				
Functional	5	0	2				
Process	2	0	1				
Behavioral	5	0	2				

(Morgan column marked as DATUM; Arnold column marked as DATUM)

The interpretation of Arnold's scores is as follows:

For technical, Arnold scored 0, because the interviewer found Arnold's technical competency is on par with Morgan's.

	Weight	Morgan	Arnold	Emily	James	Clifton	Ruth
Technical	4	0	0	1	2	1	0
Domain	3	0	-2	-2	1	2	2
Functional	5	0	2	1	-1	0	1
Process	2	0	1	2	1	0	2
Behavioral	5	0	2	0	-2	2	-1

For domain, Arnold scored -2, because the interviewer found Arnold's domain competency two notches below (worst) Morgan's.

For functional, Arnold scored 2, because the interviewer found Arnold's functional competency two notches above (best) Morgan's.

For process, Arnold scored 1, because the interviewer found Arnold's process competency one notch above (better) Morgan's.

For behavioral, Arnold scored 2, because the interviewer found Arnold's behavioral competency two notches above (best) Morgan's.

Likewise, all the cells have been populated.

Step-3

Next, multiply the weights by each of the candidate's scores.

For Arnold,

Technical Score	= 4 x 0	= 0
Domain Score	= 3 x (-2)	= -6
Functional Score	= 5 x 2	= 10
Process	= 2 x 1	= 2
Behavioral	= 5 x 2	= 10
Total		= 16

Likewise, all the cells have been summed and populated.

Next, based on the descending order of the scores, rank them.

In this example, Clifton is the candidate to be hired. If Clifton declines the offer, who is the second-best to being hired?

	Weight	Morgan	Arnold	Emily	James	Clifton	Ruth
Technical	4	0	0	4	8	4	0
Domain	3	0	-6	-6	3	6	6
Functional	5	0	10	5	-5	0	5
Process	2	0	2	4	2	0	4
Behavioral	5	0	10	0	-10	10	-5
Total			16	7	-2	20	10
Rank			2	4	5	1	3

(Morgan column = DATUM / DATUM)

PROBABILISTIC DECISION-MAKING TREE

Probabilistic decision-making is a visual model or representation which discretizes sequential decision problems under uncertainty by attaching probabilities to each possible outcome, decision, or event.

Models of decision trees incorporate ideas like nodes, **branches, terminal values, strategy, payoff distribution, specific equivalents,** and the **technique of rollback.**

Type of Node	Symbol	Details
Decision Node	■	Square
Event Node	●	Circle
Terminal Node	| or ▷	Bar or Triangle

Still Using Gut Feeling for Making Decisions?

A **decision node**, which is shown as a square, is a place where a decision must be made.

Decision branches are the branches that emerge from a decision node, and each branch represents one of the potential choices or courses of action.

These sets of choices or alternatives have to be mutually exclusive and collectively exhaustive (all possible alternatives must be included).

An **event node**, sometimes known as a "chance node," is depicted as a circle.

The **event set** is made up of the **event branches** that emerge from an **event node**, with each branch representing a possible outcome or an event.

Again, these events must be mutually exclusive and exhaustive collectively.

A subjective probability is given to each occurrence, and the total probability for all the events in a set must be equal to 1.

A **terminal node**, which represents the outcome (dead end) of a series of choices and events, is the third type of node.

The terminal nodes of a decision tree are its endpoints; they are shown as a triangle or vertical bar.

Can you identify the nodes and branches that are highlighted with question marks?

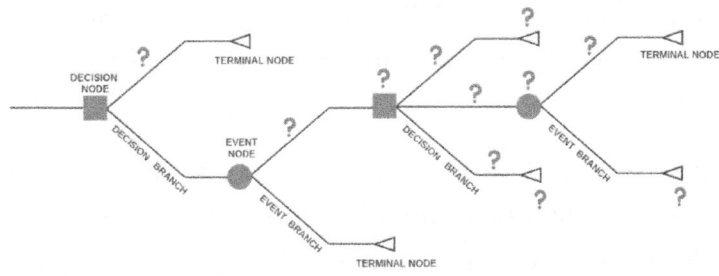

The Secrets of Design Thinking Mindset

Let's see an example.

A sales EVP (supplier) in a multinational conglomerate wants to onboard a client by offering them a free integration service for a three-month window hoping that the client will sign-up for a paid service.

This three-month window will cost the supplier $75,000 (USD) for the free resources (manpower, technologies, etc.). If the client signs up after three months, the supplier will get an advance payment of $200,000 (USD) to execute the project.

The supplier uses three integrators viz., MuleSoft, Informatica, and SnapLogic. The MuleSoft integration would cost $120,000 (USD), Informatica would cost $25,000(USD) and SnapLogic would cost $75,000(USD).

The solution architects after having the discovery call with the client are cent percent sure that MuleSoft would be the best solution followed by a possible success by using Informatica and a more likely possibility of success by using SnapLogic.

Let's help the sales EVP to make the right decision.

Step-1

From the first decision node (A) (controllable), emerges two decision branches – the sales EVP either signs up for a free service or he doesn't.

If he signs up, then it will cost him $75,000. If he doesn't, then it is not going to cost him anything ($0) at that point of the decision. This is the dead end of the decision and hence a terminal node (B) is placed at the end of this branch.

Next, if he signs up (for the event) then the event branch emerges out of the event node (C) (uncontrollable) with two mutually exclusive and mutually exhaustive events – either the client goes ahead with the paid

Still Using Gut Feeling for Making Decisions?

service or not. If the client goes for the paid service, the EVP (supplier) will receive an advance payment of +$200,000 (E), else $0. This branch is again the dead end and hence a terminal node (D) is placed.

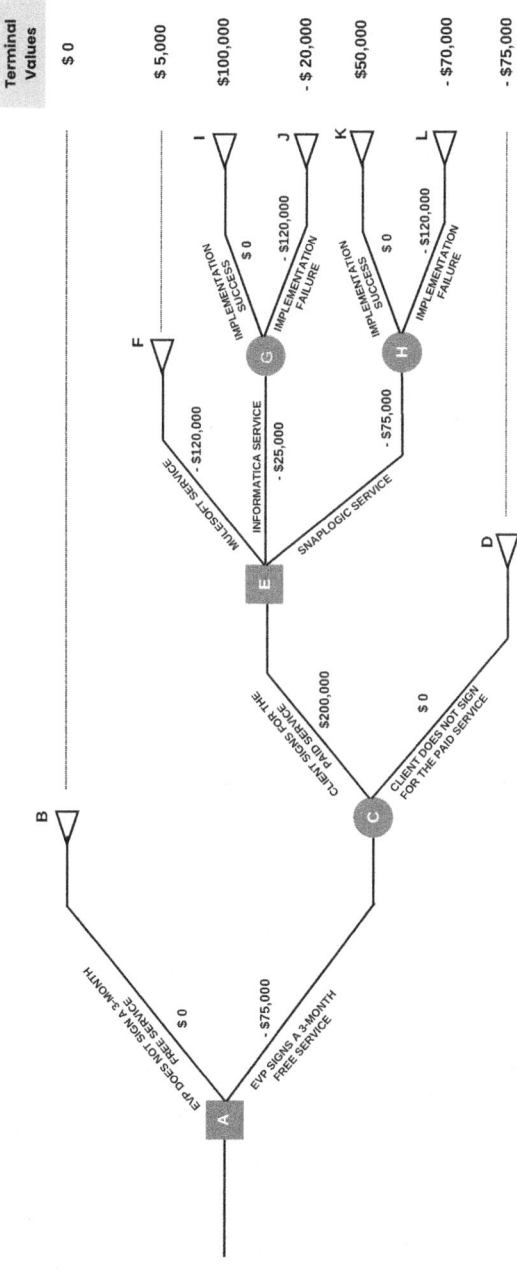

The Secrets of Design Thinking Mindset

Further, since the client is now on board, the supplier has a choice of three integrators, MuleSoft (F), Informatica (G), and SnapLogic (H), which is going to cost the supplier $120,000 (USD), $25,000(USD) and $75,000(USD) respectively.

As you see in the last paragraph of the example, the solution architects are 100% confident that the MuleSoft integrator would be a success, hence a dead end – a terminal node is placed.

Similarly, calculate the values for the other event branches.

Step-2
How to Calculate the Terminal Values?

Branch	Branch Indicator	Cash Flow	Terminal Value
	A-C	-$75,000	
A-C-E-F	C-E	+$200,000	$ 5000
	E-F	-$120,000	
	A-C	-$75,000	
	C-E	+$200,000	
A-C-E-G-I	E-G	-$25,000	$ 100,000
	G-I	$0	
	A-C	-$75,000	
	C-E	+$200,000	
A-C-E-G-J	E-G	-$25,000	-$ 20,000
	G-J	-$120,000	
A-C-E-H-K	?	?	?
A-C-E-H-L	?	?	?
A-B	?	?	?

Step-3

Now, the last part is to assign probabilities and calculate the nodal rollback values.

Till now, the tree that you have learned is a decision tree. In this last part, we will assign the probability to each event branch to make the decisions more meaningful.

Consider each circle (which represents an area of uncertainty) and calculate the probability of each possible outcome. If you are using percentages, each circle's total must equal 100 percent. If fractions are used, they must total up to 1. Making accurate probability estimates may be possible if you have data on previous occurrences. Alternatively, write down the best estimate.

Based on the evidence or past data, the EVP thinks there is a 60% (0.6) chance the client will sign up for the paid service and 40% (0.4) of not.

The solution architects think there is a 100% (1) chance of delivering the project successfully with the MuleSoft integrator. A 50% (0.5) chance of successful delivery through Informatica and a 70% (0.7) chance of successful delivery through SnapLogic.

Let's put all these probability values on the decision tree and calculate the **nodal rollback values** at the nodes A, C, E, G, and H.

How to Calculate Rollback Values?

- At the event node, the rollback value is calculated using the expected value or probability-weighted average, which means multiplying the respective branch probability by the successor rollback value, and the products of these are added.
- At the decision node, the rollback value is maximum on the immediate successor node.

The Secrets of Design Thinking Mindset

After substituting all the nodal values on the tree, the decision path (A-C-E-G-I) is a clear winner that the EVP has to follow to get the maximum from the business deal. However, if the Informatica service fails, then they have to resort to the MuleSoft service.

Terminal Node	Terminal Values
B	$ 0
D	- $ 75,000
F	$ 5000
I	$ 100,000
J	- $ 20,000
K	$ 50,000
L	-$ 70,000

Rollback Node	Formula	Substitution	Nodal Value
G Branch G-I and G-J	(Terminal value at node I x Probability value) + (Terminal value at J node x Probability value)	(100,000 x 0.5) + (-20,000 x 0.5)	$40,000
H Branch H-K and H-L	(Terminal value at node K x Probability value) + (Terminal value at L node x Probability value)	(50,000 x 0.7) + (-70,000 x 0.3)	$14,000
E Branch E-F, E-G and H-F	Max(F, G, H)	Max(5,000; 40,000; 14,000)	$40,000
C Branch C-E and C-D	(Value on C-E x Probability value) + (Value on terminal node D x Probability value)	(40,000 x 0.7) + (-75,000 x 0.3)	$5,500
A	Max(B,C)	Max(0, 5,500)	$5,500

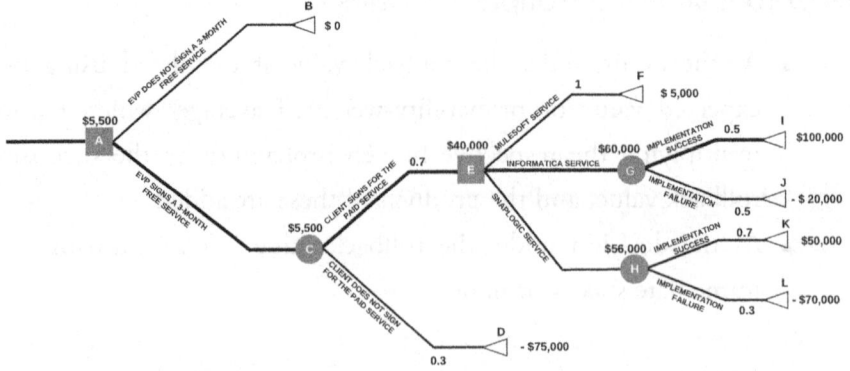

WHAT IS YOUR DECISION-MAKING STYLE?
A Self-Assessment

There are many different approaches to decision-making, and picking one can be just as challenging as making the choice itself!

You may need to make decisions on your own from time to time, but you don't want to come off as being a dictator or autocratic to the rest of the team (particularly in situations where you need their input). Other times, it's preferable to decide based on group agreement, although doing so can consume valuable time and resources. **So how do you select the most effective strategy?**

I strongly recommend answering these seven **Vroom-Yetton-Jago** decision-making model questions before proceeding to the detailed section on understating and interpreting the styles.

1. Is the quality of the decision on this problem very important? YES NO

2. Are team members/stakeholders' collaboration and commitment important for the decision that you are taking? YES NO

3. Do you have sufficient information to make this important decision yourself? YES NO

4. Has the problem been accurately identified such that it is clear what has to be done and its implications? YES NO

5. Is it feasible to expect that the team/stakeholders will unanimously agree or welcome or be sufficiently engaged and driven to accept your decision if you make this decision alone? YES NO

6. Are the team's or business unit's objectives in line with those established by the organization to determine what constitutes a successful solution? YES NO

> 7. If your team/stakeholders had to make this decision, are conflicts expected on the decision taken by you alone and its associated solution or outcome? YES NO

Keep reading from here to understand what your style of decision-making is. Along the way, you will discover the significance of each question and its implications.

VROOM-YETTON-JAGO DECISION-MAKING MODEL

The **Vroom-Yetton-Jago decision model** helps you choose the strategy. **Victor Vroom** and **Phillip William Yetton** devised the **Vroom-Yetton-Jago Decision Model** in 1973, and **Arthur G. Jago** contributed enhancements to it 15 years later.

The **Vroom-Yetton-Jago model** can be followed by anyone – from an intern to a leader.

Understanding the following three factors is important to comprehend the **Vroom-Yetton-Jago model.**

1. Quality of the Decision

The decision's quality is of paramount importance in decision making which depends on its potential influence and how crucial it is to come up with the best answer. And also, the quality of the decision is directly proportional to the number of members, time, information, and cross-functional teams involved in decision-making.

2. Collaboration and Team Work

The next important factor is collaboration and team commitment. While some of your decisions may significantly affect your team/stakeholders and hence collaborating with your team/stakeholders becomes imperative to enhance the decision's quality.

Some decisions that you take may not impact your team/stakeholders directly and hence, may not be necessary to include them in those decisions so that the process of decision-making is quicker.

For instance, if swiftness and decisiveness are required, this will probably push you in the direction of an **authoritarian** or **autocratic approach**. If cooperation is required, it will push you in the direction of a more **democratic procedure**.

3. Time Constraints

Time restraints refer to how much time you have to make a specific decision. If you're short on time, you can't include a team member or stakeholder in the decision-making process. However, if you have a lot of time, you can consult with the other members of your team before making a choice.

When the subject in question isn't time critical, you have more luxury to explore your alternatives and incorporate others, which will assist to increase the quality of your decision. However, if you are short on time, it might not be possible to include others or do in-depth research.

The Five Decision-Making Styles of V-Y-J Model

1. **Autocratic I Style (A1)** – In this style, you as an individual will make your own decision by not considering or consulting your team members or stakeholders. In short, you will take the decision and you tell your decision to the stakeholders.

2. **Autocratic II Style (A2)** – In this style, again, the choice is made independently by you in the situation as well, but unlike autocratic style 1, you or the leader has a little more time and obtains data from the team or other sources.

    The team members/stakeholders are not aware of why you are requesting the information from them. You talk to your team/

stakeholders to get the precise facts you want before making the final choice.

3. **Consultative I Style (C1)** – In this style, you brief your team/stakeholder on the issue and solicit each one's viewpoint or opinion separately and you don't bring the team together for this exercise; however, the final decision is made by you.

   Your approach here is consultative to actively take the initiative to solicit each team member's/stakeholder's viewpoint on the issue at hand.

   Compared to the autocratic decision-making method, the level of team participation is higher in this style. You are still in charge of making the final choice, and you are free to reject the team's suggestions and opinions unless they impact your understanding of the problem at hand.

4. **Consultative II Style (C2)** – In this style, you assemble a team for a group discussion and brainstorming, as opposed to the first consulting style, where the leader solicits the team members'/stakeholders' ideas.

   At this meeting, thoughts and ideas are requested and you will ultimately be the one to take the decision.

5. **Group II (G2)** – In this style, the decision is made by the entire team. You explain the situation and the problem to the team and suggest potential solutions. You don't enforce your ideas onto the group.

   You only serve as a facilitator, accepting the team's choice without expressing your perspective or vision.

Still Using Gut Feeling for Making Decisions?

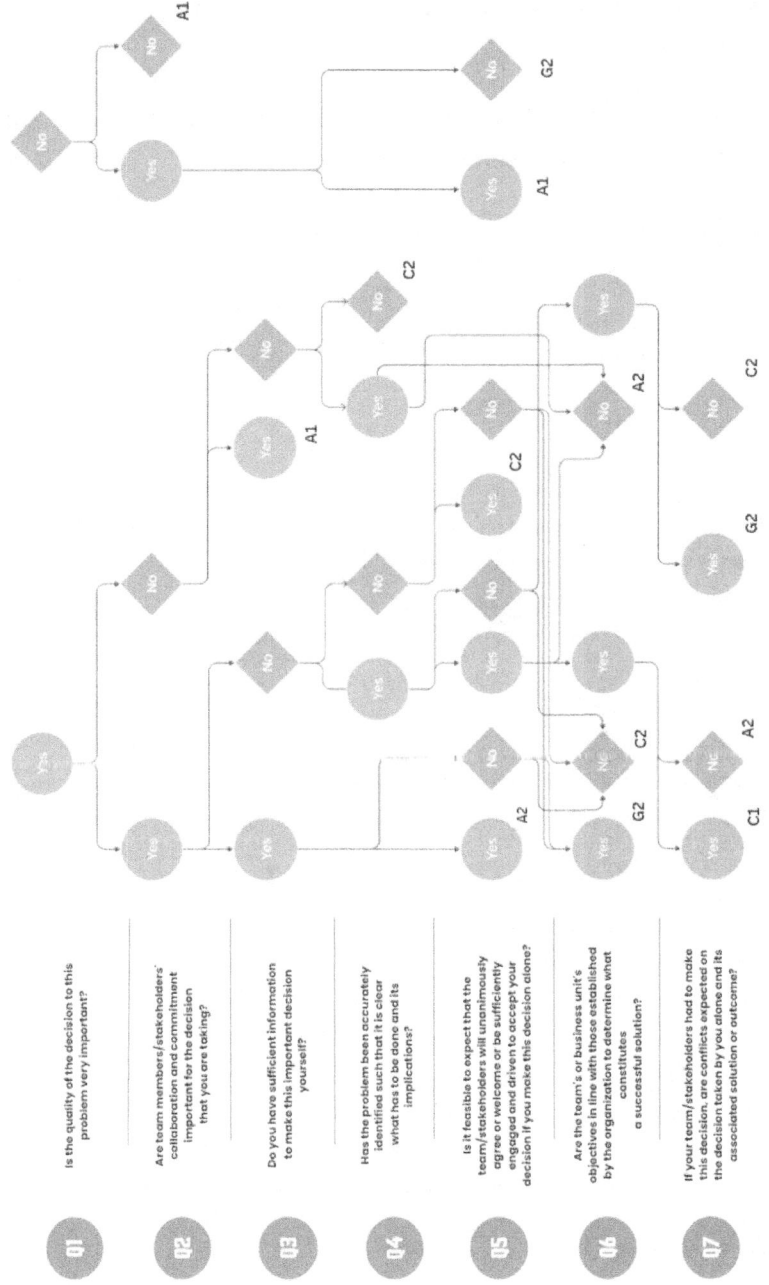

The decision tree that you see is the **Vroom-Yetton-Jago Decision-Making** tree.

The Secrets of Design Thinking Mindset

Based on the 7 answers to the questions (at the beginning of this section), you will see here what type of decision would be best.

Example: Say, the following are your answers to those seven **Vroom-Yetton-Jago Decision-Making** questions:

Q1 – Yes   Q4 – Yes

Q2 – Yes   Q5 – Yes

Q3 – No   Q6 – Yes

Q7 – No

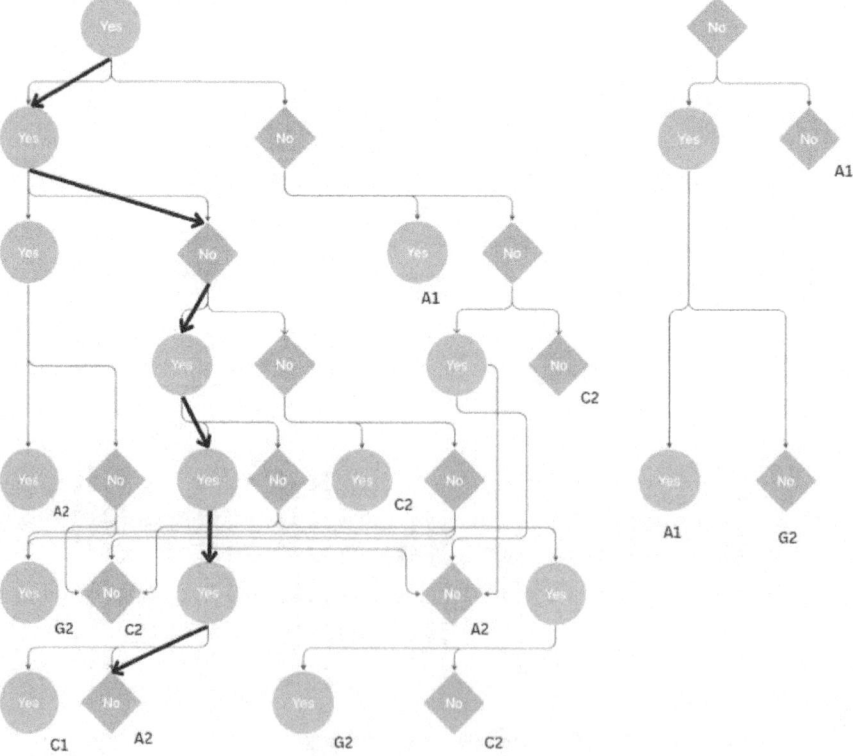

After traversing all seven rungs, you have reached the last leaf which is pointing at the A2 style of decision-making. This means the current problem at hand or the issue, assuming all your responses were thoughtful and apt, can be solved with the Aristocratic II (A2) style (refer to the description of the A2 style at the beginning of the section).

>  You are asked by your management to decide whether your team can start working from the office all five days as the CoViD-19 lockdown rules have been relaxed.
>
> You take up **Vroom-Yetton-Jago's** seven questions and the following are your answers:
>
> Q1 – Yes Q5 – No
>
> Q2 – Yes Q6 – Yes
>
> Q3 – No Q7 – No
>
> Q4 – No
>
> What is the decision-making style you need to follow for the above set of answers?

SIMPLE DECISION MATRIX (SDM)

A set of options can be compared against a set of criteria using the effective quantitative tool known as the **Simple Decision Matrix (SDM)**.

One important assumption that is done in **SDM** is to treat all the potential and qualifying criteria as having equal importance. Now, what if each of these criteria is of varying importance? You will learn that in the next section – **Weighted Decision Matrix (WDM)**.

When you have to select the best alternative and must carefully analyze a wide set of independent variables, parameters, choices, and alternatives, it is a really helpful tool that you can adopt.

With the use of a decision matrix, you can give the decision-making process a structured framework that eliminates uncertainty and emotion. Decision-making becomes logical and unbiased as a result of this.

You can use the matrix to refer back to your choices in conversations, gatherings, or presentations where you have to justify the basis or rationale of your decision.

How to Apply SDM?

The following are the three steps in adopting the SDM.

1. Freeze on the problem statement
2. Identify the selection or performance criteria
3. Brainstorm and list the choices or alternatives
4. Follow a grading scale
5. Construct the Decision Matrix

Step-1

First, you need to finalize the exact problem statement or the issue that you or your stakeholders are facing for which you would like to take a decision.

You can refer to the chapter on problem-solving in this book where a detailed section on how to build a problem statement is explained.

Let's take an example.

ABC Pvt. Ltd. company wants to buy a CRM tool that is apt for their type of business.

One of their competitors is using Microsoft Dynamics CRM. Should ABC Pvt. Ltd. company also buy Microsoft Dynamics?

Let's follow the **SDM** steps to arrive at a decision and help ABC Pvt. Ltd. company buy a best-fit CRM for their business style.

Problem statement: Finding an apt CRM for ABC Pvt. Ltd. for the nature of their business model.

Refer chapter-2 for a detailed discussion on the formulation of a good problem statement.

Step-2

Next, you need to identify the selection criteria against which you will compare the choices (Step-3).

The ABC Pvt. Ltd. company identifies the following parameters:

1. Employee Tracking
2. Built-in Social Media Features
3. CRM Analytics
4. Sales Forecasting
5. Third-Party Integration Ease

For the nature of business, the company has chosen the above five critical parameters the CRM must possess. They are not looking at the cost of the CRM as it will be taken care of by the angel investors.

Step-3

Now, the company has to list down the CRM software providers. After many deliberations and due diligence they have shortlisted the following CRMs that are the best fit for their business:

1. Salesforce
2. Microsoft Dynamics
3. SAP
4. Zoho
5. Oracle

Step-4

In this step, you have to prepare a grading scale. You can use a 3-point, 5-point, or 7-point based on the fineness of the comparison you would like to do.

ABC Pvt. Ltd. company chooses the following 5-point scale.

    1 – Very Poor   4 – Good

    2 – Poor   5 – Very Good

    3 – Fair

Step-5

	Employee Tracking	Social Media Feature	CRM Analytics	Sales Forecasting	Ease of Integration
Salesforce					
Microsoft Dynamics					
SAP					
Zoho					
Oracle					

Construct a **decision matrix** as shown. The selection criteria are arranged column-wise and the alternatives or choices, are row-wise.

In the blank cells, the scores are populated based on the expert's advice or based on the team's collective wisdom using the 5-point scale that was chosen at the beginning of step-4.

	Employee Tracking	Social Media Feature	CRM Analytics	Sales Forecasting	Ease of Integration
Salesforce	4	3	4	5	3
Microsoft Dynamics	3	2	4	3	3
SAP	3	4	5	4	4
Zoho	4	3	2	2	3
Oracle	1	2	4	4	2

The team thinks that for the Salesforce CRM, the Employee Tracking feature is GOOD, and hence from the 4 has been allocated.

Similarly, ABC Pvt. Ltd. company has to evaluate each of the parameters and score them.

	Employee Tracking	Social Media Feature	CRM Analytics	Sales Forecasting	Ease of Integration	Total Score	Ranking
Salesforce	4	3	4	5	3	19	2
Microsoft Dynamics	3	2	4	3	3	15	3
SAP	3	4	5	4	4	20	1
Zoho	4	3	2	2	3	14	4
Oracle	1	2	4	4	2	13	5

Next, add all the scores along each of the alternative CRMs and rank them based on the scores in descending order. Descending order of the total score to the ascending order of the ranking.

	Employee Tracking	Social Media Feature	CRM Analytics	Sales Forecasting	Ease of Integration	Total Score	Ranking
Salesforce	4	3	4	5	3	19	2
Microsoft Dynamics	3	2	4	3	3	15	3
SAP	3	4	5	4	4	20	1
Zoho	4	3	2	2	3	14	4
Oracle	1	2	4	4	2	13	5

And you can see that SAP scores 20 points which is the highest among the 5 alternatives. Hence, ABC Pvt. Ltd. company should shortlist SAP and do further in-depth analysis with the experts and take a call.

WEIGHTED DECISION MATRIX (WDM)

In the Simple Decision Matrix (SDM), all the selection criteria are considered to have equal importance and hence have equal weight.

In some cases, each of the selection criteria can have different importance, and accordingly, their weights have to be taken into consideration.

Weights can be assigned in two formats viz.,

1. Percentage such that the sum of all weights is equal to 100% or 1.
2. A weight-scaled natural number similar to the scoring parameters (as in step 4 in SDM) with their qualitative definitions.

How to Apply WDM?

The following are the steps in adopting the **WDM**.

1. Freeze on the problem statement (same as SDM).
2. Identify the selection or performance criteria (same as SDM).
3. Brainstorm and list the choices or alternatives (same as SDM).
4. Follow a grading scale (same as SDM).
5. Define the weight scale.
6. Construct the Decision Matrix.

We will use the same example of ABC Pvt. Ltd. company. Since steps 1,2,3 and 4 are the same as SDM, we will not repeat the process here.

Step-1 Refer to SDM for this step

Step-2 Refer to SDM for this step

Step-3 Refer to SDM for this step

Step-4 Refer to SDM for this step

Step-5

The company decides to use a 3-point weight scale.

1 – Not Important

2 – Neutral

3 – Very Important

The meaning of the weights is that particular selection criteria are either very important to be present in the CRM, or neutral which makes no difference if that criteria is present or absent in the CRM, or not important if the criteria is not a priority to have in the package.

Borrowing the same table from Step-5 of SDM (previous section)

Still Using Gut Feeling for Making Decisions?

	Employee Tracking	Social Media Feature	CRM Analytics	Sales Forecasting	Ease of Integration
Salesforce	4	3	4	5	3
Microsoft Dynamics	3	2	4	3	3
SAP	3	4	5	4	4
Zoho	4	3	2	2	3
Oracle	1	2	4	4	2

The company has assigned the weight 3 to two of the selection criteria (Employee tracking and Sales Forecasting) which is very important (qualitative definition) for them based on their current business scenario.

	Employee Tracking	Social Media Feature	CRM Analytics	Sales Forecasting	Ease of Integration
Weight	3	1	2	3	2
Salesforce	4 x 3 = 12	3 x 1 = 3	4 x 2 = 8	5 x 3 = 15	3 x 2 = 6
Microsoft Dynamics	3 x 3 = 9	2 x 1 = 2	4 x 2 = 8	3 x 3 = 9	3 x 2 = 6
SAP	3 x 3 = 9	4 x 1 = 4	5 x 2 = 10	4 x 3 = 12	4 x 2 = 8
Zoho	4 x 3 = 12	3 x 1 = 3	2 x 2 = 4	2 x 3 = 6	3 x 2 = 6
Oracle	1 x 3 = 3	2 x 1 = 2	4 x 2 = 8	4 x 3 = 12	2 x 2 = 4

Next, each of the scores has to be multiplied by their respective weights. It can also be noted that **SDM is a special case of WDM** where the weights for each criterion are equal to 1.

Now, add the new scores (Total Score) and rank (Rating) them.

	Employee Tracking	Social Media Feature	CRM Analytics	Sales Forecasting	Ease of Integration	Total Score	Ranking
Weight	3	1	2	3	2		
Salesforce	4 x 3 = 12	3 x 1 = 3	4 x 2 = 8	5 x 3 = 15	3 x 2 = 6	44	1
Microsoft Dynamics	3 x 3 = 9	2 x 1 = 2	4 x 2 = 8	3 x 3 = 9	3 x 2 = 6	34	3
SAP	3 x 3 = 9	4 x 1 = 4	5 x 2 = 10	4 x 3 = 12	4 x 2 = 8	43	2
Zoho	4 x 3 = 12	3 x 1 = 3	2 x 2 = 4	2 x 3 = 6	3 x 2 = 6	31	4
Oracle	1 x 3 = 3	2 x 1 = 2	4 x 2 = 8	4 x 3 = 12	2 x 2 = 4	29	5

You will observe that in the **weighted decision matrix** Salesforce has emerged as a winner with more points based on relevance and importance.

	Employee Tracking	Social Media Feature	CRM Analytics	Sales Forecasting	Ease of Integration	Total Score	Ranking
Weight	3	1	2	3	2		
Salesforce	4 x 3 = 12	3 x 1 = 3	4 x 2 = 8	5 x 3 = 15	3 x 2 = 6	44	1
Microsoft Dynamics	3 x 3 = 9	2 x 1 = 2	4 x 2 = 8	3 x 3 = 9	3 x 2 = 6	34	3
SAP	3 x 3 = 9	4 x 1 = 4	5 x 2 = 10	4 x 3 = 12	4 x 2 = 8	43	2
Zoho	4 x 3 = 12	3 x 1 = 3	2 x 2 = 4	2 x 3 = 6	3 x 2 = 6	31	4
Oracle	1 x 3 = 3	2 x 1 = 2	4 x 2 = 8	4 x 3 = 12	2 x 2 = 4	29	5

 As mentioned in this section, weights can be assigned in two formats viz.,

1. Percentage such that the sum of all weights is equal to 100% or 1.
2. A weight-scaled natural number similar to the scoring parameters (as in Step-4 in SDM) with their qualitative definitions, construct the same WDM with the percentage weight which when added will add up to 100% or 1.
    a. Employee Tracking (0.25)
    b. Built-in Social Media Features (0.15)
    c. CRM Analytics (0.10)
    d. Sales Forecasting (0.20)
    e. Third-Party Integration Ease (0.30)

WHAT IF YOU HAVE INFINITE CHOICES?

The previous techniques are essentially applied if the number of choices is not more than five to seven. What if the alternatives or choices to choose from are more, say, 10? How do you deal with such a large number of choices?

The upcoming sections will discuss how to identify **vital few from trivial many**.

N/3 VOTING

This technique is also known as **multi-voting** or **dot-voting**.

N/3 voting is a relatively straightforward **elimination technique** that may be used to assist a team in choosing among several possibilities or alternatives.

If the number of choices is more, then before using more complex decision-making tools like **Paired Comparison** and/or **Decision Matrix**, it is very helpful to swiftly narrow down a long list of possibilities to a manageable amount.

$$\text{Voting (V)} = \frac{N}{3}$$

Where **N** is the number of options/choices/alternatives that we would like to trim down to a manageable number (say, 5)

How to Apply N/3 Voting?

Step-1

Identify all the choices that you have for solving the current issue or the problem.

The ABC Pvt. Ltd. company had close to fifteen CRMs which they trimmed down to five.

Those fifteen CRMs were as follows:

1. Salesforce
2. Monday Sales
3. Pipedrive
4. Zendesk
5. Oracle
6. HubSpot
7. SAP
8. SugarCRM
9. Zoho
10. Sage
11. Freshsales
12. Insightly
13. Microsoft Dynamics
14. Adobe
15. NetSuite

Step-2

It becomes increasingly difficult to use the paired comparison or Pugh matrix for these fifteen alternatives.

Form a Cross Functional Team (CFT) as this is a group or team exercise.

With the team's help, we need to trim down to the vital few CRMs.

Assume there are six team members for this exercise. Each team member will get N/3 votes to vote for their choice.

$$\text{Voting (V)} = \frac{N}{3} = \frac{\text{Number of Choices}}{3}$$

$$= \frac{15}{3}$$

$$= 5 \text{ Votes each}$$

Each member will have 5 votes they can use to vote for the CRM that he/she thinks is a better fit.

If the number of votes turns out to be decimal, like 4.3 or 6.45, etc., accordingly round them off.

So, for a team size of six, there will be a total of **5 x 6 = 30 votes**.

The team members cast their votes based on the expert knowledge they have of the CRMs and the company's business model.

There is no veto power to any individual even if the EVP is participating in the voting unless they have substantial knowledge about the CRM which others are not aware of.

Try to avoid an individual casting all his/her votes to only one CRM. **One vote: One choice.**

Step-3

Next, count the votes and select the top voted choices for your further scrutiny which is proceeding with other sophisticated decision models discussed in this chapter.

The number of stars are the votes which on adding up will sum to 30 which is equal to the value arrived in step-2.

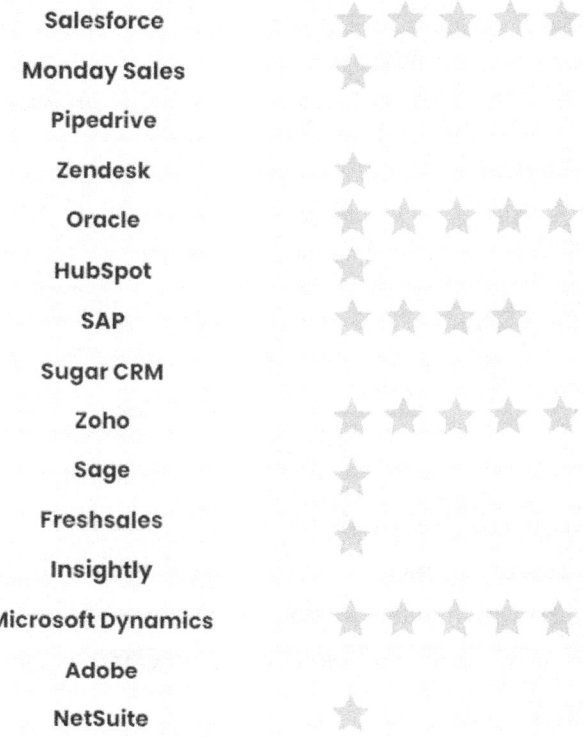

Salesforce	★★★★★
Monday Sales	★
Pipedrive	
Zendesk	★
Oracle	★★★★★
HubSpot	★
SAP	★★★
Sugar CRM	
Zoho	★★★★★
Sage	★
Freshsales	★
Insightly	
Microsoft Dynamics	★★★★★
Adobe	
NetSuite	★

From the above voting, we have SF, Oracle, Zoho, Microsoft Dynamics as vital few with 5 stars.

This is how you reduce to a vital few from a trivial many. From here you can apply other advanced decision models on the vital few to decide or narrow it down to 1 winner.

EASE-BENEFIT MATRIX

The **Ease-Benefit matrix** can be another potential tool to taper down the number of choices to fewer.

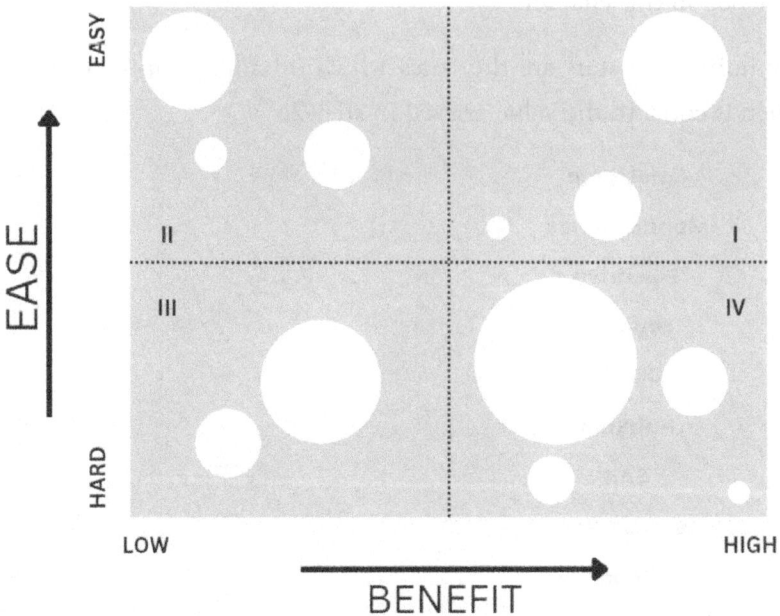

The **Ease-Benefit matrix** has the **benefit** on the **x-axis** and **ease** (of implementation, accomplishment) on the **y-axis**. Additionally, there are circles of varying sizes which indicate either the number of days required to complete the task or the number of resources required or the cost involved in completing the task, etc.

For example, the position of the circle in the first quadrant depicts high benefits and is easy to implement. However, the size of the circle cautions that it would take a greater number of days or resources to accomplish it.

So, one can use this **E-B matrix** to cut down on the number of choices from trivial many to a vital few.

PLUS-MINUS-INTERESTING (PMI)

Edward de Bono created the **Plus-Minus-Interesting (PMI)** technique as a tool for decision-making. However, this tool can also be used for critical thinking and brainstorming.

PMI, which is a **three-columned decision-making** or thinking strategy, fosters the inquiry of views and opinions from multiple angles and examines the benefits (plus), drawbacks (minus), interesting, or fascinating details of an event. **PMI** can help evaluate concepts alone or in combination to generate an opinion or alternative. Further, it also enables us to make judgments fast by analyzing and balancing the advantages and disadvantages.

Following are the definitions of **PMI**:

Plus: Any positive characteristic, favorable aspects or elements, expected advantages, consequences, or outcomes are listed under the plus grid with positive weights.

Minus: Any negative characteristic, unfavorable aspects or elements, predicted issues, or effects are listed under the minus grid with negative weights.

Interesting: Any perspective that takes into account various viewpoints, other than plus and minus which could be out-of-the-box aspects or by combining the plus and minus aspects can be a part of this grid.

This grid encourages creative thinking during the decision making process that otherwise is not captured in the conventional pros and cons or advantages and disadvantages. Here the weights can range from negative to positive.

The points on the **PMI grid** can be weighted from -3 to +3.

Attach qualitative definitions to -3,-2,-1,0,1,2,3.

How to Apply PMI?

Step-1

Invite the team for this decision-making session. Again, you can use the flipcharts for physical settings or the PDAs for online collaborations.

The team could be a team of experts or stakeholders and they should be aware/ briefed about the problem statement.

Let's say, your management wants to buy an LMS and you need the teams' input on whether should they buy or not.

Step-2

Draw the PMI grid

PLUS	MINUS	INTERESTING
Score =	Score =	Score =

Step-3

Allow the team to write down all the plus points first. Everyone in the team must contribute to plus points only. Once the team thinks it has exhausted the plus points, then the minus points are addressed again by the entire team.

Here, the team should contribute equally to plus and minus points.

Once the plus and minus are done, the team can now look at the interesting points which could not fit into the plus and minus grid. These interesting points could be a combination of the point from a plus grid and a minus grid or between the same grids which can be listed along with the weights ranging from -3 to +3.

PLUS	MINUS	INTERESTING
Better learning (+3)	Course-centric than student-centric (-3)	Can we build it in-house? (+2)
Automation of attendance (+2)	Dedicated admin needed (-3)	Assign it as an internal project? (+2)
Tracks learner's progress (+3)	Integration issues (-2)	Takes longer time to develop (-3)
Any time learning (+2)		
Score =	Score =	Score =

Step-4

Now, calculate the score for each of the grids and re-evaluate the options by combining them with other columns or girds to take a final decision.

PLUS	MINUS	INTERESTING
Better learning (+3)	Course-centric than student-centric (-3)	Can we build it in-house? (+2)
Automation of attendance (+2)	Dedicated admin needed (-3)	Assign it as an internal project? (+2)
Tracks learner's progress (+3)	Integration issues (-2)	Takes longer time to develop (-3)
Any time learning (+2)		
Score = 10	Score = -8	Score = 1

Seeing the scores, the PLUS outweighs the other two, hence, the management can go ahead with buying the LMS.

PICK CHART

PICK is an acronym for **Possible, Implement, Challenge**, and **Kill**. The **PICK chart** is a 2x2 visual method for classifying your ideas or choices/alternatives for better judgment and decision-making.

The **PICK chart** is also an effective tool that can be very effective after brainstorming or a brainwriting session. Brainstorming and brainwriting generate a vast set of choices/ideas/alternatives which is then mapped onto the **PICK chart** and can be tapered down from trivial many to a vital few.

PICK charts are frequently used to assist a person or group in determining which concepts have the highest likelihood of success.

The Secrets of Design Thinking Mindset

The following are the definitions:

P (Possible) – those alternatives or choices that are doable and easy to implement, yet with low payoffs or returns.

I (Implement) – those alternatives or choices with high payoffs or returns that are simple to implement and execute.

C (Challenge) – those alternatives or choices that are challenging to implement and with high payoffs or returns.

K (Kill) – those alternatives or choices with the poor payoff or returns and higher difficulty in implementing and should be killed.

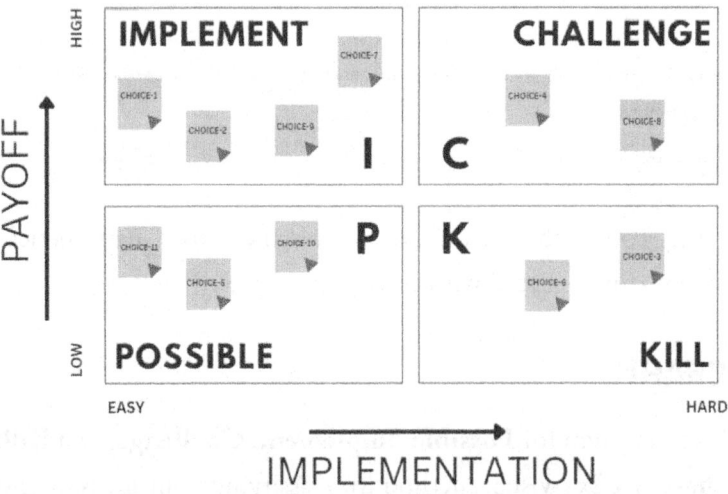

Consider one of your decision-making exercises, brainstorm alternatives with your team, and use the **PICK chart** to narrow down the choices for effective decision-making. After the **PICK chart** exercise, you can use **paired comparison method** or **Pugh method**, or **decision tree** to make your final decision.

For your current project/work, perform the PICK analysis.

Possible (Easy to Implement, Low Payoff)

List down your choices here:

_____

_____

_____

Implement (Easy to Implement, High Payoff)

List down your choices here:

_____

_____

_____

Challenge (Hard to Implement, High Payoff)

List down your choices here:

_____

_____

_____

Kill (Hard to Implement, Low Payoff)

List down your choices here:

_____

_____

_____

KJ ANALYSIS

KJ analysis is another technique much like other **pre-processor techniques** like the **PICK chart, N/3**, or **PMI** which helps you to taper down from **trivial many to vital few** choices or alternatives generated from a brainstorming or brainwriting session. Once your vital few are identified, you can further apply other advanced methods to take a decision.

KJ method also known as the **affinity diagram** or **affinity mapping** or **thematic** or **cluster analysis** was developed by Japanese anthropologist **Jiro Kawakita** in the 1960s. In Japanese, they put the last name first, and hence the initial **Kawakita Jiro (KJ)** is named after him.

How to Apply KJ Method?

Step-1

Like other decision-making techniques, the problem statement has to be well-defined using the tools discussed in the problem-solving chapter in this book.

Once the problem statement is framed, you can move to Step-2.

Step-2

In this step, assemble a Cross Functional Team (CFT)/SMEs to contribute to the exercise so that you can come out with a quality decision towards the end.

If worthy alternatives or choices are not identified, then the quality of the final decision will be hampered. So, it is extremely important to have SMEs in these sessions.

Capture all the alternatives or choices from all the participants.

Still Using Gut Feeling for Making Decisions?

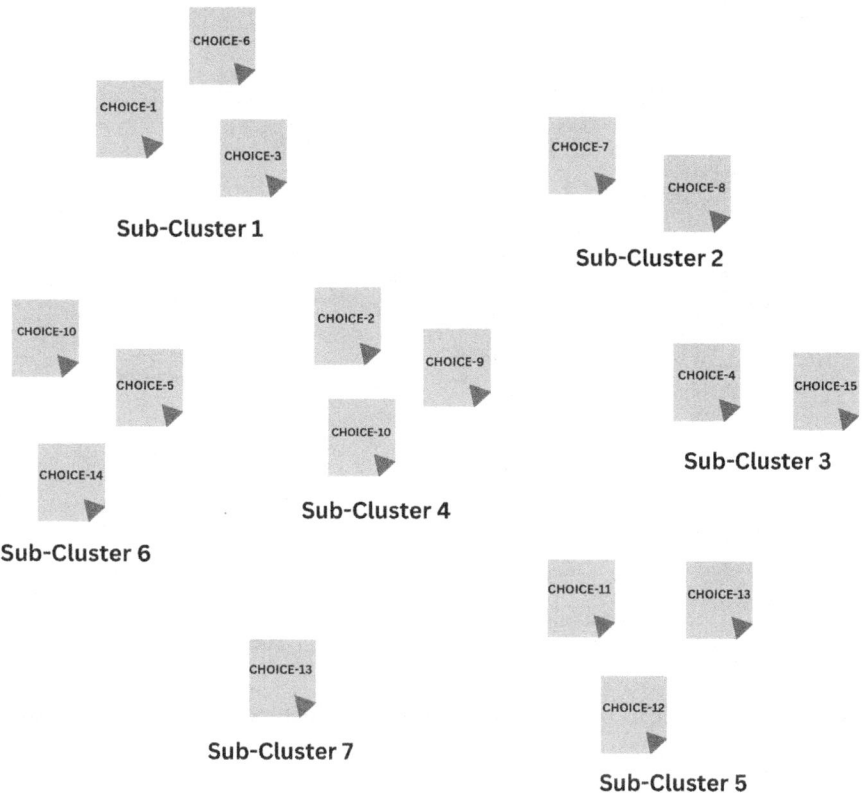

Step-3

Once the team is exhausted with identifying the potential choices or possibilities, the next phase is to group them.

Look for the choices that have relationships between or among them and accordingly group them. During this grouping, no discussion among the team members is allowed.

After some time, the cluttered ideas start forming sub-clusters that are logically connected.

The Secrets of Design Thinking Mindset

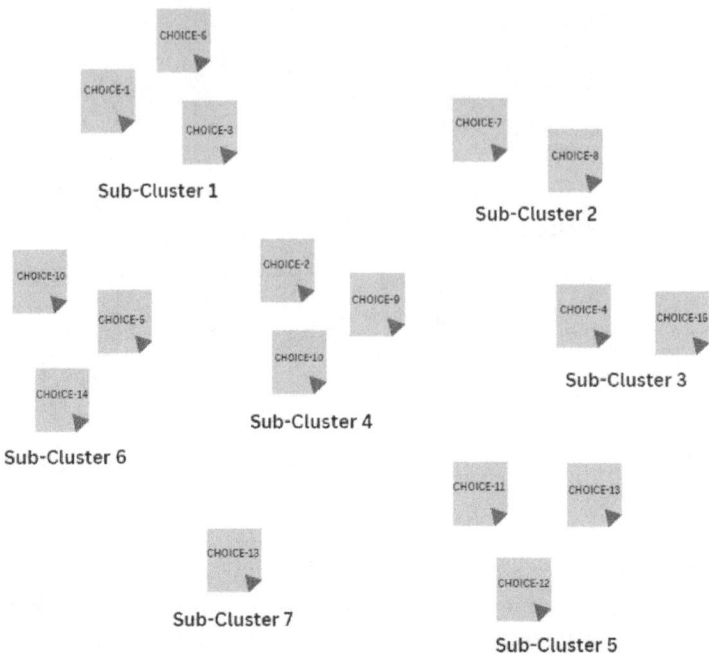

Again, find relations between or among sub-clusters to form main clusters or groups.

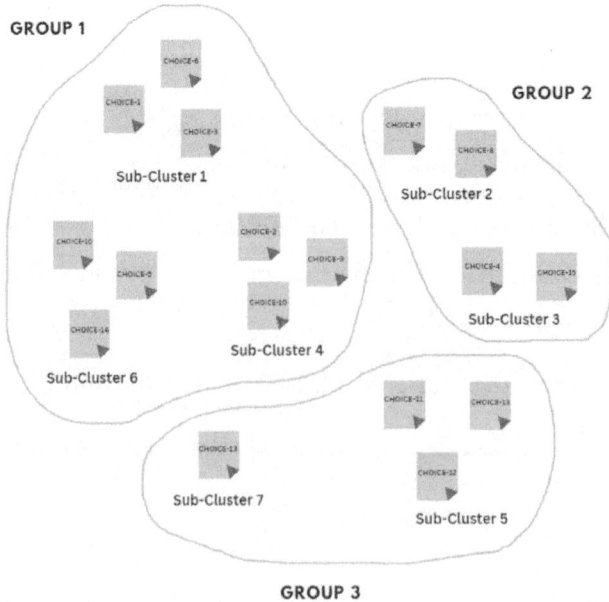

Step-4

Now, open the discussion among the team members to label these groups based on their functionality and operation.

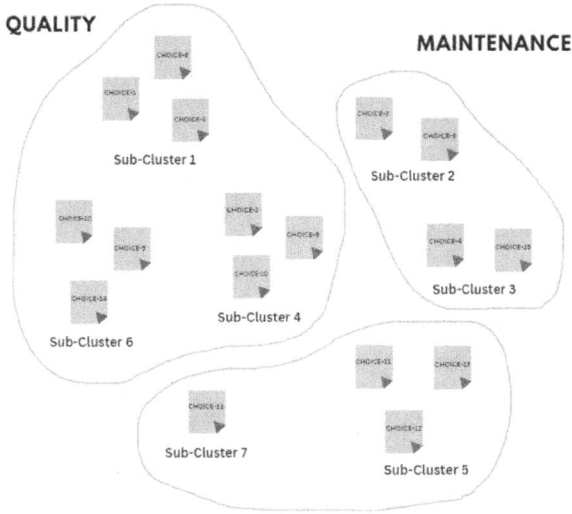

You can observe that the several choices with which the exercise started have now been reduced to 3 groups which can further be processed using any of the advanced decision-making techniques discussed in this chapter.

>  Can you use the following combinations and assess the quality of the decision?
>
> 1. PMI as pre-processor and decision tree as processor.
> 2. KJ method as pre-processor and paired comparison as processor.
> 3. N/3 as pre-processor and WDM as processor.
>
> What are the challenges that you face during applying these combinations? Discuss with your team.

"It's not the customer's job to know what they want"

– **Steve Jobs**

5

HOW TO CREATE WOW PRODUCTS FOR YOUR CLIENT?

HAVE YOU BEEN IN KEVIN'S SITUATION?

Kevin has been appointed as the head of Global Product Research (GPR) in a reputed fortune 500 company.

Kevin wants to launch an innovative, first-of-its-kind product and invites the global team to share ideas to incorporate into the (software) product.

In one month, he received a flurry of ideas and he selects the 20 best and most promising ideas for detailed scrutiny.

At this stage, Kevin is unable to decide which idea to implement as all 20 seem to be the best. On the other hand, he cannot stuff all 20 features in 1 product keeping the cost and size of the (software) product/service in mind.

Have you been through Kevin's situation, unable to decide which features to implement while creating a WOW product/service for your clients or buyers?

In this chapter, we will explore the technique which keeps the buyer/customer/client at the fore while implementing or deciding which features to add to the product/service to create those incredible and delightful moments during your client presentations.

FIND THAT X-FACTOR TO ADD TO YOUR PRODUCT

You are working on a project and this client is very important to your business. You want to give the best to your client with respect to the service you are offering or the (software) product you are selling.

Like every marketing, innovation, product, or brand manager, you could also be encountering significant hurdles as a result of new (software) product/feature and service advancements.

The most crucial query is, "Which feature(s) affect(s) your clients/customers/buyers' satisfaction, and which feature creates that WOW moment when you reveal that feature/product/service to them?"

Your team could be having innumerable ideas, but not all of them can be developed or implemented.

Keep reading to learn the technique of designing a customer-centric (software) product or a service by deploying only those features that your client/customer/buyer will never mind paying extra dollars for.

THE KANO REACTION MODEL

Who is Kano?

Dr. Noriaki Kano, (pronounced "Kah-no"), a professor of quality management at the Tokyo University of Science, published the **Kano Analysis Model** in 1984.

Kano Analysis Model is the technique widely used to help enhance the product/service based on customers' emotions.

The **Consumer Delight vs Implementation Investment** technique, also known as the **Kano Analytical Model** or the **Kano's Model**, is an analysis tool that helps you to comprehend how customers' emotional responses to goods, products, services, or features may be quantified and examined.

What is the Kano Model?

Kano's Model uses the following five emotional response types:

1. Must-be (or must-have) features
2. Performance features

How to Create Wow Products for Your Client?

3. Attractive features
4. Indifferent features
5. Reverse features

You can see how these 5 response types are depicted on the graph.

To understand the Kano Reaction Model, it is imperative to know the axes which are **Feature Functionality** (X-axis) and **Customer Satisfaction** (Y-axis).

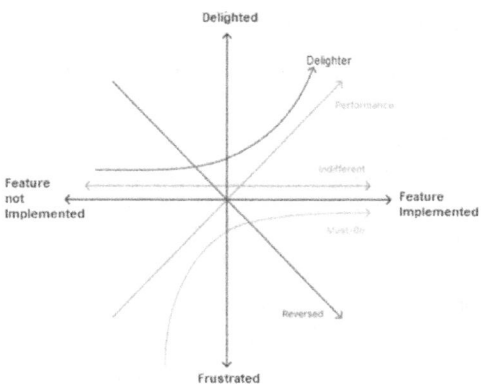

Let us deconstruct the graph and understand each element and its correlation with customer reactions.

X-Axis Spectrum

Dr. Kano created a **Feature Functionality scale** (X-axis) which on the extreme left indicates a particular feature in the product not implemented, (moving one notch towards the right) to some features being implemented in the (software) product or service, (moving one notch towards right) to

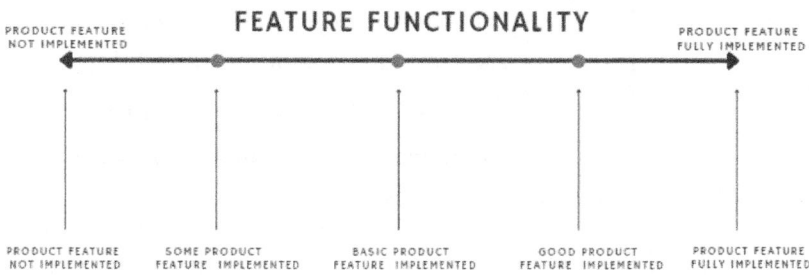

basic features implemented in the (software) product or service, (moving one notch towards right) then to good features being implemented, and finally on the extreme right, to the full implementation of the features in the (software) product or service.

Y-Axis Spectrum

Dr. Kano created a **Customer Satisfaction scale** (Y-axis) which at the lowest end indicates the customer is frustrated because a particular feature is not included/present in the (software) product/process or because that particular feature is still present/included in the (software) product/process.

Moving one notch higher on the scale, the customer is dissatisfied again because of the presence or absence of a particular feature in the (software) product/process.

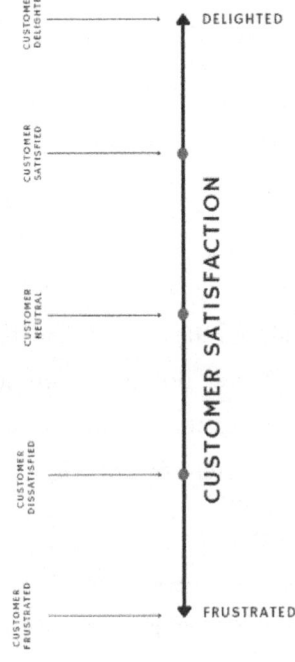

Again, moving one notch higher which is the center of the Y-axis (on the scale), the customer is in a neutral state (neither frustrated nor delighted) despite the feature being present or absent in the (software) product or process or service.

Moving one more notch higher on the axis, the customer is satisfied because of the presence or absence of that particular feature in the (software) product or process, or service.

Finally, moving to the extreme top on the axis, the customer is fully delighted or ecstatic because of the presence or absence of that particular feature present/included in the (software) product or process, or service.

How to Create Wow Products for Your Client?

This is how the combined X and Y axes a.k.a. Kano's **Feature Functionality and Customer Satisfaction** axes look.

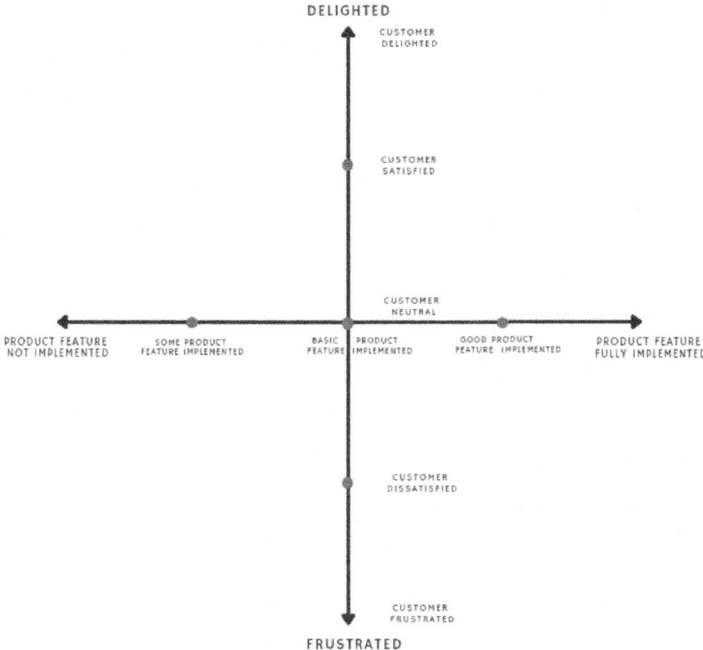

ANATOMY OF THE KANO MODEL

Let us understand the different features' emotional responses in the model.

1. Must-be (or must-have) Features
2. Performance Features
3. Attractive or Excitement Features
4. Indifferent Features
5. Reverse Features

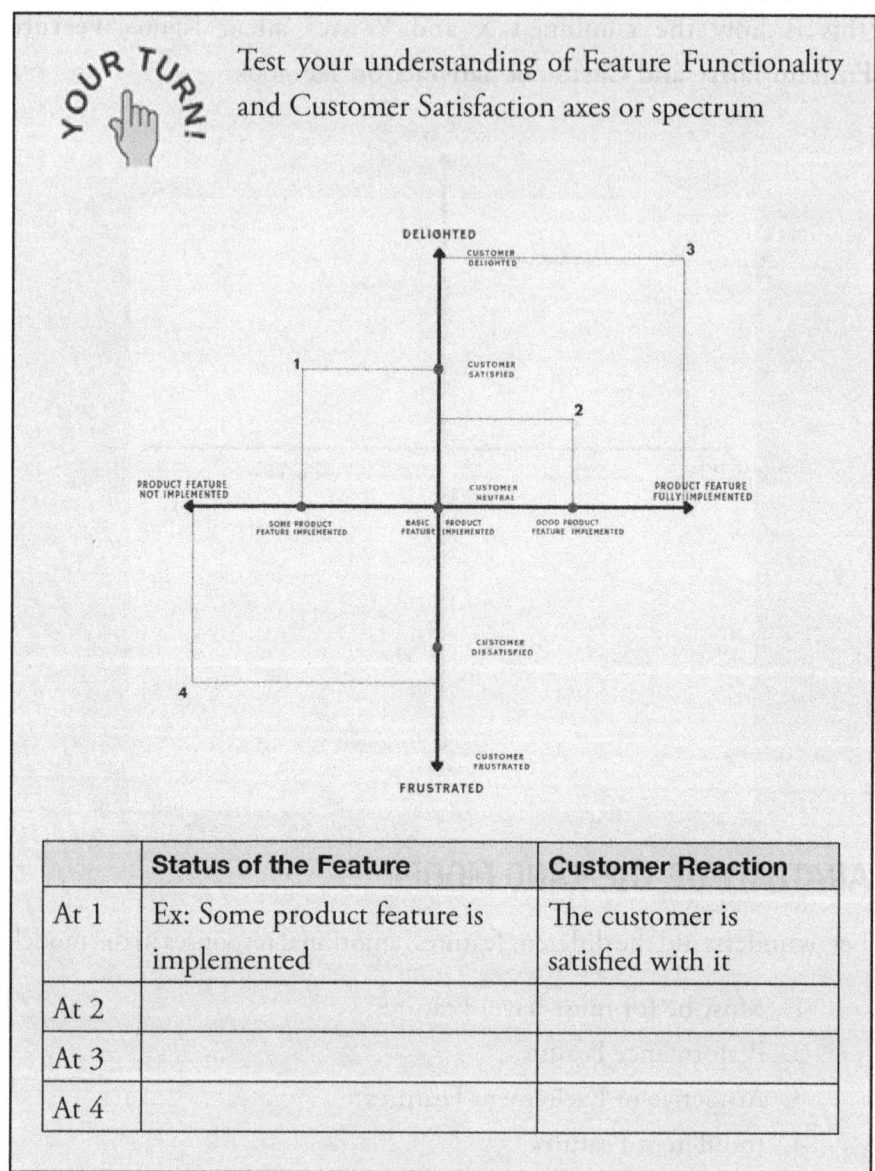

	Status of the Feature	Customer Reaction
At 1	Ex: Some product feature is implemented	The customer is satisfied with it
At 2		
At 3		
At 4		

1. Must-be (Basic or Must-have) Features

Under this category, customers anticipate/expect a (software) product or service to have some **fundamental** or **basic** or **must-be** or **must-have** features, which are represented by the **must-be curve** on the Kano graph.

How to Create Wow Products for Your Client?

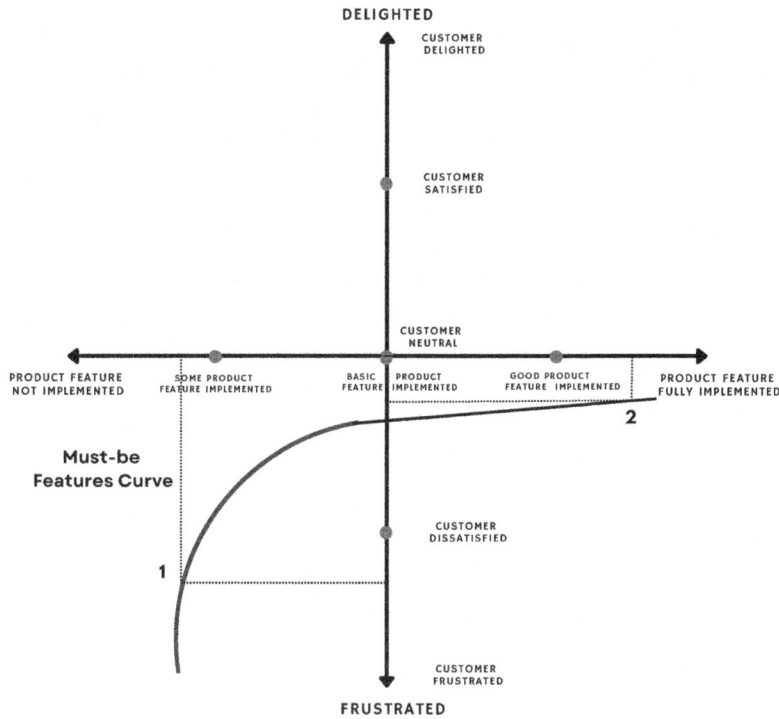

This is also referred to as threshold attributes a (software) product or service MUST have by default.

It is very important to note that if these basic or **must-have** features are included in the product or service, the customer is likely to be neutral (refer to the Y-axis or Customer Satisfaction axis and locate where is the Customer Neutral range) about them (refer point-2 on the graph). And also having these **basic must-be** features or having them in abundance won't likely add more customer satisfaction or customer ecstasy.

On the contrary, the absence of these **basic** or **must-be** features in the product or service will cause tremendous dissatisfaction (refer to point-1 on the graph). That is why the curve steeply stoops around point-1.

Let us take an example: Suppose you are going on a vacation and you have booked a hotel for a week. You arrive at the hotel, step into your suite or room and notice that the bedspreads and blankets are missing. How would you feel? You will be immediately dissatisfied with the service or get frustrated (similar to point-1 on the graph).

On the contrary, you step into your suite or room and notice that there are 5 bedspreads and 5 blankets. How would you feel? You will not feel delighted or very satisfied or excited for having these basic amenities in abundance (refer to the Customer Satisfaction axis). You would say in your mind, "hmmm…. Ok….". Even if you find 20 bedspreads and 20 blankets, your reaction will be the same.

What is the inference? Your product MUST have **must-haves** or **basic features** even though it does not create any delightful or exciting moments for your client. However, if the same basic features are missing, your client will lose his/her cool instantly and it may lead to an unpleasant situation (you might lose the client).

On the other hand, if you stuff these **basic features** in abundance in your product or service, you know what will be the client's reaction. So, keep the **must-have** features to a minimum.

2. Performance Features

Performance features in your product or service have a linear relationship or correlation to customer satisfaction.

The lesser these features are in your product or service, the lesser satisfied your customers are. The more of these features are in your product or service, the higher will be customer satisfaction. They must meet client expectations and be of comparable caliber to the same features as your competitors.

How to Create Wow Products for Your Client?

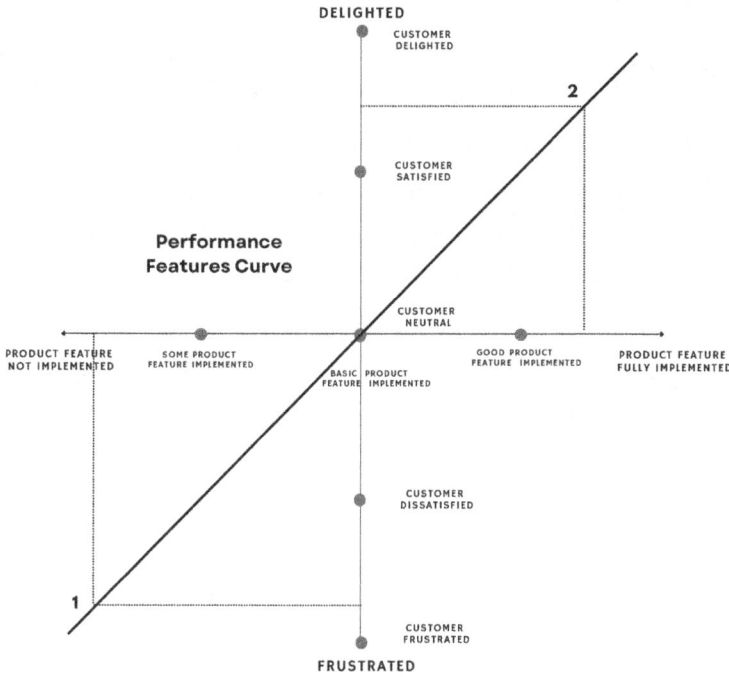

Related to the **Performance Attribute** or **Performance Features** line on the Kano graph, **performance features** are desired features that customers want to have to add to their enjoyment of the product or feature.

Kano described **performance features** as 'one-directional', as they increase satisfaction and excitement, and functionality upwards (refer to point-2 on the performance feature line). This means if there are a lot of **performance features** in your product or service, then customer satisfaction or excitement will enhance in response.

On the contrary, if these **performance features** are not present or they are fewer in your product or service, customer satisfaction or excitement will also reduce proportionately (refer to point-1 on the performance feature line).

The Secrets of Design Thinking Mindset

- Can you find or identify those features in your product or service or process that give a WOW moment to your customer?
- Alternatively, can you identify those features, which if you do not include in your product or service or process, the customer or client would be frustrated (or escalate the issue or return the product or withdraw the services)?
- For your product or service, plot the loci pertaining to those features on the performance feature curve.

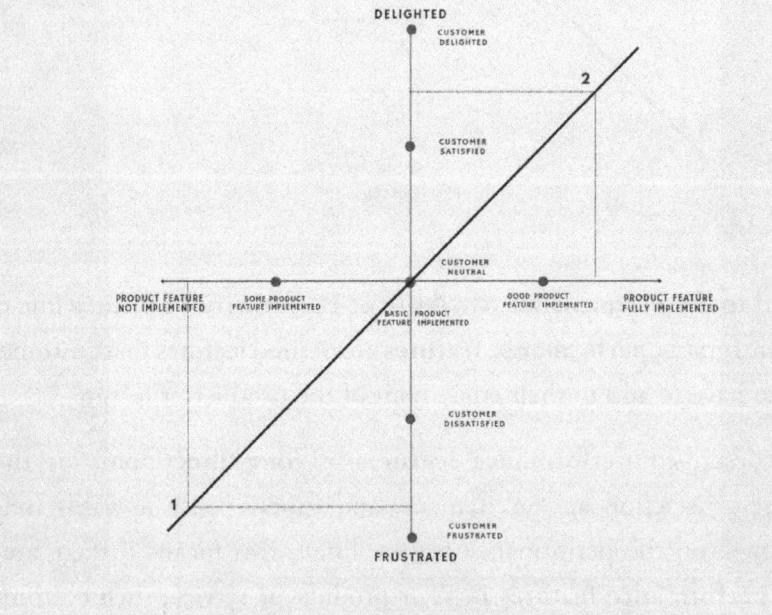

3. Attractive or Excitement Features

Attractive features or **capabilities**, if present in your product or service, will have exponential customer delight or excitement. The **wow factor** traits that can provide you with a competitive edge are called excitement attributes.

Although your buyers or clients do not anticipate these features, they are welcomed if they are offered. Your customer's ecstasy or pleasure is not adversely impacted if they are absent (refer to point-1 on the excitement feature curve). However, if these features are included in your product or service, then it will help you stand out from the competitors.

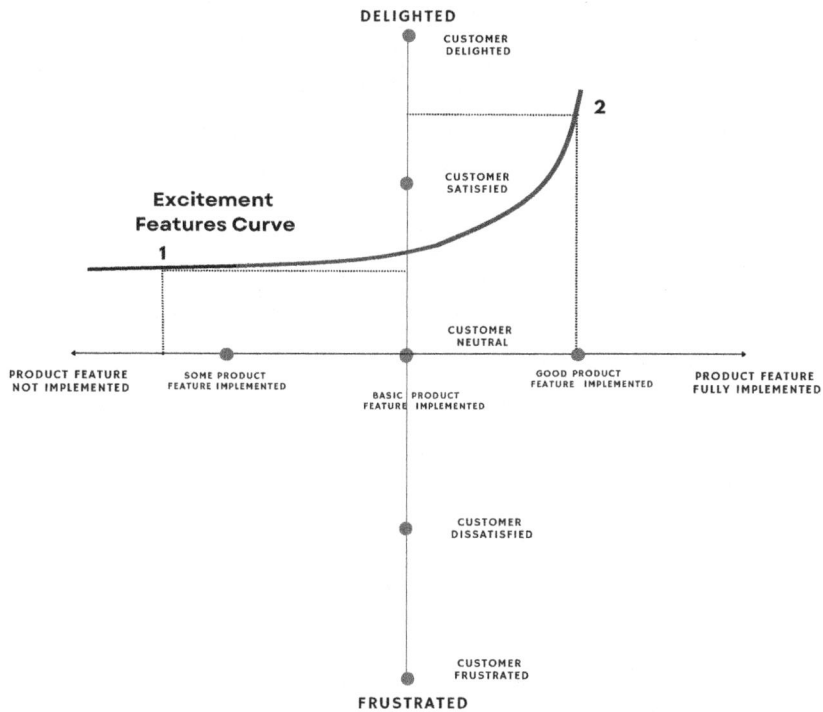

Given that you don't need many of these features to achieve high levels of customer satisfaction, they can be smart investments.

- Can you find or identify those features, when implemented in your product or service, or process, can excite your customer?
- Alternatively, can you identify those features in your product, which even if not included in your product or service or process, the customer is OK with it?
- For your product or service, plot the loci pertaining to those features on the excitement feature curve.

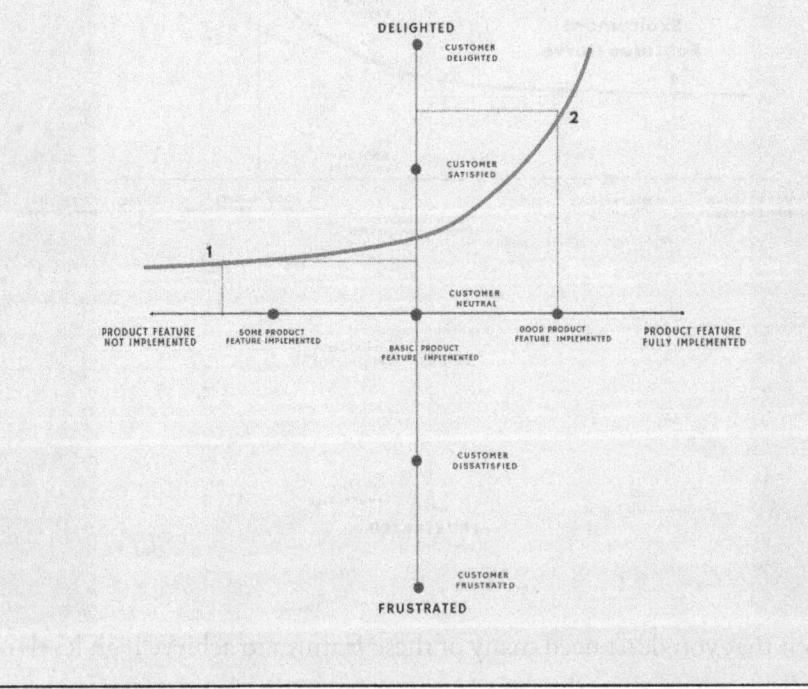

Product features that excite or thrill clients distinguish your product or service from the competitors.

Let us take an example: Suppose, again, you are on a vacation trip and book a hotel that has basic amenities in the room or suite. You step into the room and to your pleasant surprise, you find an attached mini bar counter along with an open kitchen.

What effect would it have on your excitement? Very obviously, you will be very delighted and ecstatic (refer to point-2 on the excitement curve) as you did not expect this feature in the room or suite you had booked, but the hotel management has given it to you because of various reasons. Maybe, you are their 100th customer or the suite that you had booked was not available once you arrived at the hotel.

4. Indifferent (Neutral) Features

As the name indicates, these are the features or capabilities which do not add value for your customers. In addition, they also do not have any impact on satisfaction, either when present or absent.

Features that are neutral don't elicit either satisfaction or dissatisfaction (refer to point-1 and 2 on the Kano line). They are inconspicuous elements that have no bearing on the customer.

Let us take an example: In the same suite that you had booked in a hotel, you step in and find there is a wooden cupboard to keep your clothes and luggage.

Now, whether the cupboard is wooden or metal, would it make any difference to you? If it is a wooden cupboard, your reaction will be the same as if it had been a metal cupboard.

Therefore, while deciding on these **neutral features** or capabilities for your product, be judicious. Too many of these **neutral features** are not going to impact the customer's emotion, however, it will add up to your product cost. Think about it!

The Secrets of Design Thinking Mindset

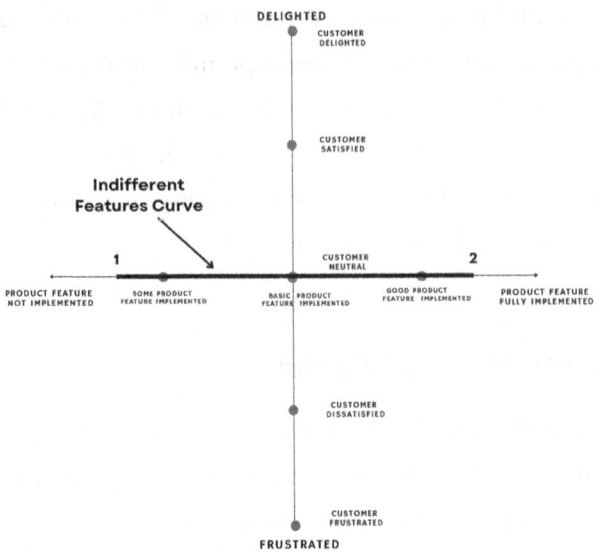

- Can you find or identify those features, when implemented in your product or service, or process, can excite your customer?
- Alternatively, can you identify those features in your product, which even if not included in your product or service or process, the customer is OK with it?
- For your product or service, plot the loci pertaining to those features on the excitement feature curve.

5. Reverse Features

When the presence of any feature or capability in your product or service causes clients to be dissatisfied while the removal of these features causes them to be satisfied, it is said to be a **reverse feature**.

You want to detect these and exclude them from your design. Implementing such features raises design and development expenses while lowering the product's value in the eyes of the client.

How to Create Wow Products for Your Client?

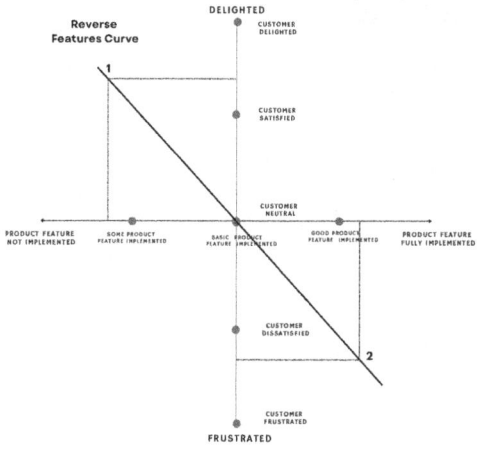

- Can you think of a generic example of a feature in a product that can be classified as a reverse feature?

- From the reverse figure line on the model, can you identify a capability in your process that can be placed at point-1 (feature if absent, causes near delight) and point-2 (feature if present, causes near frustration)?

- For your product or service, plot the loci pertaining to those features on the reverse feature curve.

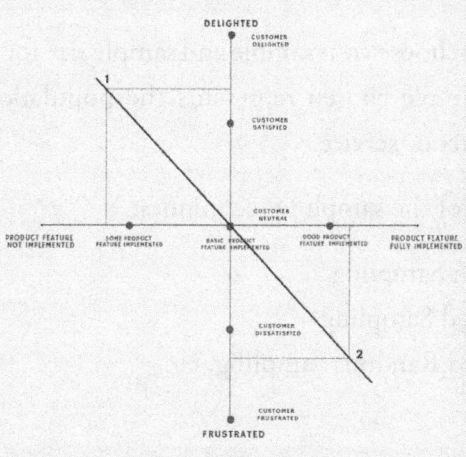

PUTTING IT TOGETHER

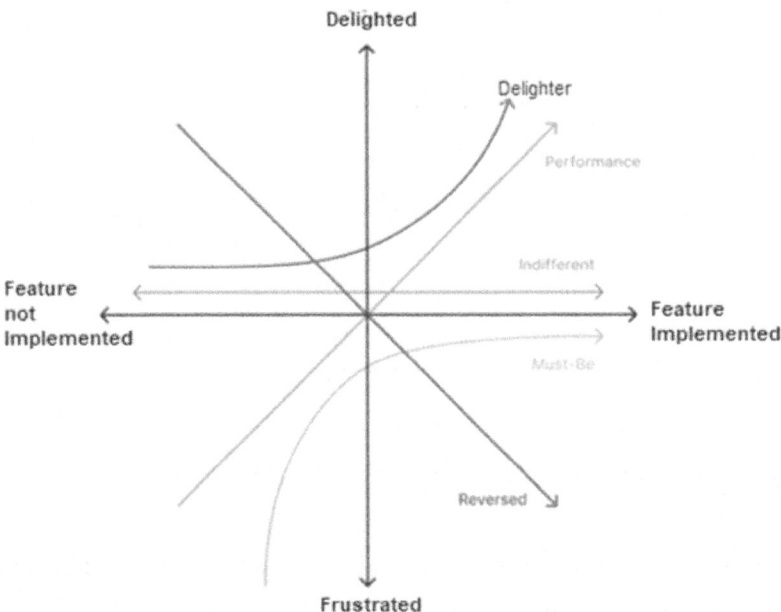

How to Apply Kano Model to your Products?

Step-1 List and select all the features that you would like to incorporate into your (software) product/service/process.

Step-2 Carefully choose your sample and sample size for the feature survey such that the sample chosen represents the population that uses your (software) product or service.

You can use any of the sampling techniques:

    i. Random Sampling
   ii. Clustered Sampling
  iii. Stratified Random Sampling, etc.

How to Create Wow Products for Your Client?

You can learn more about these probabilistic and non-probabilistic sampling types from a good Applied Statistics book and adopt a suitable method for your survey.

Let us learn how to conduct the standardized Kano survey and finalize features for your product.

	Love it	Expect it	Don't Mind	Tolerate it	Hate it
FUNCTIONAL QUESTIONS					
How do you feel if the product has XYZ feature?					
How do you feel if the product has more of XYZ feature?					
DYSFUNCTIONAL QUESTIONS					
How do you feel if the product does not have XYZ feature?					
How do you feel if the product has less of XYZ feature?					

Your survey must have both questions – **functional and dysfunctional** – for every feature that is being surveyed.

Step-3 Once the responses are collected, you can use the following grid and matrix to decode the customer's reactions or responses.

FUNCTIONAL		DYSFUNCTIONAL		FEATURE CLASSIFICATION
LOVE IT	+	HATE IT	=	PERFORMANCE FEATURE
LOVE IT	+	DON'T MIND	=	DELIGHT FEATURE
EXPECT IT	+	HATE IT	=	MUST-BE FEATURE
DON'T MIND	+	DON'T MIND	=	INDIFFERENT FEATURE
HATE IT	+	EXPECT IT	=	REVERSE FEATURE

Kano's Response Evaluation Grid

Populating the responses in a matrix form for all the combinations of the responses for the feature:

		DYSFUNCTIONAL RESPONSES				
		LOVE IT	EXPECT IT	DON'T MIND	TOLERATE IT	HATE IT
FUNCTIONAL RESPONSES	LOVE IT	Q	D	D	D	P
	EXPECT IT	R	Q	I	I	M
	DON'T MIND	R	I	I	I	M
	TOLERATE IT	R	I	I	Q	M
	HATE IT	R	R	R	R	Q

Kano's Response Matrix

Q: Questionable Response   P: Performance

M: Must-Have   I: Indifferent

D: Delighter   R: Reverse

Step-4: After doing the basic formulation of the responses, you can do:

i. A Discrete Response Analysis
ii. A Continuous Response Analysis (beyond the scope of the book)

- ## Discrete Response Analysis

The **discrete response analysis** is also called a **mode analysis table** or **frequency analysis table**.

Here the percentages of responses are collected and calculated as shown in the table.

The **discrete response analysis** has a few challenges, but it's a fantastic place to start and gives us a general understanding of the outcomes.

Imagine, you are a product manager who is responsible to incorporate features in your company's new phone that will be launched one year from now.

Certainly, you would like to know which features the customers hate the most to have in the phone and which features they are delighted or excited to have. You conduct a survey following the procedure mentioned in step-1, step-2, and step-3.

From the survey of your sampling, you will tabulate the following discrete responses.

	MUST-HAVE	PERFORMANCE	DELIGHTER	INDIFFERENT	REVERSE	FEATURE TYPE
CHARGER	20% (500)	40% (650)	23% (690)	13% (500)	4% (550)	PERFORMANCE
TOUCH SCREEN	73% (600)	3% (650)	6% (650)	12% (575)	6% (506)	MUST-HAVE
500 HRS BATTERY	4% (587)	32% (450)	45% (395)	9% (434)	10% (500)	DELIGHTER
FITNESS TRACKER	24% (543)	23% (399)	5% (600)	40% (593)	8% (632)	INDIFFERENT
50 GB CLOUD SPACE	20% (429)	19% (387)	51% (650)	3% (613)	7% (619)	DELIGHTER

From the responses gathered, what is your inference? Discuss it with your team.

In discrete response analysis, along the mathematical process, a lot of meaningful information is lost and we fail to understand the variance in the responses collected.

Hence, the continuous response analysis is preferred which is mathematically intense where we use statistical concepts; hence, restricting our scope of study to discrete response analysis and keeping this book math-light.

Step-5 Now, prioritize the features that you would like to incorporate into your product.

   i. First concentrate on **must-have** or **must-be features** in your product
   ii. Try to use as many **performance features** as possible considering the final product cost in mind
   iii. You can comfortably neglect the **indifferent features** as they are not adding any value
   iv. Eliminate all the **reverse features** from your product

 For the product that you are developing, do the following along with your team:

1. Identify all the features that you would like to include in your product.
2. Create a Kano's reaction survey questionnaire.
3. Prepare a Kano's response matrix.
4. Analyze the responses using the discrete response analysis method.
5. Finalize the features that you would like to include based on Step-5 guidelines.
6. Plot these features on Kano's reaction graph (use sticky notes).

"The key is not to prioritize what's on your schedule, but to schedule your priorities."

– **Stephen Covey**

6

HOW TO PRIORITIZE YOUR PRIORITIES?

HAVE YOU BEEN IN SOPHIA'S SITUATION?

Sophia has secured a software testing job in a multinational company recently. She has about one year of prior experience in testing at a small firm.

While testing software in her new job, she comes across the following errors:

1. User Interface Errors
2. Boundary Related Errors
3. Control Flow Errors
4. Calculation Errors
5. Testing Errors
6. Hardware Errors

Out of these six errors, she has to recommend to the developer team which of the errors have to be solved on a priority and immediate basis.

To Sophia, all six errors seem equally important and she is confused about what she should convey to the development team in the team meeting.

Have you been in this situation where you were in two minds on which problem or error to tackle first?

In this chapter, you will discover some tools and techniques to help you rank which task or problem to solve.

WHAT IS COOKING IN YOUR PROJECT?....R I C E?

You are working as a product manager and you are supposed to make informed decisions on the implementation of features in your product and prioritize them.

Of late, you are stressed and confused, unable to offer your expert advice or justify which feature to be ranked first… second… third… etc. to the management.

If you are finding yourself in a similar situation then you are not aware of the **R I C E** scoring model of prioritization that can help bail you out in such an awkward situation.

WHAT IS R I C E?

R I C E is an acronym for **Reach**, **Impact**, **Confidence**, and **Effort**.

With the **RICE** model, you may objectively evaluate each feature of a product concept, which also aids in balancing costs and advantages.

When deciding which features or project ideas should be focused on first, product managers may more easily classify them using the **RICE** score. It helps product managers quantify the projected value of a feature or project concept.

The R I C E Equation

$$\text{RICE Score} = \frac{R \times I \times C}{E}$$

where R = Reach, I = Impact, C = Confidence, E = Effort.

- **REACH**

The **reach** factor is a projection of the number of relevant consumers/customers that a given idea or product could reach over a specified timeframe.

You are in charge of defining the users in this case as well as the scope of the **reach**. This might be the impact that a feature concept will have on any particular market group that is pertinent to your product, whether it is made up of current or potential customers.

Here is how you can use the **reach** score. As you are the product manager and your team is developing an app feature that will be accessible to all customers who consistently log in to check their bank balance at the end of each month.

Suppose there are 200 users each month, for a total of 600 users per quarter.

Alternatively, you have 800 customers reach and only 40% of them avail of the services or buy your product. Then your **reach** will be 800 x 40% x 3 months = 960 customers is your **reach** for a quarter.

You can do this exercise with your product team. No team member's score should influence the scoring pattern of the rest. Collect all these scores and take the mean or average, and you will get your **reach score**. If any of your team members have very low or high **reach scores** – please investigate the variance and try to keep it as closer to zero as possible. This confirms the unanimity of the team's **reach scores.**

- **IMPACT**

The **reach** score makes a good faith effort to answer the question: How many people will this new concept or feature affect? The **impact score** makes an effort to answer the subsequent question: By how much?

Impact refers to how much you believe a particular concept or feature could influence a particular objective for a particular client. For example, as you are the product manager, the **impact** is defined as the potential influence of a concept on the possibility that a single prospective client would become a long-term paying customer.

How to Prioritize Your Priorities?

Alternatively, for your product which is listed on the e-commerce website, anticipate that out of the one million visitors to the site over 30 days, 10,000 will purchase a product. The impact is measured overall by the 10,000 individuals.

Setting a quantifiable objective is made easier by **impact.** What are your objectives, such as conversions, acquisition of new clients, fostering customer loyalty, etc.? The "why" a consumer makes a decision is difficult to ascertain from statistics alone, making this indicator more challenging to quantify.

The **impact scoring** method has five levels viz.,

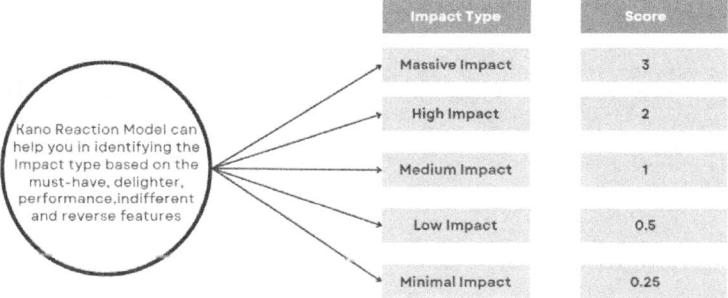

Again you can do this exercise with your product team. No team member's score should influence the scoring pattern of the rest. Collect all these scores and take the mean or average, and you will get your **impact score.** If any of your team members have very low or high impact scores – please investigate the variance and try to keep it as closer to zero as possible. This confirms the unanimity of the team's **impact scores.**

- **CONFIDENCE**

For unduly optimistic **reach** and **impact scores** that you may have given, a **confidence score** serves as a bias damper. How confident are you in the **reach, impact**, and **effort scores** (in the next section) that you assigned to each idea/concept/feature that may be quantified by **confidence**?

Let's imagine you have quantified the **reach**, **impact**, and **effort scores**, but you still believe that you lack the necessary data or information to be confident in those ratings. This uncertainty is taken into account in the RICE formula by including a **confidence score**.

Here is the **confidence scale**. The confidence score is always in the percentage.

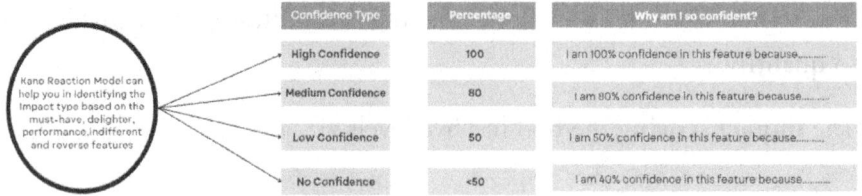

For example, Medium Confidence is 80%; hence in the calculation it should be used as 80/100 = 0.8.

The obvious limitation that comes from low confidence is that you as a product manager have not researched much on this idea/concept or the feature.

This will propel you to do enough research on the idea or the feature that you are planning to implement.

Hence, the **C** in **R I C E** plays a vital role in prioritization. High levels of **confidence** ratings should be anchored in user context and statistics, such as research and experimentation. Your confidence has to be based on authentic and scientific data.

- ## EFFORT

This is the quantity of labor or time required for your team to develop a feature or finish a project. You can also use **effort** as a function of time or budget to calculate the **RICE scores**.

How to Prioritize Your Priorities?

>  Can you find those ideas or features in your product that have a high impact and reach scores, but the confidence level of your team on the success of this new feature is low?
>
> If you have such features with a low confidence level score, can you investigate what are the reasons for the low score?
>
> In addition, can you also investigate why some of your team member's scores are way above or below the average team's confidence scores?

However, referring to the RICE equation, you should know that the **effort** is inversely proportional to the RICE score. The higher the value of **effort**, the lower will be your **RICE score**, and vice-versa. Accordingly, that feature or idea may take a lower rank in the prioritized feature list which you will learn in the next section.

The other elements in the RICE equation are directly proportional to the RICE score which means that the higher the value of R, I and C, the better will be the ranking of the concept or feature on the priority list and vice-versa.

You should consider how many individuals (in terms of man-hours or man-weeks or man-months) it will take to implement the feature or complete the project, as well as how long it will take them to calculate your **effort score**.

If you carefully notice, the **effort** scoring pattern is the same as the **reach** scoring which is the number of people per unit time frame. To calculate the **effort score**, determine how many resources will be required to finish the product or feature over a particular time frame.

For instance, if it takes 7 individuals working for 10 weeks to complete the product feature or project, then your **effort score** will be 7.

You should make sure that the unit of time (10 weeks) is constant throughout your **effort scores** across all the features on your priority list.

PUTTING R I C E TOGETHER

Your team is working on introducing the following features in a watch:

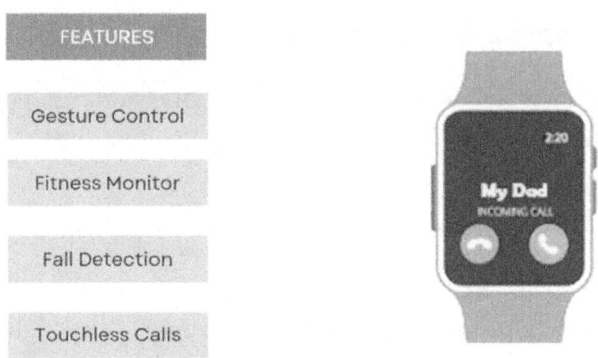

You have followed all the steps explained in the previous sections, and now, this is what your feature RICE grid looks like.

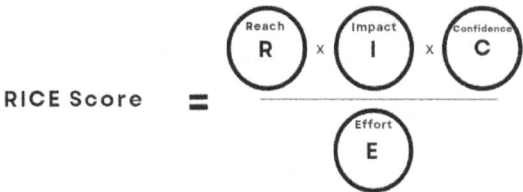

Please note the confidence values are taken as percentage for calculation.

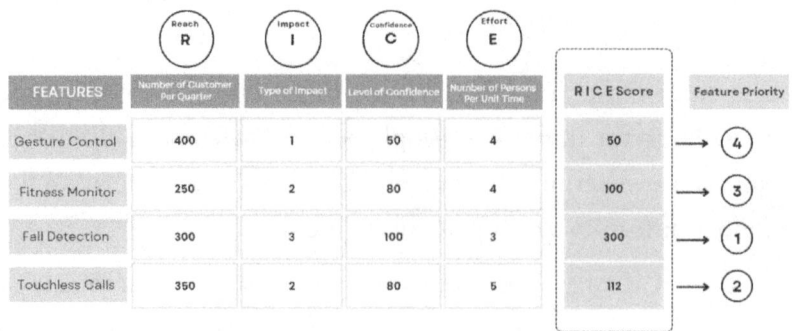

What is your inference from the above grid? Which feature will you prioritize to work on first, then second, and so on?

>  Use the R I C E technique to prioritize which features you and your team will propose to your management to implement in the next product release or launch.

VITAL FEW AND TRIVIAL MANY TECHNIQUE

- 80% of your company's revenue is from 20% of your clients
- 20% of your team members do 80% of the work.
- 80% of the complaints are from 20% of clients.
- 20% of your products generate 80% of your profits
- 20% of the world's population holds 80% of the world's wealth

The above proportion of 80% and 20% is called the 80:20 rule or widely known as **Pareto's principle**.

Who is Pareto?

Vilfredo Pareto, an economist from Italy, observed in 1906 that just 20% of the population in his nation controlled 80% of the land. He conducted more research and concluded that Europe as a whole had the same uneven wealth distribution.

The official definition of the 80-20 rule is as follows: Around 80% of a nation's wealth or total income is believed to be held by the richest 20% of its people.

About 40 years after it was first published, in 1937, Romanian-American management thinker Joseph Juran came upon Pareto's work. After that, Juran changed the 80:20 rule's name to "Pareto's Principle of Unequal Distribution."

How to Apply Pareto's 80:20 Rule?

Let us go back to Sophia's error-handling issues that we saw at the beginning of the chapter and help Sophia to prioritize her work.

Following are the errors that she is grappling with and unable to prioritize:

1. User Interface Errors
2. Boundary Related Errors
3. Control Flow Errors
4. Calculation Errors
5. Testing Errors
6. Hardware Errors

Sophia should use the following steps to discover which are the top errors that she has to recommend to her development team to work on first and prioritize the errors.

Step-1

For all the six errors, Sophia has to prepare a frequency table i.e., the number of times these errors have occurred in a given time frame i.e., one month, one quarter, one year, etc.

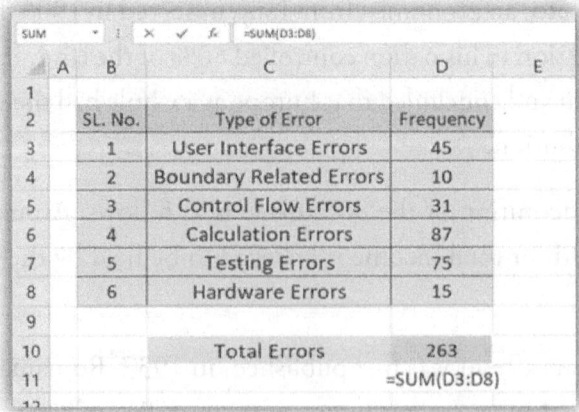

Step-2

Next, Sophia has to calculate the errors in percentage as shown in the screen grab.

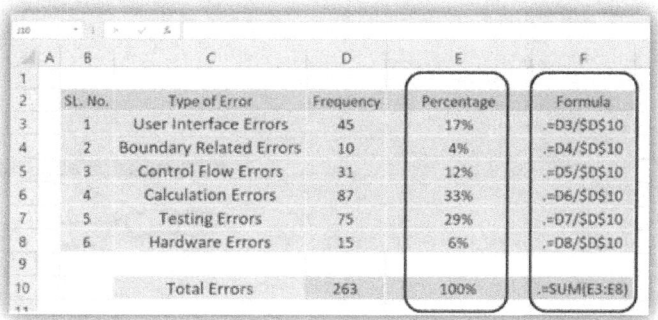

These percentages are calculated by individual error frequency divided by the sum of total errors (263). The formula column displays the formula used.

It is very important to notice that the sum of the percentages in column-E should add up to 100%; if not, the values are erroneous. Please check your formula and calculations.

The values in Column-E are rounded off for the illustration purpose.

Step-3

Now, Sophia has to sort these errors in descending order (higher value to lower value) of percentage errors.

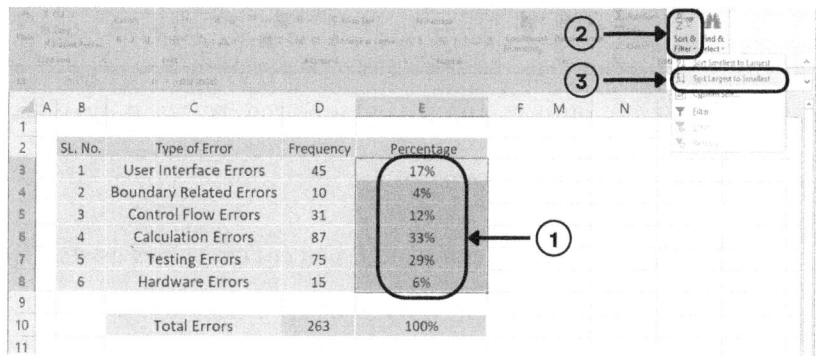

1. Select the cells with percentage values (E3:E8).
2. Click on Sort and Filter.
3. Click on Largest to Smallest.

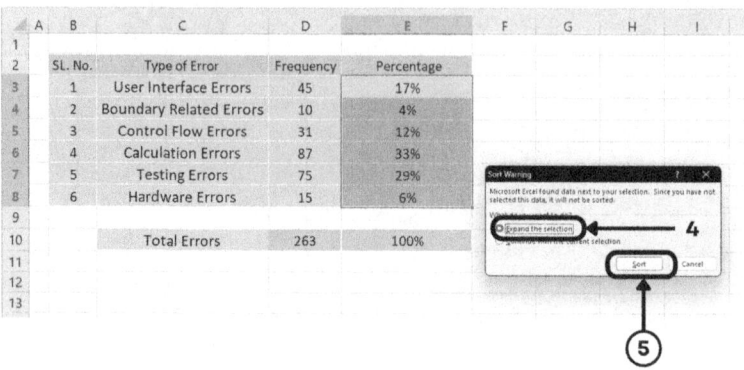

4. Expand the selection.
5. Next, click on Sort.

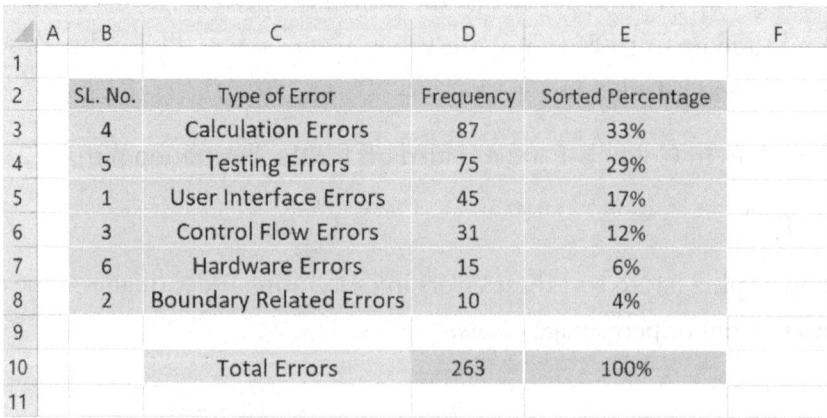

Now, you can see column-E. The values are sorted in ascending order.

Step-4

Now, Sophia has to find the cumulative percentage values as shown in column-F.

How to Prioritize Your Priorities?

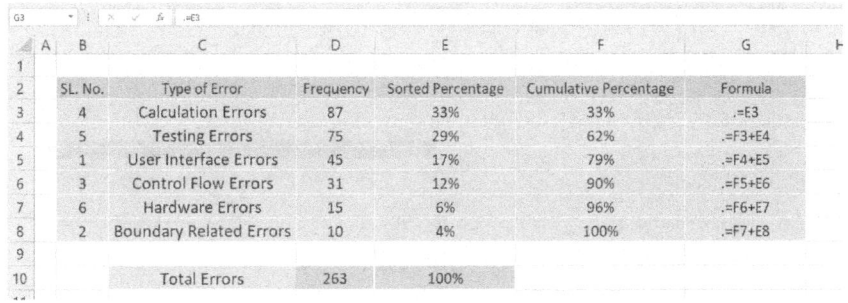

Step-5

Next, the combo graph has to be plotted. Follow the steps.

1. Select the **Type of Error** column, next (press and hold the CTRL key) select the **Frequency** column, next (keep the CTRL key pressed) select the **Cumulative Frequency** column.

2. Next, click on **Insert** and click on the Bar graph icon (as shown in 5).

3. Now, click on **More Column Charts...**

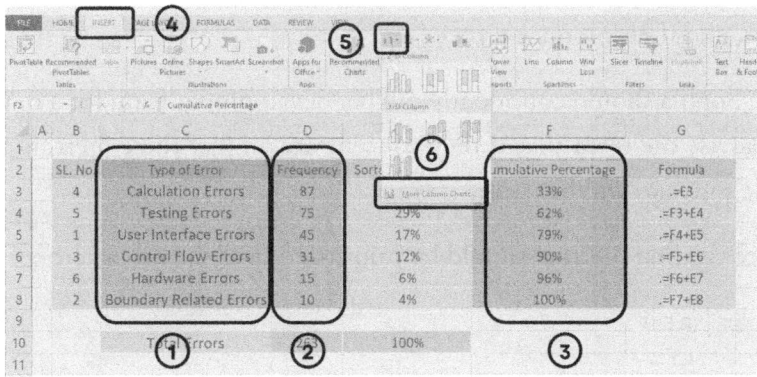

4. Next, click on **Combo**, then **check** the **Secondary Axis**.
5. Finally, click on **OK**.

The Secrets of Design Thinking Mindset

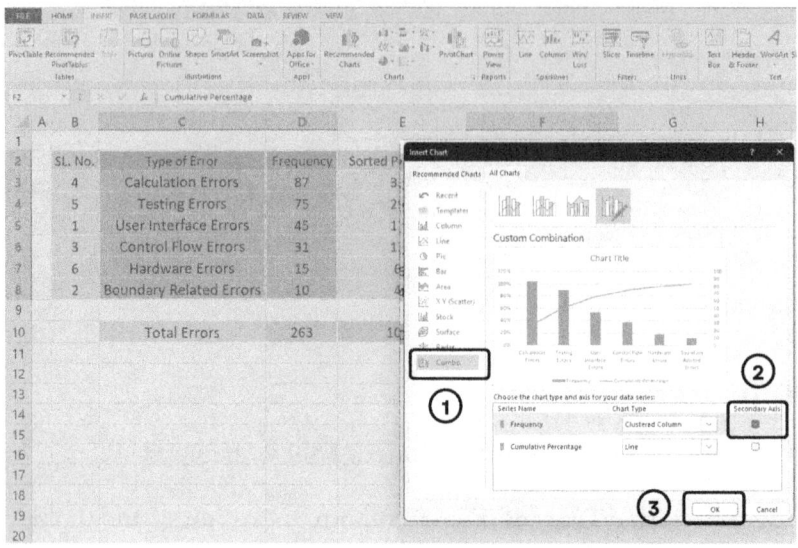

Step-6

This chart is called the **Simple Pareto Chart**.

What do you observe from the chart? You can see that 79% of the issues in the software are caused by these 3 errors viz., calculation errors, testing errors, and user interface errors.

Now, Sophia should confidently call her development team for a meeting and advise the team that if they concentrate on just these 3 errors, 79% of the software will be clean.

Hence the first 3 errors should be prioritized over the other errors.

Simple. Isn't it?

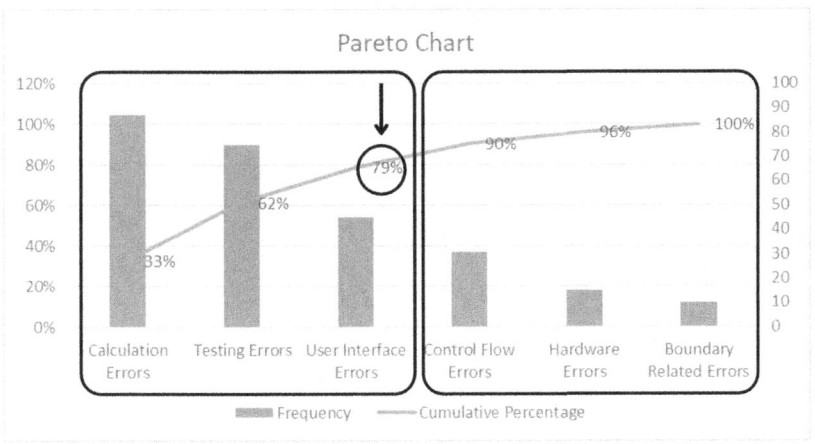

However, this method has some reservations as it does not consider either the priority or the impact or severity of each error.

For more accurate prioritization, you will learn **Weighted Pareto Analysis** in the next section. Keep reading.

WEIGHTED PARETO ANALYSIS

With this technique, an additional dimension will be added to the table which is called the **weights** and these weights will be a function of either the priority and/or the impact and/or severity of each error.

In the Simple Pareto Analysis, it is assumed that each of the errors is having the same impact or priority, or severity. In the weighted Pareto analysis, you assign weights.

Let's go to Step-1 and redefine the error-frequency table.

Step-1

In the **Weighted Pareto Analysis**, we consider, say, the impact of the error on the usage or cost of the software that has all the errors in question.

The Secrets of Design Thinking Mindset

Let us borrow the impact scores from the **R I C E framework** which you learned at the beginning of this chapter.

Impact Type	Score
Massive Impact	3
High Impact	2
Medium Impact	1
Low Impact	0.5
Minimal Impact	0.25

The score in the R I C E framework will be the weights in the **Weighted Pareto Analysis**.

Here, each of these errors has varying impacts on the software's functioning. Column-E is the **impact weights** added. The **weighted scores** are calculated, which is every cell of column-D multiplied by the corresponding cell in column-E.

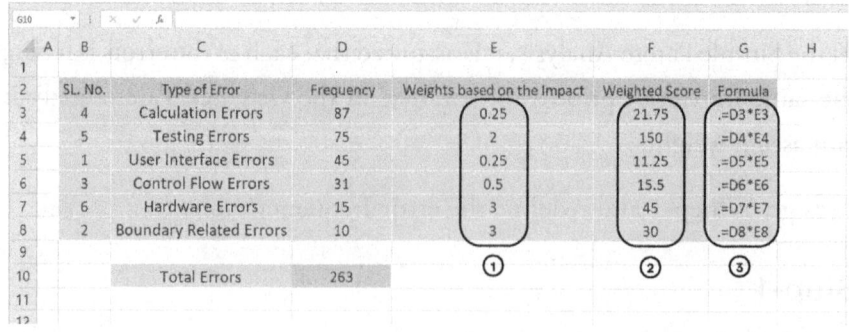

Now, the treatment that we gave to column-D (Frequency column) will be given to column-F which is the **weighted score**.

Step-2

In this step, we will calculate the percentages of column-F.

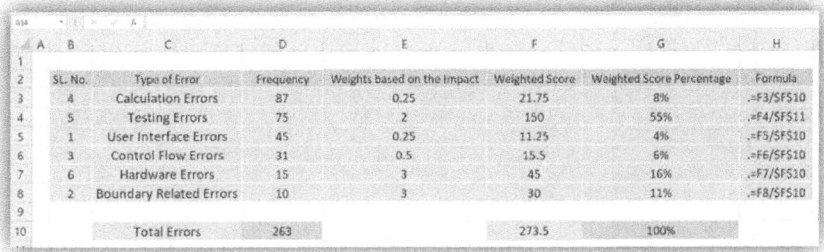

Step-3

Next, sort the **weighted score percentage** (column-G) in descending order (higher value to lower value) of percentage errors.

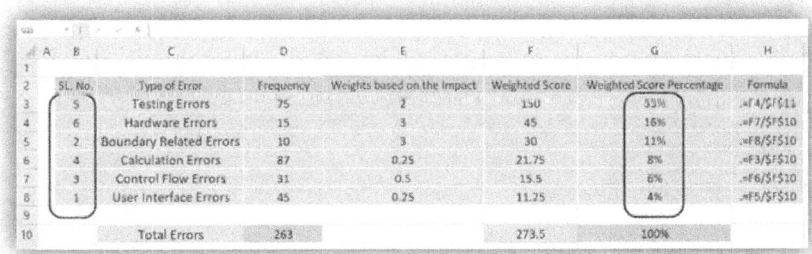

Step-4

Now, find the weighted score cumulative percentage values.

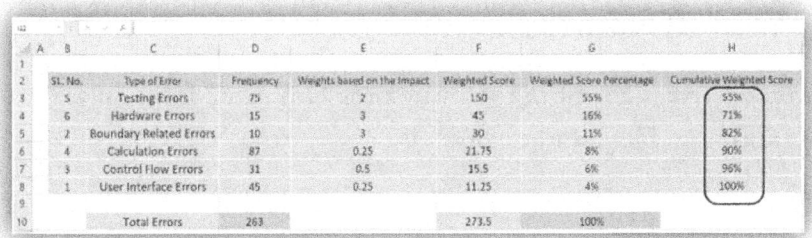

Step-5

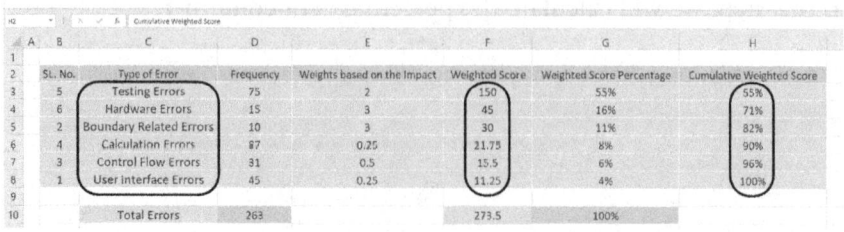

Select the **Type of Error**, **Weighted Score**, and **Cumulative Weighted Score** for plotting the **Weighted Pareto Chart**.

Step-6

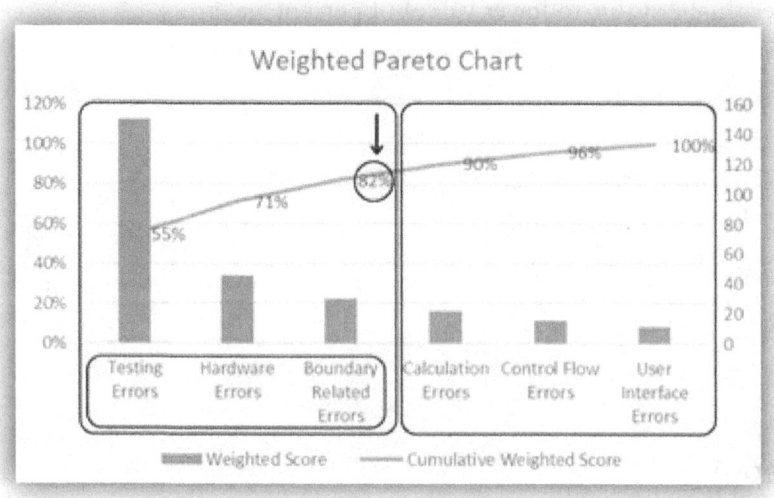

Investigate the changes in the top 3 errors from the **Simple Pareto Chart** and **Weighted Pareto Chart**.

If you observe, 71% of the software problems come from only 2 errors viz., testing and hardware errors.

How to Prioritize Your Priorities?

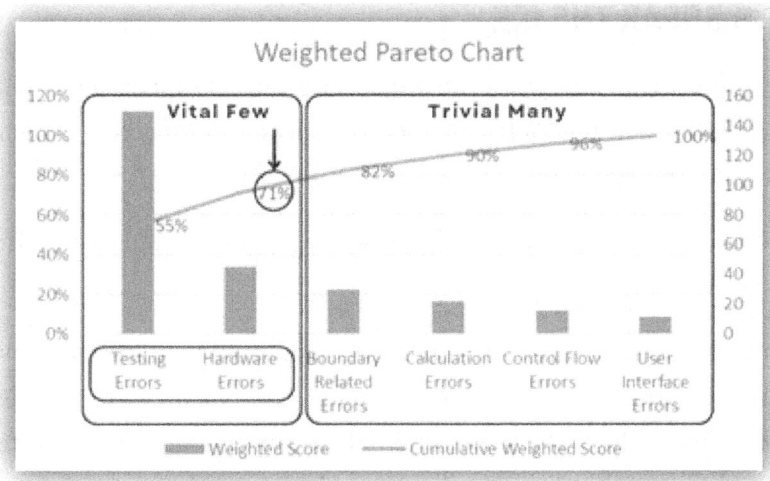

 Following were the errors that were detected while auditing a Fortune 500 company's blog along with their frequency of occurrences and weights.

SL. No.	Blog Errors	Frequency	Weights based on the impact
1	Misplaced Hyperlinks	62	2
2	Wrong Capitalization	78	0.25
3	Pixelated Images	31	3
4	Grammatical Errors	45	0.5
5	Meta Description Missing	15	3
6	Citations Missing	54	0.25

Following is the Weighted Pareto Chart:

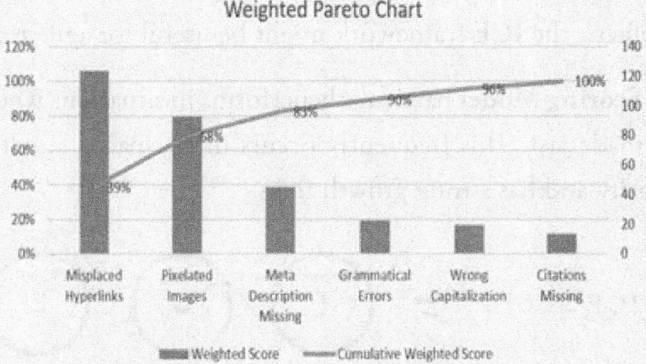

Verify if the analysis is correct.

LET'S BREAK THE ICE

You are the scrum master for the project and you are supposed to facilitate the backlog grooming (or backlog refinement) session/meeting along with your other stakeholders.

As you know, most of the time these meetings are restricted to 45 minutes to 1 hour.

Before the backlog grooming meeting, you and your product owner should undertake some informal backlog refinement with the subject matter experts (SMEs) and stakeholders to confirm they are prioritizing the user stories with the most significant business value.

You, as a scrum master along with the product owner, should start prioritizing the user stories that will eventually fill the sprint backlog when the user story refinement and estimation are complete.

Can you advise the product owner about which user story has to be picked on a priority basis?

You can do it with the **I C E prioritization framework**.

How to Apply the I C E Frameworks?

ICE is an acronym for **Impact, Confidence,** and **Ease**. Due to its speed and simplicity, the **ICE** framework might be useful for agile teams.

The **ICE Scoring Model** particularly performs in situations when choices must be made fast. This frequently occurs in fast-paced situations. It is high-velocity and has strong growth rates.

How to Prioritize Your Priorities?

- **IMPACT**

The **impact** of the ICE is the same as that of the RICE technique. **Impact** determines the initiative's or feature's potential impact on your existing or prospective customer base. Will the user be benefited from this new feature, and if so, how much?

You can use a rating from 1 to 6, or 1 to 10 making sure that the consistency remains the same throughout the model.

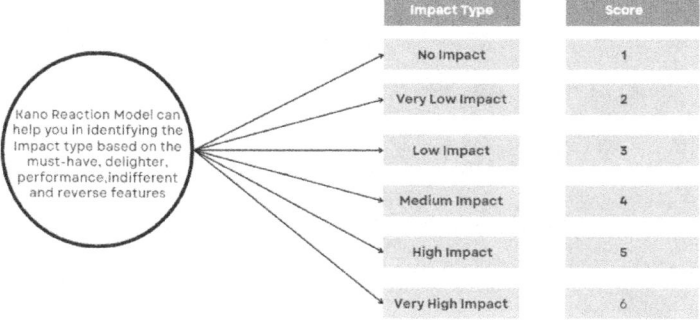

- **CONFIDENCE**

Similar to the **confidence** of the RICE technique, your **confidence score** might be supported by the data from related prior projects or user stories.

How confident are you that this user story will be favorably received? How critical is it to devote time and resources to this project?

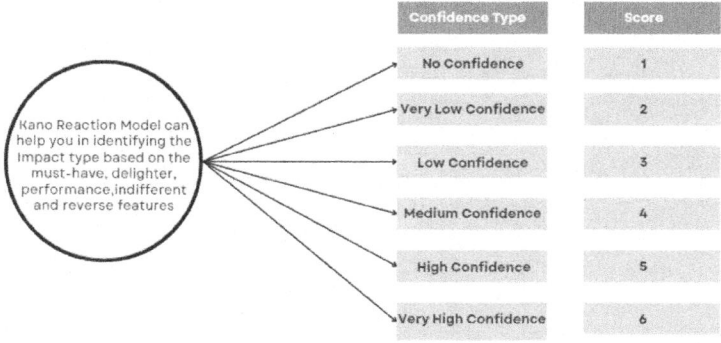

EASE

In simple terms, **ease** means how easily or how comfortably we can work on the user story or feature.

The **ease** of incorporating the user story depends on the team's competences and competencies.

Ease Type	Score
Very Hard	1
Hard	2
Medium	3
Easy	4
Very Easy	5

Putting the ICE Together

$$\text{ICE Score} = \text{Impact (I)} \times \text{Confidence (C)} \times \text{Ease (E)}$$

USER STORY	Type of Impact	Level of Confidence	How Hard is the Task?	ICE Score	User Story Priority
User Story -1	1	5	2	10	4
User Story -2	2	2	4	16	3
User Story -3	6	4	3	72	1
User Story -4	2	3	5	30	2

Now with this **ICE scoring** framework, you can advise your product manager that User Story-3 can be picked on high priority, subsequently, User Story-4, User Story-2, and User Story-1.

Use the impact and confidence scores from the RICE model and, the impact and confidence scores of I C E to prioritize the website errors.

SL. No.	Website Errors	Frequency
1	Wrong Capitalization	78
2	Pixelated Images	31
3	Misplaced Hyperlinks	62
4	Meta Description Missing	15
5	Grammatical Errors	45
6	Citations Missing	54

Do you find any difference in the priority sequence?

Discuss this with your team.

WHICH IS THE CAPITAL OF RUSSIA?

Yes, you are right. It is indeed Moscow.

In this section, you will be learning about a different **MoSCoW** – another prioritization model you can use for comparative study.

Dai Clegg initially introduced the abbreviation **MSCW** (must, should, could, won't) in 1994. The abbreviation was then made pronounceable by adding two 'o's.

The **MoSCoW** approach aids in sorting and ranking the components of your product to get a good outcome. The approach is based on your team's subject matter expertise. It's quick and simple to finish, and it establishes the order of importance for further developments.

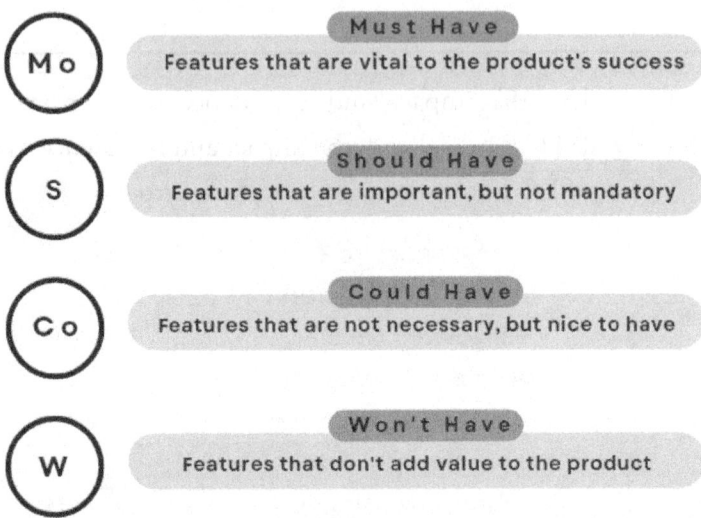

How to Apply MoSCoW for Products/Services?

Step-1

Identify all stakeholders responsible for your product design which can have representatives from your technical team, product team, project team, sales team, and/or customer success team.

Set up a meeting, giving them the agenda of this meeting or discussion.

Step-2

If this meeting is face-to-face, then make sure you choose a meeting place that has a large board. Have some pens and flip charts or sticky notes handy.

If the meeting is online, then you can use any of the digital collaboration or whiteboarding tools like Google docs, Miro or Mural, etc.

How to Prioritize Your Priorities?

With all the stakeholders in the room, list down all the features that you would like to incorporate into your new product.

The rule is one feature on one sticky note.

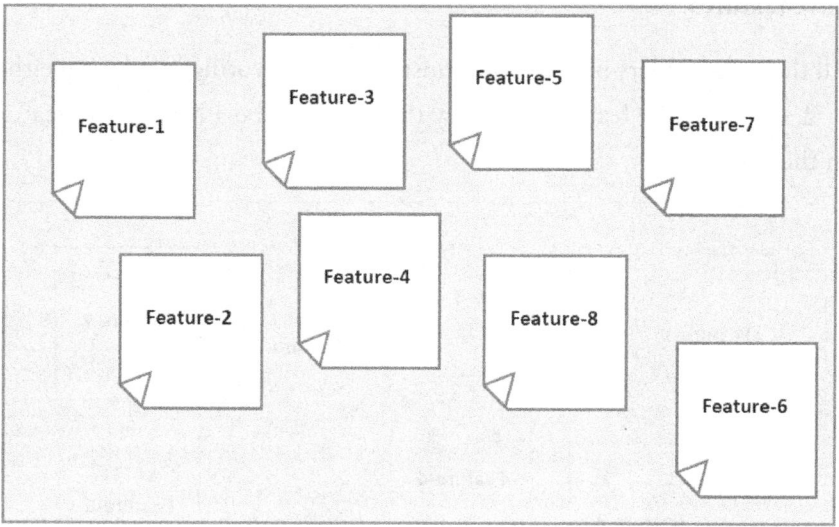

Next, we will be using the dot-voting technique in this exercise.

Weight =1   **Weight =2**   **Weight =3**

You will distribute these 3 dots (stickers) to each of the stakeholders in the meeting room.

These weights could mean high impact or high reach or high cost etc – you can choose an appropriate parameter.

Step-3

In the **MoSCoW model**, you begin with **Must-have features**, then, **Should-have features**, then **Could-have features**, and finally, **Won't-have features**.

All the stakeholders in the room must do the dot voting by placing either 1, 2, or 3 on each feature that they think should be a **Must-have** feature in the product.

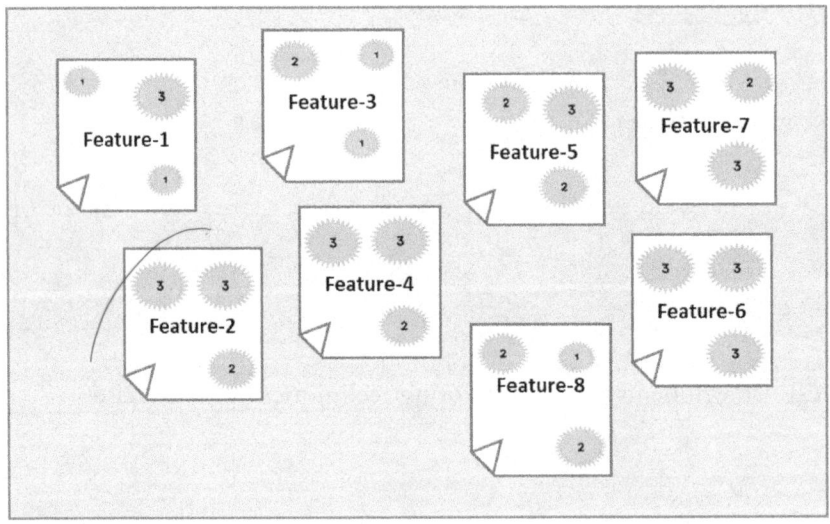

The following rules should be used during voting:

1. One stakeholder can vote only once for one feature.
2. All the stakeholders should vote.
3. All the stakeholders should know of each of the features, or else they can refrain from voting.
4. There is no veto power given to any stakeholder unless he or she is a direct customer/client.

Step-4

Now, tabularize the features by the votes. Here is how to do it.

How to Prioritize Your Priorities?

The team can decide how many features to include in the **must-have** category.

For illustration, all features with scores 9 and 8 get shortlisted as **must-have** features.

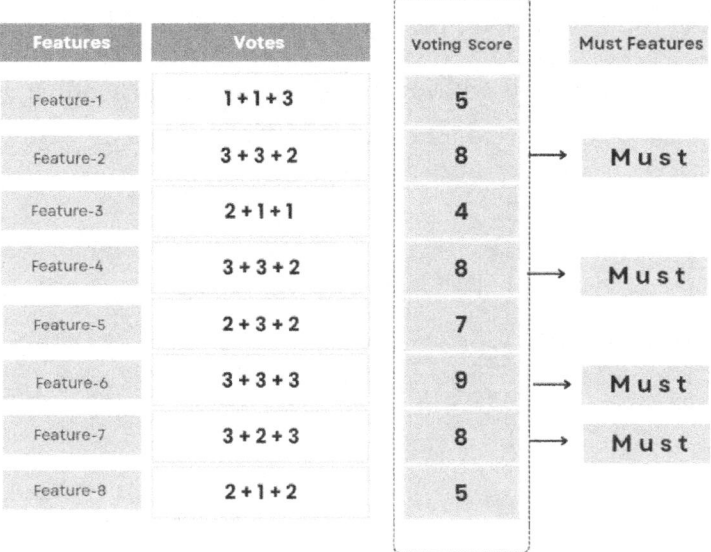

Therefore feature-2, feature-4, feature-6, and feature-7 are considered **must-have** features.

Pro Tips:

- It should not be misconstrued that the lower scores are eligible for **should-have**, **could-have**, and **won't-have** features. There will be separate voting for these categories.
- Some features like feature-1 may have a voting conflict: 2 stakeholders have rated 1 and only 1 stakeholder has rated 3.

You need to check why there is an internal disparity in the voting and have a legitimate reason for the extremely divided opinion before proceeding to the next step.

The more unanimity in the voting weights within each feature, the more certain you will be that the feature is being considered for that category.

Now, from the collaboration board, clear off the **must-have** features.

Step-5

Now, the voting will be for the next category – **should-have** features.

Again, the stakeholders will vote based on their understanding of which features can be considered for the **should-have** category.

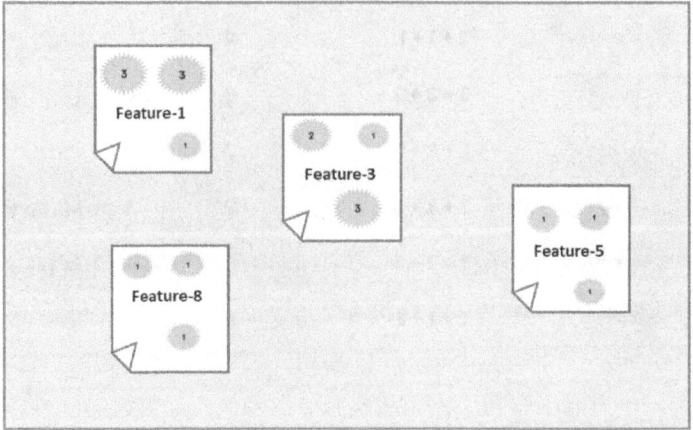

Tabularize the **should-have** feature voting. Here you find feature-1 has the highest score and hence this feature will be considered in the **should-have** category.

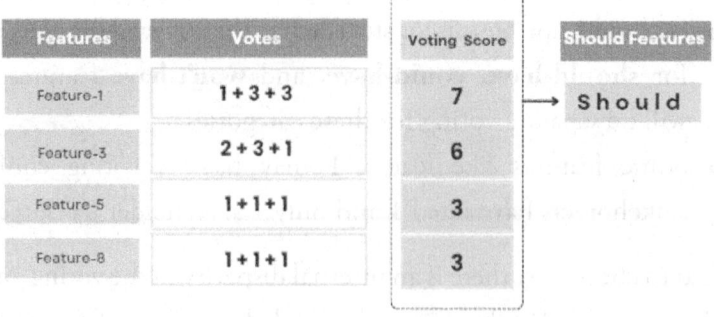

You can also consider feature-3 in the **should-have** category. This exercise is just for illustration.

Again, we see extreme voting in feature-3, which means the stakeholder cohort is divided in their opinion. You again need to investigate why a stakeholder considers it as 1 (low priority) and the other stakeholder considers it as 3 (high priority).

Now, clear off the **should-have** category features from the collaboration board.

Step-6

Next, the voting will be for the next category – **could-have** features.

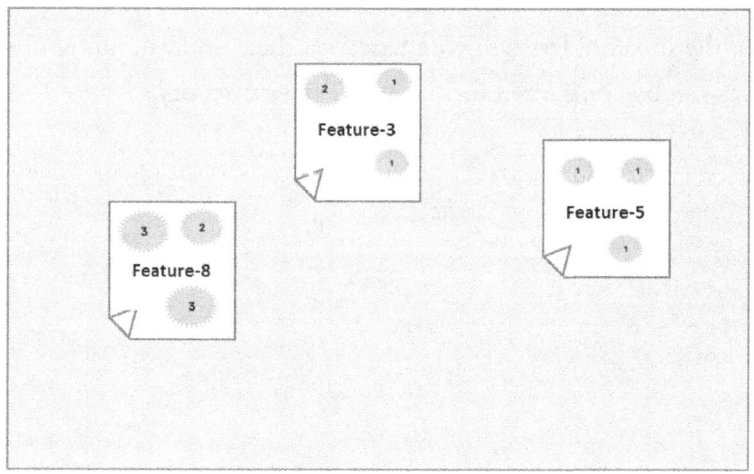

Here, you can see that feature-8 gets qualified for the **could-have**.

Step-7

Tabularize the feature voting pattern.

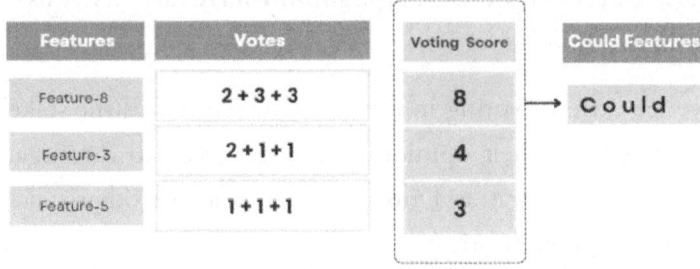

Now, clear off the Could-have category features from the collaboration board.

Step-8

Next, the voting will be for the next category – **Won't-have** features.

Again, the stakeholders will vote based on their understanding of which features can be considered for the Won't-have category.

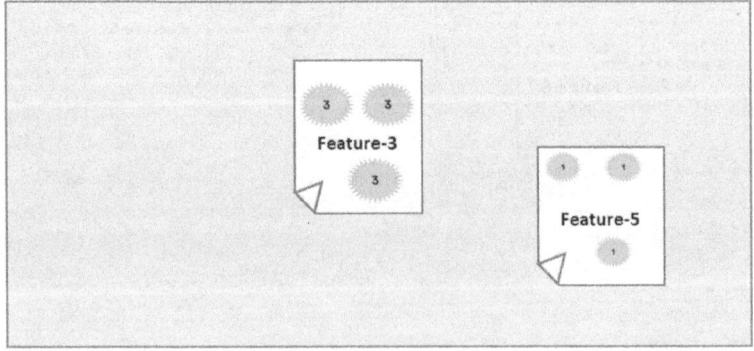

From the table, you infer that the stakeholders have unanimously voted out feature-3 from the list. This means all the stakeholders agree that feature-3 must be eliminated from the list.

How to Prioritize Your Priorities?

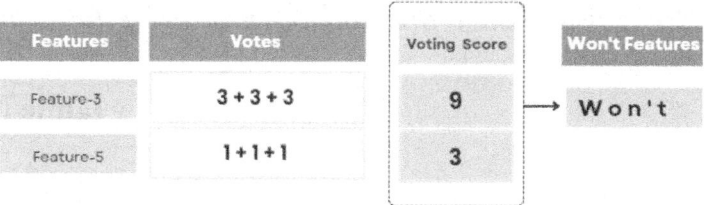

But, there is an interesting voting antipattern you can see for feature-5. All the stakeholders have given the least weight for feature-5 which means they are not sure if they want to eliminate the feature from getting deployed.

In such cases, you can further investigate the reasoning for low scores and re-visit feature-5 if it has to be included in other categories of MoSCoW.

> **YOUR TURN!**
>
> 1. Compare the MoSCoW with the Kano Model. 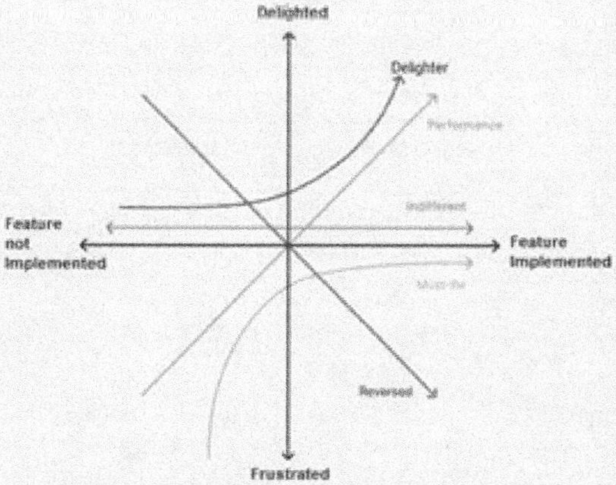
>
> [Kano Model diagram showing Delighted/Frustrated axis vs Feature not Implemented/Feature Implemented axis, with curves labeled Delighter, Performance, Indifferent, Must-be, and Reversed]
>
> 2. Attaching the weights to MSCW (M-1, S-3)

"Innovation is a change that unlocks new value (of a product, service, or process)."

— **Jamie Notter**

7

FALLING SHORT OF PRODUCT IDEAS AND INNOVATION?

HAVE YOU BEEN IN LOGAN'S SITUATION?

Logan is a product manager in a multinational corporation. Logan is responsible for encouraging innovation in his team and the organization to come up with better and more innovative products.

His client wants to launch the product by creating value for their customers by adding some innovative features to the product and has entrusted Logan's company with this task.

The client he is working with is not happy with the new ideas that Logan is coming up with. There have been many escalations around this. Logan and his team have suggested a couple of new product features/ideas and now they feel like he is exhausted with the ideas.

Every client call is becoming challenging for Logan as he is unable to suggest an innovative product solution.

If you find yourself in Logan's shoes and his story sounds similar to your daily struggle, then this chapter will share some tools and techniques to overcome it.

INNOVATIONS AHEAD OF THE PACK

Joseph Schumpeter, an Austrian economist, first used the phrase "creative destruction" in 1942. In his *book Capital in the Twenty-First Century*, Schumpeter defined creative destruction as "**the process of industrial mutation that ceaselessly revolutionizes the economic structure from within, endlessly destroying the old one, relentlessly introducing a new one.**"

Your endeavor should be incessantly working on innovative products that create a big splash in the market when introduced for your product and services.

The Secrets of Design Thinking Mindset

Now, is there any framework that can aid innovative thoughts?

Yes.

Keep reading.

SCAMPER

Alex Faickney Osborn, who is credited with creating many of the questions used in **SCAMPER**, founded the program in 1953. In his book *SCAMPER: Games for Imagination Development*, written in 1971, **Bob Eberle** grouped the questions and created the term **SCAMPER**.

SCAMPER is an acronym and stands for:

> **S**ubstitute
>
> **C**ombine
>
> **A**dapt
>
> **M**odify (Also magnify and minify)
>
> **P**ut to another use
>
> **E**liminate
>
> **R**everse (Rearrange, Reorder)

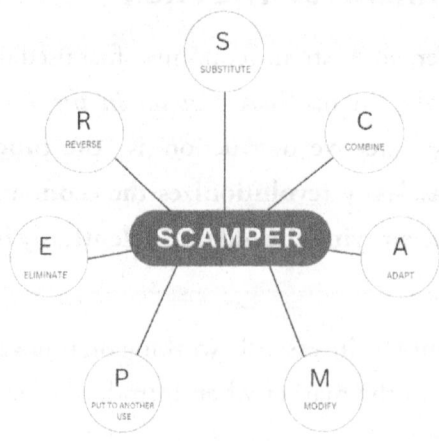

Falling Short of Product Ideas and Innovation?

The **SCAMPER** approach provides a guided framework for you and your team to ask seven distinct sorts of questions, which will help you comprehend how you can innovate, ideate, and enhance existing goods, services, issues, and ideas. This tool helps you to come up with ideas for new products and services.

In the next section, you will learn how to apply **SCAMPER** for your existing product, services, problems etc.

How to Ideate Using SCAMPER?

Let's look at a wristwatch; apply **SCAMPER** and understand the nuances of the technique.

To begin this technique, first, you should have an existing product or an issue, or a service that you wish to enhance.

Let's say you are the product manager of the watch company which looks like in the picture.

Your clients are asking for a new design – could be functional or aesthetic.

Apply **SCAMPER**.

Note: The **SCAMPER** technique works best when you involve your team or SMEs in all the phases till it culminates in the WOW factor of design.

- **Substitute**

You can ask this basic question: What can I **substitute** in the current product to enhance its features? Hands? Dial? Color? Keep making the list and encourage your team too. There are no right or wrong answers at this phase.

You can use PDAs (Personal Digital Assistants) or sticky notes to record the ideas.

> ### Additional Guiding Questions
> - Can I **substitute** the location, the time, the resources, or the person/on the project?
> - Can I **substitute** its appearance, color, texture, sound, etc.?
> - What materials can I **substitute** to enhance the product or design or service?
> - What step of the procedure may be **substituted** without having an impact on the entire project?
> - Can I **substitute** other techniques or methods?
> - What will happen if we **substitute** one project component for another?
> - Can I **substitute** a less complicated procedure in its place?

For our watch example, assume that you decided to **substitute** the dash dial with California format – Roman, Arabic and stick numerals. And also, **substitute** a metal strap with a leather strap; or, **substitute** the analog dial with a digital one.

You can see how you can work with the design changes. This example is just for illustration and to understand the application of the concept, however, various factors like cost, durability etc. will be crucial during the design changes.

Alternate words you can use for a **substitute** are – imitate, replace, alternate, dummy, supplement etc.

- ## Combine

Here, you can ask this basic question: How can I **combine** a feature or features in the current product to get better results? Alarm? Display light? Calculator?

Keep building the list of features you would like to **combine** to give that WOW factor to your customers. Again, to remind you, it is a team activity and there is no right or wrong idea(s).

> ### Additional Guiding Questions
> - Can I **combine** two products' working in one product?
> - What elements can you **combine** to improve the outcome?
> - Can two or more processes be **combined**?
> - Can two or more properties be **combined**?
> - Can people, teams, or businesses be **combined**?
> - Can two or more concepts be **combined**?
> - Can two or more technologies be **combined**?

Coming back to our watch example, assume that you decided to **combine** two products working in one, i.e., instead of having 1 watch and 1 calculator – combine them. Now, your new watch has a calculator feature in it.

The Secrets of Design Thinking Mindset

Alternate words you can use for **combine** are – make one, connect, intermix, link, mingle, bundle, unite, amalgamate, link, relate, conjoin etc.

- **Adapt**

Here, you can ask a question like: What can I **adapt** in my current product or process or service imitating an established concept or procedure to improve the idea?

Brainstorm with your team and list what features you will **adapt** to our watch in the example.

List your ideas here:

1._____

2._____

3._____

4._____

You can use the following hints:

- Get inspiration from existing products.
- Get fresh insights from your product's history.
- Get ideas from a few other products.
- Get ideas from the offerings from industry peers.

> ### Additional Guiding Questions
>
> - Can I **adapt** to an outdated method, system, or component?
> - Can the current product be **adapted** to incorporate a new method or technology?
> - Can I **adapt** a tried-and-tested method to enhance speed, efficiency or effectiveness?
> - Can I fix this issue by **adapting** to an idea that has previously proven successful?
> - What concepts from outside the framework of my product can I **adapt**?
> - Which concepts from the competitor's products may I **adapt**, duplicate, or borrow without breaching the law?

Alternate words you can use for **adapt** are – alter, make alterations to, change, adjust, make adjustments to, convert, transform, restyle, reorganize, tweak etc.

- **Modify (Magnify, Minify)**

Under this, you can ask a question like: What can I **modify** in my current product or process or service imitating an established concept or procedure to improve the performance (our watch example)? **Minimize** the size of the battery? **Maximize** the display time? **Minimize** the dial?

> ### Additional Guiding Questions
>
> - What can I **widen** or **magnify**?
> - What can I **reduce** or **remove**?
> - Could I **emphasize** or **highlight** the size, colors, or buttons?
> - What may be **increased** in height, size, or strength?

Back to our watch example, you can see one of the modifications – the display and strap have been **minimized** (sleek). The time numerals (08:45) are **magnified** (oversized).

Alternate words you can use for **modify** – are enlarge, oversize, boost, enhance, maximize, increase, augment, extend, expand, decrease, diminish, downsize, lessen, reduce, shorten etc.

- **Put to Another Use**

Here, you can ask a question like: What **other use can I put** my current product to? Phone calls? Messages? Measure heartbeats?

Keep listing down the ideas along with your team. Again, you can use PDAs or sticky notes to populate your ideas. Nothing is right or wrong in this state too, no matter how weird, naïve or absurd the idea may seem – keep listing.

Additional Guiding Questions

- What **other use** does it have?
- How **different personas** – children, adults, old aged, etc. – could use it?
- Which **other Business Units** (BU) in the company can utilize the product?

> - What advantages does the product have when utilized **elsewhere**?
> - Can the product be marketed to a **different** market segment?

Now, back to our watch example, assume you are putting your watch to make and receive calls.

Now you see where this technique is heading towards. From a simple analog watch, you have arrived at a smartwatch that you could be possessing.

Alternate words you can use for **put to another use** are – find a use for implement, make use of, adopt, deploy, put into service etc.

- ## Eliminate

In **eliminate**, you can ask a question like: what can I _____ _____ (fill the blank. By now you should be familiar with the questioning technique) from my current product or service? Moving parts in a watch (cogs and gears from the analog watch) or buckle in the watch strap? Charger?

> **Additional Guiding Questions**
> - What elements of a product or procedure can be **removed**?
> - Can you make the concept, procedure, or solution **simpler**?
> - What can I **eliminate** without changing its working?
> - Can I **divide** my product into **separate** components?
> - What would we accomplish if we only had only **fewer** resources?

Back to our watch example, assume you are planning to **eliminate** the buckle in the watch strap.

You can see this magnetic watch strap. You can still brainstorm with your team to ideate on different watch straps.

Alternate words you can use for **eliminate** are – simplify, delete, remove, stop using, phase out, put an end to, discard, omit, shut off, erase, get rid of etc.

▪ Reverse (Rearrange, Reorder)

Under this, you could ask what feature or process can you **reverse** or **rearrange** from your current product to achieve an innovative, yet scientific product – display the correct orientation of time even if the watch is **reversed** (upside-down) by the movement of the wrist.

You would have already witnessed this feature in your smartwatch. Now you see how a product can be innovated or enhanced to give those WOW moments to your clients.

Alternate words you can use for **reverse** are – rearrange, reorder, inside-out, upside-down, opposite, backward, reposition, etc.

Additional Guiding Questions

- Can a process be **reversed** and yet produce results?
- Can I utilize the product with the **inside-out** or **upside-down** rearrangement?
- Can I **reorder** some of the product's components to the client's advantage?
- Can some components be **reversed** to produce better results?
- Can I **reorder** the first step to the finish or the other way around?

In your current product, process, service or project that you are working on, can you use the **SCAMPER** technique along with your team to create a WOW factor in your product or service?

The more assorted your team is, the better will be the ideation process as individuals from different BU or departments can give valuable inputs. More can be achieved in fewer sittings and avoids unnecessary iterations in the process.

Your ideation team has to have members from both the upstream and downstream part of the process; or the consumers/customers (internal or external) and suppliers (internal or external) of your process/product/service.

Step-1: Mention the product/service/feature you would like to enhance

Step-2: Get your team and start brainstorming/brainwriting

| S | C | A | M | P | E | R |

Falling Short of Product Ideas and Innovation?

1. For Apple's magic mouse, can you apply the SCAMPER technique and discuss the enhancements over the 1st generation mouse?

2. For your computer keyboard, apply the SCAMPER technique and discuss why the keys on the keyboard are not in alphabetical order.

"When the trust is high, communication is easy, instant, and effective."

– **Stephen Covey**

8

HOW TO BUILD AND REPAIR TRUST WITHIN THE TEAM?

HAVE YOU BEEN IN NOEL'S SITUATION?

Noel recently took over as head of a software development team as he has been having the longest tenure in the company.

But Noel is from a software testing background all his career and has no skills in software development. As he is the head of the team, he has been attending client discovery calls where he is supposed to take decisions on SoW and day-to-day operations.

He has been relying on his team members for these decisions.

After a couple of weeks, the team members lost their confidence and trust in Noel's decisions as he was not an SME in software development. Gradually, the team members stopped sharing all the technical information with Noel because of his limited knowledge.

Team members now had started making and executing decisions on their own without Noel's consent which was annoying Noel.

The crack within the team was visible and the team was falling apart.

Have you been in such situations where the team members lost trust in you or you lost that trust in your team member(s)?

In this chapter, you will discover some tools and techniques to help you rank which task or problem to solve.

WHAT IS TRUST EQUILIBRIUM?

Everything begins with trust and ends with a lack of trust. Lack of trust within the team or with your client or at the workplace lowers productivity and effectiveness.

The Secrets of Design Thinking Mindset

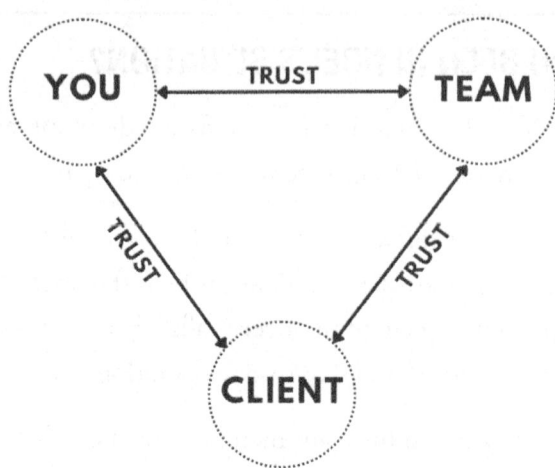

This is the **trust equilibrium** that has to be present in your project ecosystem to be efficacious and efficient. If this molecule of trust is replicated in all the teams across all the business units of the organization, then the entire organization will be functioning full throttle and would be the greatest place to work.

Like EQ (Emotional Quotient), and IQ (Intelligence Quotient), TQ is the Trust Quotient which is of paramount importance in a close-knitted pocket of an ecosystem (trust with the team, trust with the client, trust with family members, etc.).

If your team members are not communicating or showing concerns about collaborating or withholding information from each other are some of the key symptoms of a lack of trust.

HOW TO BUILD AND REPAIR TRUST?

Charles H. Green in his book *The Trusted Advisor* introduces The Trust Equation.

The **Trust Equation** has four variables that affect your trustworthiness within the team, team-client relation, etc. – **Credibility**, **Reliability**, **Intimacy**, and **Self-Orientation**.

$$T\uparrow = \frac{C\uparrow + R\uparrow + I\uparrow}{S\downarrow}$$

The **trustworthiness** of an individual or a team is based on the intensity of each of these **four variables**.

For example: If your team member(s) is/are not sharing the information or knowledge within your team that they should, then you need to identify which of the four (C-R-I-S) variables(s) is/are low or missing. It's time to repair your **trustworthiness**.

On the other hand, say, you have inherited a new team as a lead or a manager – how can you be treated as a trustworthy person?

Again, you need to work on each of these four variables individually to build your trustworthiness.

$$\text{TRUSTWORTHINESS}\uparrow = \frac{\text{CREDIBILITY}\uparrow + \text{RELIABILITY}\uparrow + \text{INTIMACY}\uparrow}{\text{SELF-ORIENTATION}\downarrow}$$

Let's learn what each of these variables means and how to use them to gain optimum or high trustworthiness.

WHAT IS CREDIBILITY?

Credibility in simple terms means being a subject matter expert in the area of your work.

Credibility is directly proportional to gaining trust either within your team, across the team, or with the client. This means if your **credibility** is high, the chances of you being trusted by your stakeholders are high.

Ask these simple questions to yourself – Are you Mr. or Ms. dependable on the outcome or results in your field of expertise? Can your stakeholders rely on you with the decisions you take?

For example, you have recently inherited a managerial or HoD position in an AWS-based project. But your expertise does not coincide either with AWS or any other cloud-based services. Your team members, though less experienced than you, have all their years of experience on AWS.

The million-dollar question now is: Can your team members trust you in the decision that you make on AWS? The answer is NO, which translates that the team has less or no trust in your decision and this trust starts eroding as days pass. Eventually, there will be discontent and disconnect between you and your team members which leads to a less productive team.

$$T \uparrow = C \uparrow$$
$$T \downarrow = C \downarrow$$

Now, what is the solution? How to build trust or repair the lost trust? Start learning the skill and start gaining expertise through additional courses or certifications or other mediums to enhance your competencies and skills.

WHAT IS RELIABILITY?

Reliability in simple terms means being able to **walk the talk**. Say-do, say-do, say-do, say-do should be your rhythm or cadence. It can help you gain trust very easily across your stakeholders. Either don't say anything, or if said, or promised something – keep up to that promise.

$$T \uparrow = R \uparrow$$
$$T \downarrow = R \downarrow$$

What is your say-do ratio?

$$\frac{SAY}{DO} = 1$$

$$\frac{SAY}{DO} < 1$$

$$\frac{SAY}{DO} > 1$$

WHAT IS INTIMACY?

Intimacy in simple terms means how comfortable your team member is in sharing his/her personal information with you – could be on his/her aspirations, the discontent that he/she is going through the role, fears, failures, etc.

In the research conducted, **intimacy** was more highly correlated than any other variables of the trust equation. **Intimacy** is also closely related to security. How secure does your team member feel sharing his/her personal information with you?

In **Maslow's hierarchy of needs**, too, the safety or security needs of an individual are classified as his/her basic needs which is very important and chimes well with the **Intimacy factor** in the trust equation also.

Especially if you are a medical doctor or a lawyer where the clients share their very personal information with you which their family members may not even know.

$$T \uparrow = I \uparrow$$
$$T \downarrow = I \downarrow$$

WHAT IS SELF-ORIENTATION?

Self-orientation in simple terms means being selfish, and self-centered and all the motives or actions driven to satiate self-needs, and desires and achieve self-goals. How often do you place yourself in front of others, especially when as part of a team?

For example, your team does all the hard work and you are applauded in the town halls. When the project fails, you blame your team members, or if your project is delivered well, you take all the credit.

Self-orientation is in the denominator of the trustworthiness equation which means if you have a high level of self-orientation, it will decrease your trustworthiness.

$$T\uparrow = S\downarrow$$
$$T\downarrow = S\uparrow$$

To sum it up, you now know what variables you need to work on to build or repair your trust equation with your team/client/stakeholders.

 Let's evaluate your Trust Quotient (TQ).

Name of your client/team member: _____

Scores:

Self-Orientation: 5=Very self-oriented (Low), 1=Very client/team-oriented (High)

Credibility, Reliability, and Intimacy: 5= High, 1=Low

How to Build and Repair Trust within the Team?

Calculate the TQ

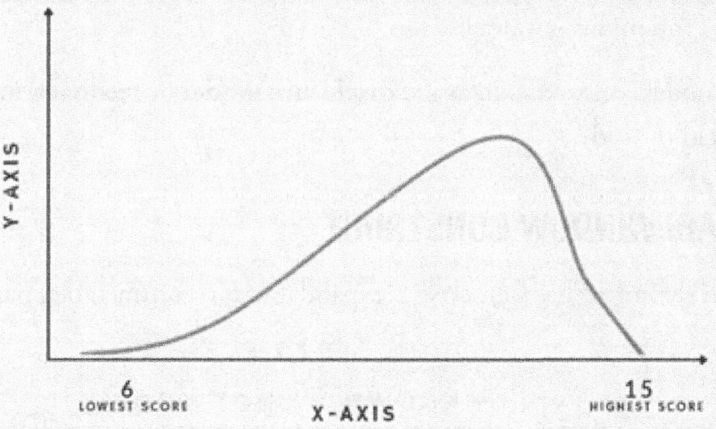

15 is the highest TQ score.

Plot your score on the TQ distribution and know how trustworthy you are. If your score is less, then identify which variable(s) of the four you have to work on to improve your score and trustworthiness.

NB: Please note the real TQ scale is left-skewed (negative skew). The above distribution is a close approximation and is considered just for illustration purposes to avoid statistical complexity.

KNOW THYSELF THROUGH JO-HARI'S WINDOW

Knowing oneself or having a high degree of self-awareness forms a basis for building trust with your team members, client, stakeholders, and family members, too.

The Secrets of Design Thinking Mindset

Jo-Hari (also referred to as Johari) window is a tool that was developed to help individuals in comprehending their relationships with both themselves and others.

Psychologists **Joseph Luft** and **Harrington Ingham** developed it in 1955.

The initial names of Luft and Ingham were combined (**Jo + Harri**) to create the tool "Johari" for their model.

This model is built on two principles:

1. Trust can be gained by sharing (more) information about you with your team members, stakeholders, etc.
2. Enhance self-learning from their feedback/advice leading to more self-awareness.

This model is also known as the **disclosure model** or **feedback model** in the field of study.

JOHARI WINDOW CONSTRUCT

Johari's window has four elastic (expandable and contractable) panes viz.,

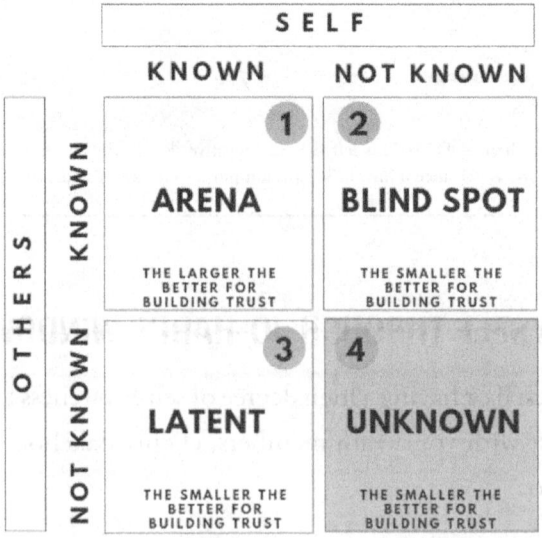

How to Build and Repair Trust within the Team?

1. Arena or Open Area of Free Self (1st quadrant)
2. Blind Spot or Blind Self (2nd quadrant)
3. Latent or Hidden Area or Hidden Self or Façade (3rd quadrant)
4. Unknown or Unknown Self (4th quadrant)

1. Arena or Open Area

It represents the knowledge or information that both you (the self) and your team/stakeholders (the others) have about you, including your traits like expertise, skill, capabilities, action, personality, emotions, and others.

SELF (YOU)   **OTHERS (YOUR TEAM)**

If this elastic pane area is larger than the rest of the three panes, it means the trustworthiness or the trust quotient is high between your team and team members or stakeholders or family members.

When does this pane area increase? It increases when there is transparency in the team which means the team members have more information about you even to an extent that they know your family members.

The bigger the area better is the trust quotient.

2. The Blind Spot or Blind Self

It represents the knowledge or information that you don't know about yourself (the self), but your team/stakeholders (the others) know about it.

Say, **for example**, while addressing a group in your office, unconsciously or unknowingly you start fidgeting with your hand and feet, with a wavering voice. These are the signs of being nervous that you are not aware of, but others know about it or notice it.

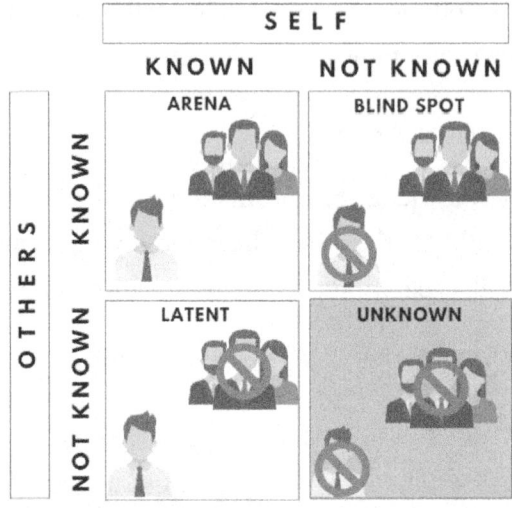

This **blind spot** is one of those panes which unconsciously communicate to the world and this pane has to be as smaller as possible.

Bigger this pane means there are more things that you don't know about yourself than others know about you. The smaller this pane, means you are very well aware of your body language and the nuances that you are communicating.

How to decrease the pane area? Ask for feedback from the team/others or do a 360-degree evaluation and you will be more aware of yourself.

The smaller the area better is the trust quotient.

3. The Latent or Hidden Self or Façade

The latent area represents the knowledge or information that you know about yourself (the self), but your team/stakeholders (the others) don't.

It is the information, feelings, secrets, and emotions that you have hidden from others and this is due to the mask that you wear, trying to show to others which in general you aren't.

Say, **for example**, you are not comfortable working with one of your team members, and an initiative has been assigned to both of you to co-work and complete. You have not mentioned to your manager that you are not comfortable working together so that he/she could realign you to another initiative or resolve the bad blood between you and the team member.

As a result, what happens? You are not able to collaborate well, have less productivity, you are trying to gloss over showing everything is ok between both of you. This is where the decline starts and things in the team start falling apart.

This window pane has to be as smaller as possible.

How to make it smaller? Tell and share with the manager, team members, or stakeholders if it is affecting your day-to-day work.

The smaller the area better is the trust quotient.

4. Unknown or Unknown Self

It represents the knowledge or information or feelings or abilities that are neither known to you nor known to others.

This could be the unexplored talents you may have, unattempted capabilities that you have which are deeply rooted at a subconscious level.

The bigger this pane, the more mysterious and unpredictable you will be which may impact your relationship at your workplace.

You have to discover yourself more and know more about your idiosyncrasies. You can identify a mentor or a coach at your workplace who can help you discover or rediscover yourself and reduce the size of this windowpane.

The smaller the area better is the trust quotient.

HOW TO INCREASE THE SURFACE AREA OF THE ARENA?

For better team dynamics, your aim should be to increase the **Open Area** or **Arena** without becoming too personal. Communication between your team members or stakeholders with a big **Open Arena** is more honest and open, leading to a higher level of trustworthiness. Therefore, the **Open Area** is a crucial quadrant since you will be more successful, productive, and cooperative while dealing with others if you have a better understanding of people in work environments.

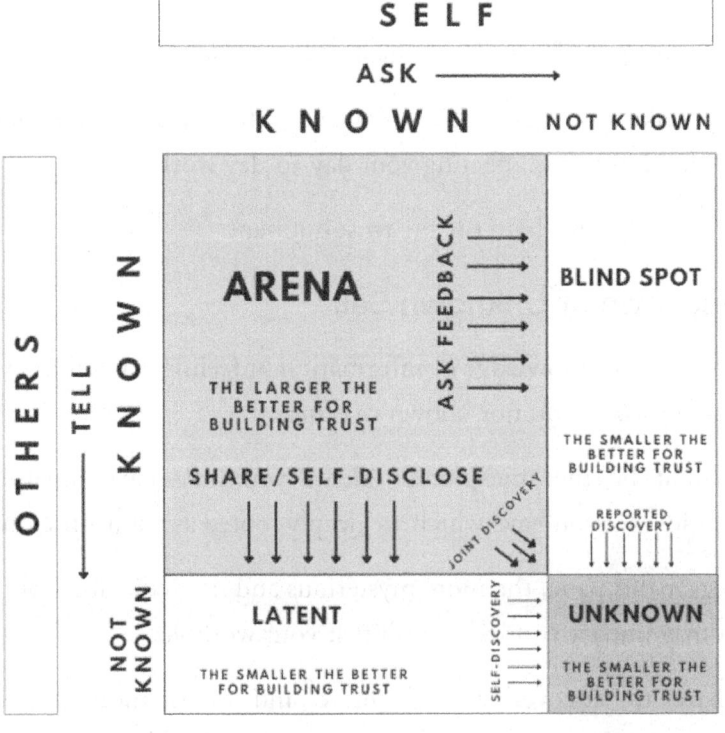

To increase the surface area of the **arena**, keep asking for feedback and be mindful of those which will reduce the **blind spot** area. On the other side of the **arena**, keep sharing information and disclosing some spheres of your personality with your team members or stakeholders which will reduce the **latent** or **hidden area**.

$$\text{SURFACE AREA OF THE ARENA} \uparrow = \text{TEAM ENGAGEMENT} \uparrow$$

The higher the surface area of the **arena**, the higher will the team engagement, productivity, and efficiency.

MORE WINDOW ANALYSIS

Can you guess what this typical window represents?

Arena and **blind spot** areas are very less compared to the **latent** and **unknown**.

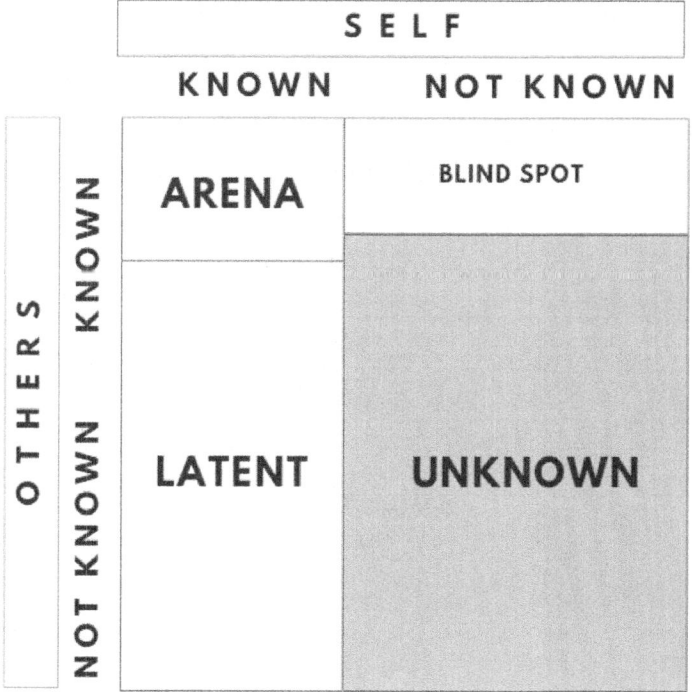

This could be either of the two cases:

1. A new team member has joined your team.

The Secrets of Design Thinking Mindset

2. You have joined a new team or inherited a new team because of a promotion or a new job.

The **arena** is the smallest because others know little about the new person who has joined your team or they know little about you if you have joined a new team.

The **blind area** is again the smallest because others still don't know about this new member who has joined your team.

The **hidden** or avoided issues and feelings are also a relatively large area.

The **unknown area** is the largest, which may be because the person lacks self-knowledge or information about the new role or belief.

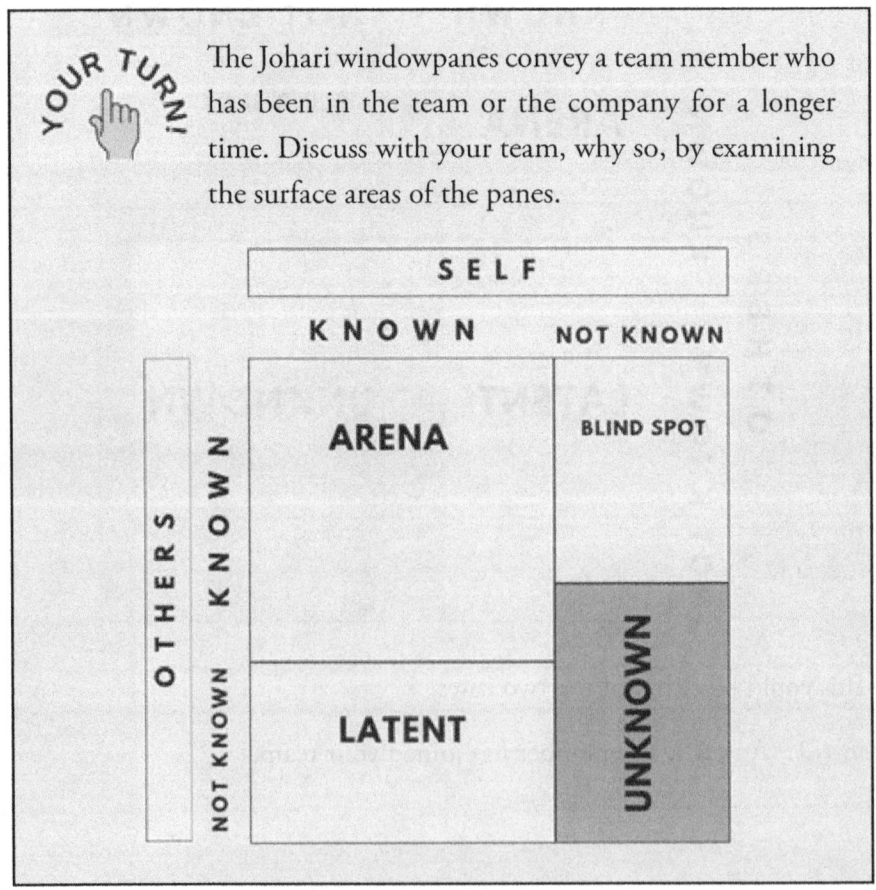

YOUR TURN! The Johari windowpanes convey a team member who has been in the team or the company for a longer time. Discuss with your team, why so, by examining the surface areas of the panes.

DISCOVER YOUR WINDOWS

Step-1

Select some team members/peers and share the list of 145 descriptors with them (next page).

Step-2

Now, write down 15 descriptors from the list that you think represents your personality completely.

Step-3

Next, ask your team member/peers to write 15 descriptors that they think represent your personality based on their observations.

Step-4

Now, all the participants will combine and reveal the 15 descriptors that they have noted down in their sheets and compare them with the 15 that you have listed in your sheet.

Do the following:

a. Those descriptors that are present in all the participants' sheets including yours, place those descriptors in the **arena pane**.
b. For those descriptors that are present in the participants' sheets but not in yours, place those descriptors in the **blind spot pane**.
c. For those descriptors that you have listed down and it is not present in any of the participants' sheet, place those descriptors in the **latent or hidden or Façade pane**.
d. The **unknown pane** is a little challenging because neither you know nor the participants know about it.

You can try to put down the hunches that you feel and also those that have appeared as a flash-in-the-pan observed by the participants in the **unknown pane.** Have a coach or a mentor to identify these traits.

The Secrets of Design Thinking Mindset

Your final Johari will look like this.

	SELF KNOWN	SELF NOT KNOWN
OTHERS KNOWN	ALOOF / AGRESSIVE / BOASTFUL / FRIENDLY / LOGICAL / DEMANDING / RASH / IMPULSIVE	HUMOROUS / IMPATIENT / INDEPENDENT / WITTY
OTHERS NOT KNOWN	TENACIOUS / RISK / NERVOUS / UNRELIABLE	INATTENTIVE / TALKATIVE / COMPLIANT

List of Adjectives and Descriptors

1. Able
2. Accepting
3. Adaptable
4. Adventurous
5. Aggressive
6. Aloof
7. Assertive
8. Autocratic
9. Autonomous
10. Aware
11. Blasé
12. Boastful
13. Bold
14. Brave
15. Callous
16. Calm
17. Caring
18. Chaotic
19. Cheerful
20. Childish
21. Clever
22. Cold
23. Complex
24. Compliant
25. Confident
26. Conscious
27. Contained
28. Courageous
29. Cowardly
30. Critical
31. Cruel
32. Cynical
33. Decisive
34. Demanding
35. Dependable
36. Dignified
37. Diplomatic
38. Dispassionate
39. Distant
40. Dominating
41. Dull
42. Embarrassed

How to Build and Repair Trust within the Team?

43. Empathetic
44. Energetic
45. Extroverted
46. Flexible
47. Foolish
48. Friendly
49. Giving
50. Glum
51. Happy
52. Helpful
53. Hostile
54. Humorless
55. Humorous
56. Idealistic
57. Ignorant
58. Impatient
59. Imperceptive
60. Impulsive
61. Inane
62. Inattentive
63. Incompetent
64. Independent
65. Inflexible
66. Influential
67. Ingenious
68. Innovative
69. Insecure
70. Insensitive
71. Inspirational
72. Intelligent
73. Intolerant
74. Introverted
75. Intuitive
76. Irrational
77. Irresponsible
78. Kind
79. Knowledgeable
80. Lethargic
81. Listener
82. Logical
83. Loud
84. Loving
85. Loyal
86. Mature
87. Modest
88. Motivator
89. Needy
90. Nervous
91. Observant
92. Open
93. Organized
94. Overdramatic
95. Panicky
96. Passive
97. Patient
98. Persuasive
99. Powerful
100. Predictable
101. Private
102. Proud
103. Quiet
104. Rash
105. Reflective
106. Relaxed
107. Reliable
108. Religious
109. Responsive
110. Risk
111. Searching
112. Self-Conscious
113. Selfish
114. Self-Satisfied
115. Sensible
116. Sentimental
117. Shy
118. Silly
119. Simple
120. Smug
121. Spiritual
122. Spontaneous
123. Stupid
124. Sympathetic
125. Systematic
126. Taker
127. Talkative
128. Tenacious
129. Tense
130. Thorough
131. Timid
132. Trustworthy

133. Unethical	138. Vacuous	143. Wise
134. Unhappy	139. Violent	144. Withdrawn
135. Unhelpful	140. Vulgar	145. Witty
136. Unimaginative	141. Warm	
137. Unreliable	142. Weak	

FIND OUT YOUR BLIND SPOT
A Self-Assessment

Carefully read each numbered item and its statements marked "A" and "B."

Assign a point value to the A and B statements as follows:
  i. The total point value for A and B added together is five (5).
  ii. If statement A is most similar to what you would do, mark 5 for A and 0 for B.
  iii. If A is not wholly satisfactory, but in your judgment better than B, mark 4 or 3 for A and 1 or 2 for B.
  iv. The converse is true: if B is best mark 5 for B and 0 for A and so on.

Example:

If I had begun to dislike certain habits of a friend to the point that it was interfering with my enjoying his/her company, I would:

***3** A. Say nothing to him/her directly, but let him/her know my feelings by ignoring him/her whenever his/her annoying habits were obvious.*

***2** B. Get my feelings out in the open and clear the air so that we could continue our friendship comfortably and enjoyably.*

1) If a friend of mine had a "personality conflict" with a mutual acquaintance of ours with whom it was important for him/her to get along, I would:

   _____ A. Tell my friend that I felt s/he was partially responsible for any problems with this other person and try to let him/her know how the person was being affected by him/her.

   _____ B. Not get involved because I wouldn't be able to continue to get along with both of them once I had entered in any way.

2) If one of my friends and I had a heated argument in the past and I realized that s/he was ill at ease around me from that time on, I would:

   _____ A. Avoid making things worse by discussing his/her behavior and just let the whole thing drop.

   _____ B. Bring up his/her behavior and ask him/her how s/he felt the argument had affected our relationship.

3) If a friend began to avoid me and act in an aloof and withdrawn manner, I would:

   _____ A. Tell him/her about his/her behavior and suggest that s/he tell me what was on his/her mind.

   _____ B. Follow his/her lead and keep our contact brief and aloof since that seems to be what s/he wants.

4) If two of my friends and I were talking and one of my friends slipped and brought up a personal problem of mine that involved the other friend, of which s/he was not yet aware, I would:

_____ A. Change the subject and signal my friend to do the same.

_____ B. Fill my uninformed friend in on what the other friend was talking about and suggest that we go into it later.

5) If a friend of mine were to tell me that, in his/her opinion, I was doing things that made me less effective than I might be in social situations, I would:

_____ A. Ask him/her to spell out or describe what s/he has observed and suggested changes I should make.

_____ B. Resent his/her criticism and let him/her know why I behave the way I do.

6) If one of my friends aspired to an office in our organization for which I felt s/he was unqualified, and if s/he had been tentatively assigned to that position by the leader of our group, I would:

_____ A. Not to mention my misgivings to either my friend or the leader of our group and let them handle it in their way.

_____ B. Tell my friend and the leader of our group of my misgivings and then leave the final decision up to them.

7) If I felt that one of my friends was being unfair to me and his/her other friends, but none of them had mentioned anything about it, I would:

_____ A. Ask several of these people how they perceived the situation to see if they felt s/he was being unfair.

_____ B. Not ask the others how they perceived our friend, but wait for them to bring it up with me.

8) If I were preoccupied with some personal matters and a friend told me that I had become irritated with him/her and others and that I was jumping on him/her for unimportant things, I would:

_____ A. Tell him/her I was preoccupied and would probably be on edge for a while and would prefer not to be bothered.

_____ B. Listen to his/her complaints but do not try to explain my actions to him/her.

9) If I had heard some friends discussing an ugly rumor about a friend of mine which I knew could hurt him/her and s/he asked me what I knew about it, if anything, I would:

_____ A. Say I didn't know anything about it and tell him/her no one would believe a rumor like that anyway.

_____ B. Tell him/her exactly what I heard, when I had heard it, and from whom I had heard it.

10) If a friend pointed out the fact that I had a personality conflict with another friend with whom it was important for me to get along, I would:

_____ A. Consider his/her comments out of line and tell him/her I didn't want to discuss the matter any further.

_____ B. Talk about it openly with him/her to find out how my behavior was being affected by this.

11) If my relationship with a friend has been damaged by repeated arguments on an issue of importance to us both, I would:

_____ A. Be cautious in my conversations with him/her so the issue would not come up again to worsen our relationship.

_____ B. Point to the problems the controversy was causing in our relationship and suggest that we discuss it until we get it resolved.

12) If in a personal discussion with a friend about his/her problems and behavior s/he suddenly suggested we discuss my problems and behavior as well as his/her own, I would:

_____ A. Try to keep the discussion away from me by suggesting that other, closer friends often talked to me about such matters.

_____ B. Welcome the opportunity to hear what s/he felt about me and encourage his/her comments.

13) If a friend of mine began to tell me about his/her hostile feelings about another friend whom s/he felt was being unkind to others (and I agreed wholeheartedly), I would:

_____ A. Listen and also express my feelings to me/her so s/he would know where I stood.

_____ B. Listen but do not express my negative views and opinion because s/he might repeat what I said to him/her in confidence.

14) If I thought an ugly rumor was being spread about me and suspected that one of my friends had quite likely heard it, I would:

_____ A. Avoid mentioning the issue and leave it to him/her to tell me about it if s/he wanted to.

_____ B. Risk putting him/her on the spot by asking him/her directly what s/he knew about the whole thing.

15) If I had observed a friend in social situations and thought that s/he was doing a number of things that hurt his/her relationships, I would:

_____ A. Risk being seen as a busybody and tell him/her what I had observed and my reactions to it.

_____ B. Keep my opinion to myself rather than be seen as interfering in things that are none of my business

16) If two friends and I were talking and one of them inadvertently mentioned a personal problem that involved me, but of which I knew nothing, I would:

_____ A. Press them for information about the problem and their opinions about it.

_____ B. Leave it up to my friends to tell me or not tell me, letting them change the subject if they wished.

17) If a friend seemed to be preoccupied and began to jump on me for seemingly unimportant things, and became irritated with me and others without real cause, I would:

_____ A. Treat him/her with kid gloves for a while on the assumption that s/he was having some temporary personal problems which were none of my business.

_____ B. Try to talk to him/her about it and point out to him/her how his/her behavior was affecting people.

18) If I had begun to dislike certain habits of a friend to the point that it was interfering with my enjoying his/her company, I would:

_____ A. Say nothing to him/her directly, but let him/her know my feelings by ignoring him/her whenever his/her annoying habits were obvious.

_____ B. Get my feelings out in the open and clear the air so that we could continue our friendship comfortably and enjoyably.

19) In discussing social behavior with one of my more sensitive friends, I would:

_____ A. Avoid mentioning his/her flaws and weaknesses so as not to hurt his/her feelings.

_____ B. Focus on his/her flaws and weaknesses so s/he could improve his/her interpersonal skills.

20) If I knew I might be assigned to an important position in our group and my friends' attitudes toward me had become rather negative, I would:

_____ A. Discuss my shortcomings with my friends so I could see where to improve.

_____ B. Try to figure out my own shortcomings by myself so I could improve.

CHARTING YOUR SCORES

SOLICITS FEEDBACK	SELF-DISCLOSURE
2B ____	1A ____
3A ____	4B ____
5A ____	6B ____
7A ____	9B ____
8B ____	11B ____
10B ____	13A ____
12B ____	15A ____
14B ____	17B ____
16A ____	18B ____
20A ____	19B ____
TOTAL ____	TOTAL ____
Plot these scores along the left axis	Plot these scores along the right axis

With the above scores, let us plot your Jo-Hari window.

On the top line of the graph, mark your score for Solicits Feedback, then draw a vertical line downward.

On the left line of the graph, mark your score for Willingness to Self-Disclose/Gives Feedback, then draw a line across horizontally (left to right).

Now, that the four windows are formed, you can take appropriate steps to enhance the surface area of Arena and reduce the surface areas of the other three.

Do this exercise for your team and adopt the correct measures to build trust within/across your team.

The Secrets of Design Thinking Mindset

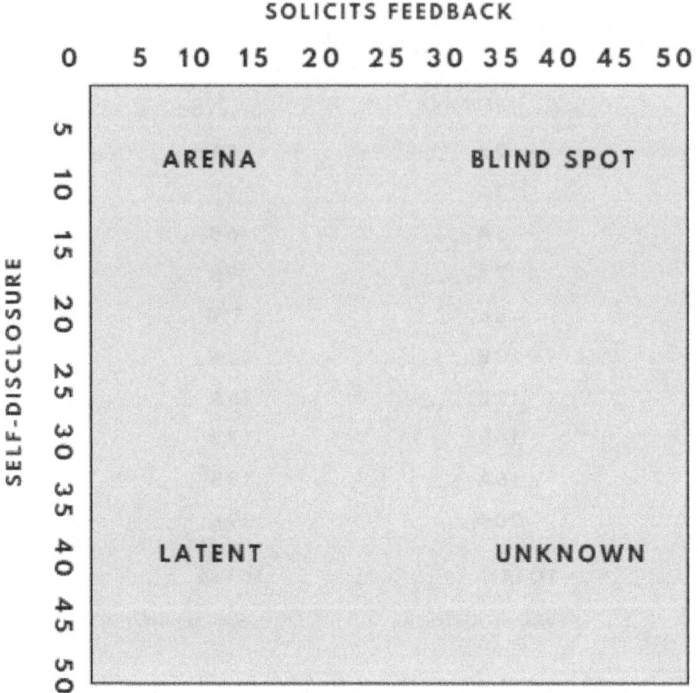

Do you know why team bonding exercises/games and outbound activities are planned by your HR team? Why is it believed that these outbound activities enhance the team's productivity?

The answer is simple. To make team members know each other better which means increasing the surface area of the **arena**. Think about it!

WHY DO YOUR TEAMS HAVE CONFLICTS?

Ivan has joined a new team recently. After some days, the team members have been experiencing a hard time working along with Ivan. Ivan is a nice person and very compliant and data-oriented, and he is making his best efforts to align with the team.

Recently, the manager summoned them for missing the deadlines and understood from the team members that they are not able to get along with Ivan, and hence there have been some heated arguments within the team.

Why do these instances happen? Is it normal?

The following is the signature lifecycle of a any newly formed team or a new member in team.

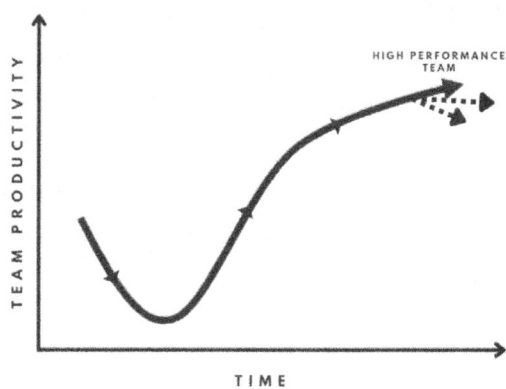

Teams go through a growth cycle. Midway through the 1960s, **Bruce W. Tuckman** created the framework that is most frequently used to describe the stages of growth of a team. Even though many authors have added to and modified Tuckman's ideas, his descriptions of **Forming, Storming, Norming, Performing, and Adjourning** offer a helpful foundation for analyzing your own team.

Understanding why things are happening on your team in certain ways can be a key step in the self-evaluation process. Each level of team growth has its own distinct, recognized sensations and behaviors.

- **What is Forming?**

Team members are often delighted to be a part of the (new) team and enthused about the work that lies ahead at the **forming stage** of team growth. The expectations that team members have for their interactions are usually extremely high in this phase. They could also experience some worry as they consider how they will fit into the team and how their performance will fare.

Numerous queries from team members may be seen during the **forming stage**, expressing both their excitement for the new team and any ambiguity or fear they may be experiencing over their position on the team.

During the **forming stage**, the team's main task is to establish a collaboration with a defined structure, objectives, direction, and duties so that members may start to develop trust. The team's mission and goals may be helped by a strong orientation or kick-off process, which can also serve to set expectations for the team's output and, more crucially, its workflow. Task completion may be below average during the **forming stage** since the team's energy is largely directed toward identifying the team members, their strengths, weakness, fitment etc.

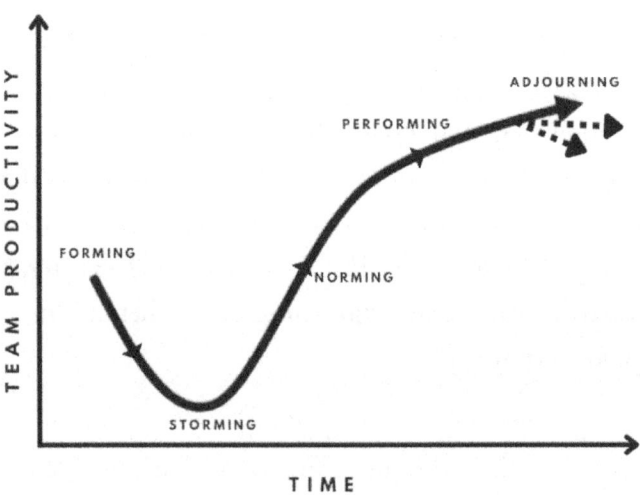

- ## What is Storming?

At this stage, team members learn that the team did not fulfill all of their original optimism and goals as they make progress toward their desired outcomes. Their attention may divert from the work at hand to sentiments of annoyance or rage at the team's performance or procedure.

The productivity of the individuals and the team as a whole starts declining. Team members could voice worries about falling short of the group's objectives which could lead to finger-pointing. Members test the team's ability to deal with conflict and respond to disagreements during the **storming stage**.

Storming stage interactions with the team/stakeholder might be less courteous than forming stage interactions, with open expression of anger or disagreement regarding objectives, expectations, roles, and duties. Members may get irritated with impediments that hinder their personal or team performance; this dissatisfaction may be noticed by other team members, the leadership of the team, or the team's manager.

To deal with this stage, and to complete team tasks during the storming stage of development, the team must be focused on its objectives and may need to divide more challenging objectives into more manageable chunks. The team may need to build abilities for managing conflict and group dynamics in addition to task-related abilities. Team members may be able to get over the dissatisfaction or misunderstanding they feel during the storming stage by redefining the group's objectives, roles, and responsibilities.

- ## What is Norming?

The team members start to reconcile the disparity they sensed between their individual expectations and the reality of the team's experience during the **norming stage** of team development. Members should feel more at ease expressing their "true" thoughts and feelings if the team is effective in creating more accommodating and inclusive standards and expectations. As they come to understand how the diversity of viewpoints and experiences strengthens the team and enhances the quality of its output, team members sense a growing acceptance of their fellow team members. It's possible and encouraged to offer constructive critique. The team might enjoy the improved group cohesion as they begin to feel like a member of a team.

Team members may actively try to settle issues and maintain peace in the group throughout the **norming stage** of behavior. Team members might talk more often and effectively, and they might be more likely to ask one another's help and exchange ideas. Team members return their attention to the task at hand and refocus on the established team standards and procedures. Teams may start to create their own language, including inside jokes and nicknames.

Members of the team become more focused on the team's objectives and exhibit a rise in productivity throughout the **norming stage**, both in their individual and group work. The team can decide that now is the right moment to assess their working methods and productivity.

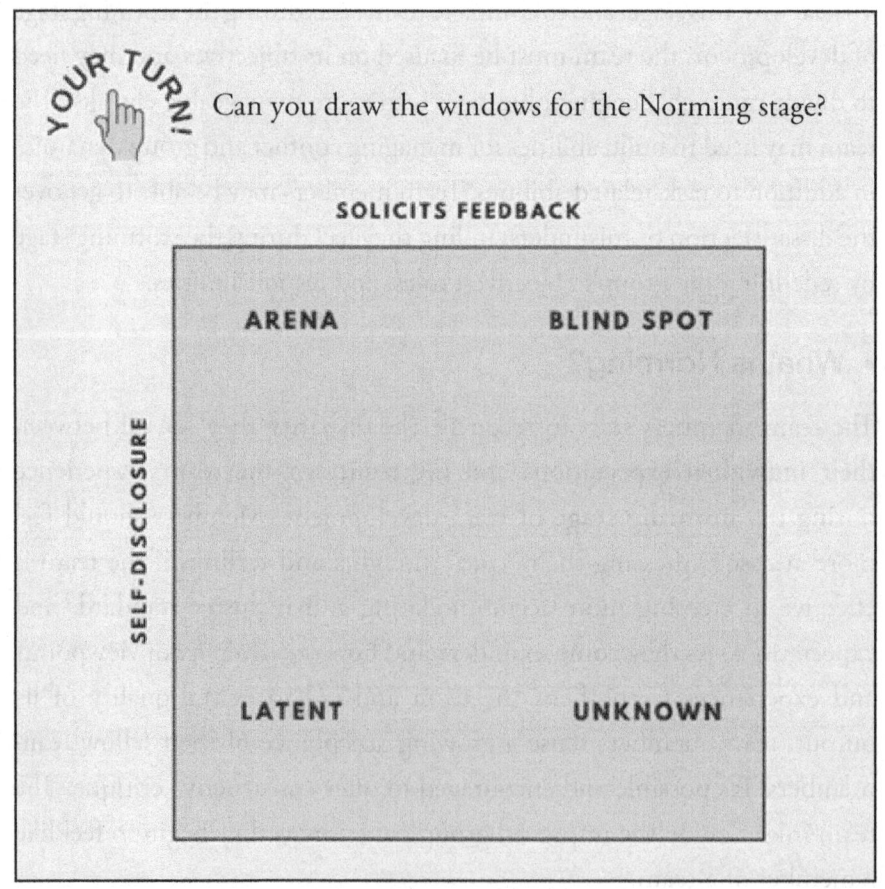

YOUR TURN! Can you draw the windows for the Norming stage?

- **What is Performing?**

Members of the team are pleased with their success throughout the **performing stage** of team development. They discuss group and personal processes and are aware of each other's and their own strengths and shortcomings. Members of the team sense a connection to the team as something that is "bigger than the sum of its parts" and take pride in the team's accomplishments. They have faith in both their own and their colleagues' talents.

Members of the team can stop or fix issues before they affect the team's workflow or development. Offers to help one another are evident, as well as a "can do" mentality. Positions on the team may have changed, with people taking on different tasks and duties as necessary. Individual member differences are valued and utilized.

The team makes considerable headway toward its objectives during the **performing stage**. There is a high level of skill on the team as well as a commitment to the team's goals. Members of the team should seek to consistently enhance team growth while also expanding their knowledge and abilities.

- **What is Adjourning?**

The majority of the team's objectives have been met as the meeting is coming to an end.

The focus is on finishing off last-minute activities and recording the work and outcomes. Individual team members may be transferred to other teams when the workload decreases, leading to the team's dissolution.

Numerous anxieties about the team's probable disintegration may be experienced by team members. Due to uncertainties over their specific roles or upcoming obligations, they could be experiencing some worry. Regarding the upcoming changes to their team connections, they can experience melancholy or a feeling of loss.

At the same time, team members could have a profound feeling of satisfaction over the group's successes. Individual members may experience all of these things simultaneously or may alternate between cycles of satisfaction and emotions of loss. Due to these competing emotions, both individual and team morale may increase or decrease during the closing period. Everyone on the team will likely be feeling a variety of emotions about anything at any one time.

"Get closer than ever to your customers. So close, that you tell them what they need well before they realize it themselves."

– Steve Jobs

9

K.Y.C. – DO YOU KNOW YOUR CLIENT ENOUGH?

> ## HAVE YOU BEEN IN JOHN'S SITUATION?
>
> Recently, John has been shunted again from his client-facing role for the 4th time in a row.
>
> Since John is perfect, methodical, courteous, patient, and systematic in his role and at his work, he has been promoted to project manager. But for some reason, in his every client-facing role as a project manager, he has not been successful.
>
> His recent client, Matthew, is a quick decision-maker and risk-taker, and expects quick turnarounds, and is a thorough gentleman. On the contrary, Jessi who is a junior on John's team is able to get a lot of accolades from the same client.
>
> John as well as his manager are unable to understand why John is failing consistently in the client-facing roles whereas there is no issue with John's behavior or work, nor any problem with the client. Yet, John is unable to get along with the clients and Jessi is doing well with the client.
>
> If John's and Jessi's story sounds similar to your daily struggle, then this chapter will share some techniques to overcome it.

LET US DISC-USS IT!

You are responsible for multiple projects assigned by your reporting manager. Hence, it becomes imperative for you to interact with multiple stakeholders of different designations and backgrounds.

Have you ever wondered why with some stakeholders you can glue well and share a good rapport, while you have a bad time interacting with others? And this sourness grows every passing day and may tend to hurt you which might result in **low collaboration** and make you **less productive**.

People are not bad, it is their style of expressing themselves when faced with a certain situation. One key aspect to getting rid of the above situation is to know yourself well as well as others.

If you are struggling with similar issues, then it's a hint that you are not aware of the **DISC language**.

Let's discuss.

DO YOU KNOW YOUR DISC PERSONALITY TYPE?
A Self-Assessment

It is highly recommended to take this behavior style assessment first before proceeding to read about DISC.

With this assessment, you will be able to know your behavior style.[1]

This test can also be used to understand the behavior style of your stakeholders, clients, boss, team members, family members, etc.

There are no right or wrong answers in this assessment, it is just to know your behavior style and understand more about yourself and your client, team members, etc.

Be honest in answering.

> **Instructions:**
>
> On a scale from 1 to 4, with 4 being the term that most accurately reflects you, and 1 being the least like you.
>
> Rank each horizontal row of words. Use each line's ranks just once.

---

[1] For a more precise evaluation, I recommend instruments using a "Most/Least" selection process which provides an expanded profile analysis.

There are no correct or incorrect responses. Instead of responding as what you believe is good/bad or should be/should not be, respond according to your personal preference.

1. **I am forceful most of the time with my team members**

   1   2   3   4

2. **Whenever I am in a social gathering, I am very lively and enjoy people's company**

   1   2   3   4

3. **Most of the time, I am modest, and unboastful of my belongings and achievements**

   1   2   3   4

4. **I am very tactful and thoughtful when I am executing my daily work**

   1   2   3   4

5. When it comes to performing my tasks, I am aggressive most of the time

   1   2   3   4

6. When I see someone in need, I get emotional

   1   2   3   4

7. I am accommodating and helpful to people around me

   1   2   3   4

8. I am consistent in delivering my tasks every time and each time

   1   2   3   4

9. **I am direct and candid with everyone around me**

    1   2   3   4

10. **I get animated and excited for small wins, gains, and news.**

    1   2   3   4

11. **I am agreeable and sincere and like to help other people**

    1   2   3   4

12. **In the tasks that I work on, I make sure it is accurate and correct**

    1   2   3   4

13. I act tough on others when trying to get results

    1   2   3   4

14. I am friendly, outgoing, and warm

    1   2   3   4

15. I see myself as a gentle person.

    1   2   3   4

16. I consider myself a perfectionist in whatever I do

    1   2   3   4

17. **I am a very daring person.**

    1   2   3   4

18. **I am a very impulsive buyer**

    1   2   3   4

19. **I usually tend to be kind to others**

    1   2   3   4

20. **I am cautious whenever I speak or execute my tasks**

    1   2   3   4

21. **I like competing**

    1   2   3   4

22. **I am very expressive in my action, talks**

    1   2   3   4

23. **I see myself as a supportive person of others**

    1   2   3   4

24. **I tend to execute tasks correctly and precisely**

    1   2   3   4

25. **I like taking risks to experience new challenges**

    1   2   3   4

26. **I am talkative and conversational, and I have no trouble sharing my thoughts with people.**

    1   2   3   4

27. **I am gentle and friendly with others; I am not stern or rough**

    1   2   3   4

28. **Before taking any decision, I always check facts before acting on it**

    1   2   3   4

29. I am argumentative with others when they don't agree with my decision or thoughts

    1   2   3   4

30. I am outgoing, fun-loving, and optimistic about life

    1   2   3   4

31. I am very patient

    1   2   3   4

32. I am logical in my thought process and work

    1   2   3   4

33. **I am bold and courageous about speaking my opinions**

    1   2   3   4

34. **I am very spontaneous**

    1   2   3   4

35. **I am stable in my thought process and emotions**

    1   2   3   5

36. **I am organized in whatever I do**

    1   2   3   4

37. I prefer to take charge and handle things because I become restless.

    1   2   3   4

38. I am optimistic, outgoing, and fun-loving about life

    1   2   3   4

39. I feel peaceful, I don't quarrel and am not easily disturbed

    1   2   3   4

40. I am conscientious and analyze things carefully

    1   2   3   4

41. **I am very candid and blunt in my approach**

    1   2   3   4

42. **Everyone describes me as a cheerful, easy-going, and pleasant individual**

    1   2   3   4

43. **Loyalty is my strength**

    1   2   3   4

44. **I don't take life seriously**

    1   2   3   4

45. I am independent and confident in my abilities

    1   2   3   4

46. I am enthusiastic and eager, and excited by challenges

    1   2   3   4

47. I try to empathize with people's emotions and listen to them.

    1   2   3   4

48. I maintain high standards

    1   2   3   4

WHAT IS DISC?

Dr. William Moulton Marston is credited with revolutionizing the **DISC** language. However, the first individual to create a psychological tool based on the Marston idea was **Walter Clark** during the 1950s.

DISC is the **universal** and **neutral language** that can help you understand the behavior and emotions of an individual. It is your behavior's language, or how you (or your team, stakeholder, client, or family member) respond or react to certain situations.

Similar-styled people frequently engage in certain behaviors that are exclusive to that style. A person's actions are a crucial and essential component of who they are.

In other words, a large portion of human conduct is influenced by both *nature* (which is inherited) and *nurture* (our upbringing). The **DISC** model only evaluates a person's behavioral style, or how they go about accomplishing things.

However, it is noteworthy to mention that **DISC** is not for gauging strengths, knowledge, educational background, beliefs, competence, or experience.

HOW CAN DISC HELP YOU ON A DAILY BASIS?

The knowledge of **DISC** can help you in the following:

1. Will help you to know yourself better and why you behave in a certain way in certain situations.
2. Forming successful teams.

3. Conflict prevention (teams, stakeholders, clients, family members, etc.)
4. Conflict resolution (teams, stakeholders, clients, family members, etc.)
5. Getting support and collaboration (teams, stakeholders, clients, family members, etc.)

WHAT IS THE DISC CONSTRUCT?

According to **DISC**, human behaviors can be classified into the following four pure behavioral styles:

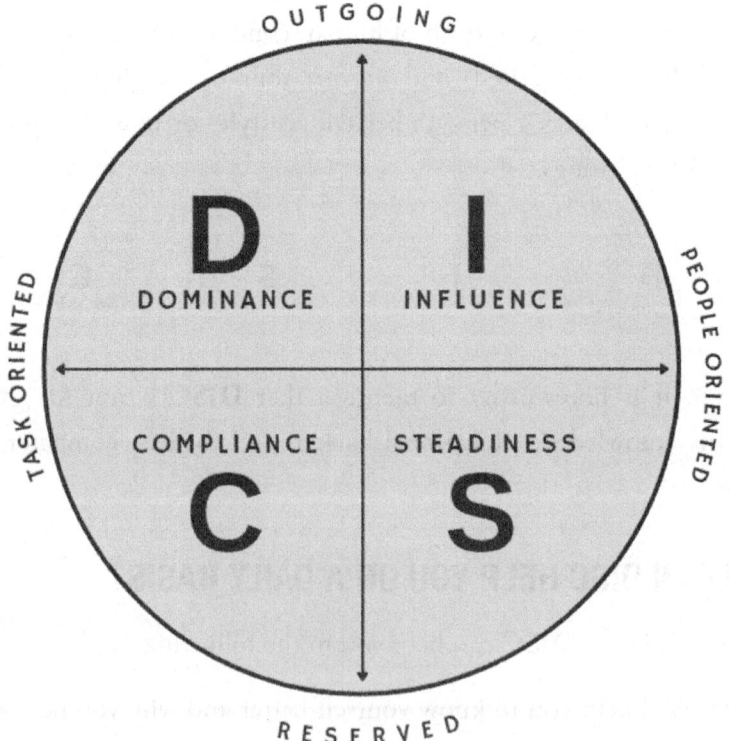

The D-Style

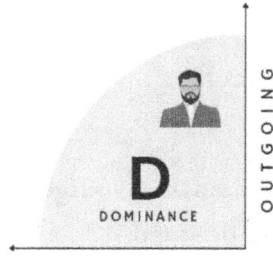

Meet Matthew, John's project client.

According to the DISC profiling, Matthew is high in **Dominance**.

What does that mean? It means he is **outgoing** (extroverted) and **task-oriented**.

He frequently exhibits **dominance** and **decisiveness behavior**. He often concentrates on the bottom line and the results.

Matthew can make judgments and decisions very quickly, commands, ensures wins, and often doesn't hesitate to voice his opinions or ideas.

Like Matthew, all the individuals with high dominance are result-oriented, action-driven, and swift in action.

How To Identify a High-Dominance Person in Your Project?

- They expect quick outcomes.
- They think big and are prepared to take risks.
- They speak assertively.
- They don't mind bending the rules for positive results.
- They are self-starters and initiators.
- They are challenge-oriented and competitive.
- They are bold, daring, and demanding.

  With the above descriptors, can you identify a high-dominant person in your team?

With the above descriptors, what are the other observable behaviors in that person you have noticed?

■ The I-Style

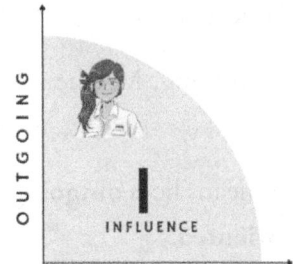

Meet Jessi, John's junior in his project team.

According to the DISC profiling, Jessi is high in **Influence**.

What does that mean? It means she is **outgoing** (extroverted) and **people-oriented**.

She is a social person and inclined towards side-of-life encounters and seeks a friendly, welcoming, and informal environment, meeting, or a setup.

Jessi is very optimistic and enthusiastic and is a creative problem solver.

Like Jessi, individuals with high-Influence love the highest degree of people contact, not very attentive to details or rules.

How To Identify a High-Influence Person in Your Project?

- They are impulsive customers, ostentatious, and quick decision-makers.
- They avoid conflict.
- No planning and goal setting, but sporadic in decision making.
- They feel good around people and hate being alone.
- They are optimistic, generous, charming and self-promoting.
- Talks a lot while working and are very social.

 With the above descriptors, can you identify a High-Influence person in your team?

With the above descriptors, what are the other observable behaviors in that person you have noticed?

The S-Style

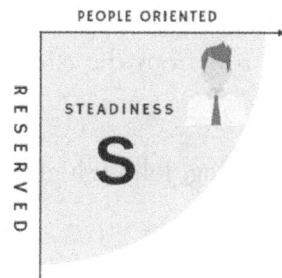

Meet Melwin, an intern in John's project team.

According to the DISC profiling, Melwin is high in **Steadiness**.

What does that mean? It means he is people-oriented and reserved.

He is often **polite** and **soft-spoken**. He makes thoughtful decisions and wants to be certain their solution is the best one before committing.

He is a great listener, a dependable team player, a logical and step-wise thoughtful person, and a low-risk taker.

How To Identify a High-Steadiness Person in Your Project?

- They are slow decision-makers.
- They are resistant to quick changes until they are convinced (process, lifestyle, etc.)
- They usually follow a standard set of rules.
- They are not good at multitasking.
- They are mild and sincere.

 With the above descriptors, can you identify a High-Steadiness person in your team?

With the above descriptors, what are the other observable behaviors in that person you have noticed?

The Secrets of Design Thinking Mindset

▪ The C-Style

Finally, meet John, our project manager who was shunted out 4 times in a row from the client-facing roles.

According to the DISC profiling, John is high in **Compliance**.

What does that mean? It means he is **task-oriented and reserved**.

He is methodical and analytical in his approach while making decisions. Instead of deviating into tangential conversations, they prefer to stick to the facts and data.

John is a critical thinker, has a few chosen friends, and his work is always of high quality and standards.

How To Identify a High-Compliance Person in Your Project?

- They always take decisions based on data and calculations.
- They are precise and accurate.
- They go by the rule book.
- They are very attentive to detail.
- They need proof and evidence to convince.

 With the above descriptors, can you identify a High-Compliance person in your team?

With the above descriptors, what are the other observable behaviors in that person you have noticed?

Now, you have learned what are DISC behaviors and how you can find the pattern from the descriptors.

In the next section, you will understand the interactions between these individuals.

JOHN AND MATTHEW'S CASE

As you know, John was a project manager and Matthew was his latest client before John was expelled for the 4th time from the client-facing role.

Can you recall their behavior descriptors? After understanding the **DISC behaviors explained in the previous section**, next what you have to be mindful of is that Matthew is not interacting with John (or vice-versa), but it is a **high-dominant person talking or interacting with a high-compliance person**.

Hope you are following!

Putting their behavior descriptors here again for quick reference.

Have a careful look at their descriptors. Do you get any hint why Matthew and John's interactions were not on good terms?

This could be happening with you in your team and among your team members.

Deconstructing the interaction between Matthew and John and understanding what could possibly have transpired which eventually may have led to the expulsion of John from the project:

Matthew: Hey, John.

John: Hey, Matthew.

The Secrets of Design Thinking Mindset

Matthew: *Have you completed the changes I asked you to do in the feature? (Seeking immediate results)*

John: *Not yet…*

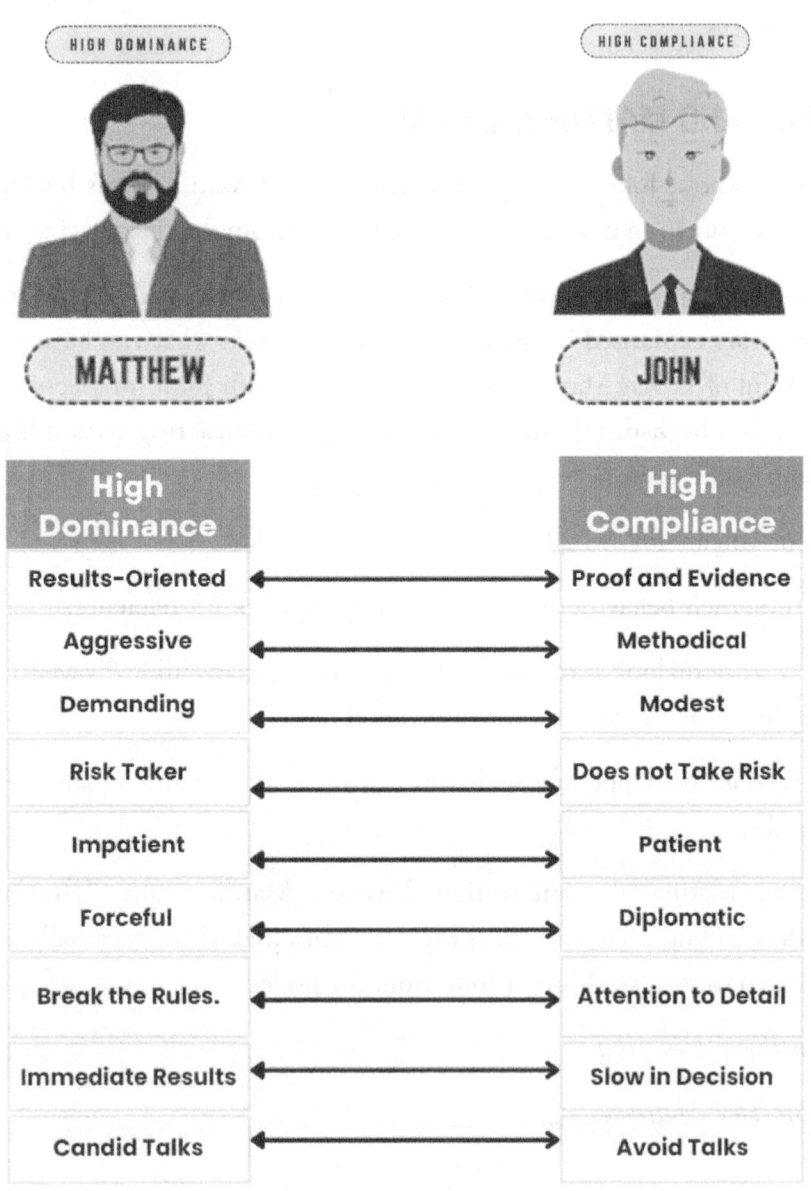

Matthew: *WHY? I told you yesterday that I need it in 24 hours. (Being forceful and demanding)*

John: *I need more data and information to make that decision. (Wants more data, proof, facts)*

Matthew: *You are the SME, you could have made relevant assumptions and could have completed it. (Break the rules)*

John: *We have completed feature-1, feature-2 and next in sequence is feature-3 as we agreed in SoW. (Being compliant)*

Matthew: *SoW is fine, but I told you to implement feature-6. You should have followed my instructions. (Being aggressive)*

John*: I can't proceed further unless I have been given enough information about feature-6 and allow me some time to understand its implications.*

You can see how the conversation is turning hostile and abrasive.

Though task orientation is a common behavior trait of the High-C (Compliance) and High-D (Dominance), speed and risk-taking are the areas where possible conflict may arise. The High-D takes more risk than the High-C who is less risky.

Taking a long time to make a judgment vs making a quick decision and with little information. Since they both have high expectations for one another, they are similar, yet this might make one of them too critical or demanding (depending on their values).

The Secrets of Design Thinking Mindset

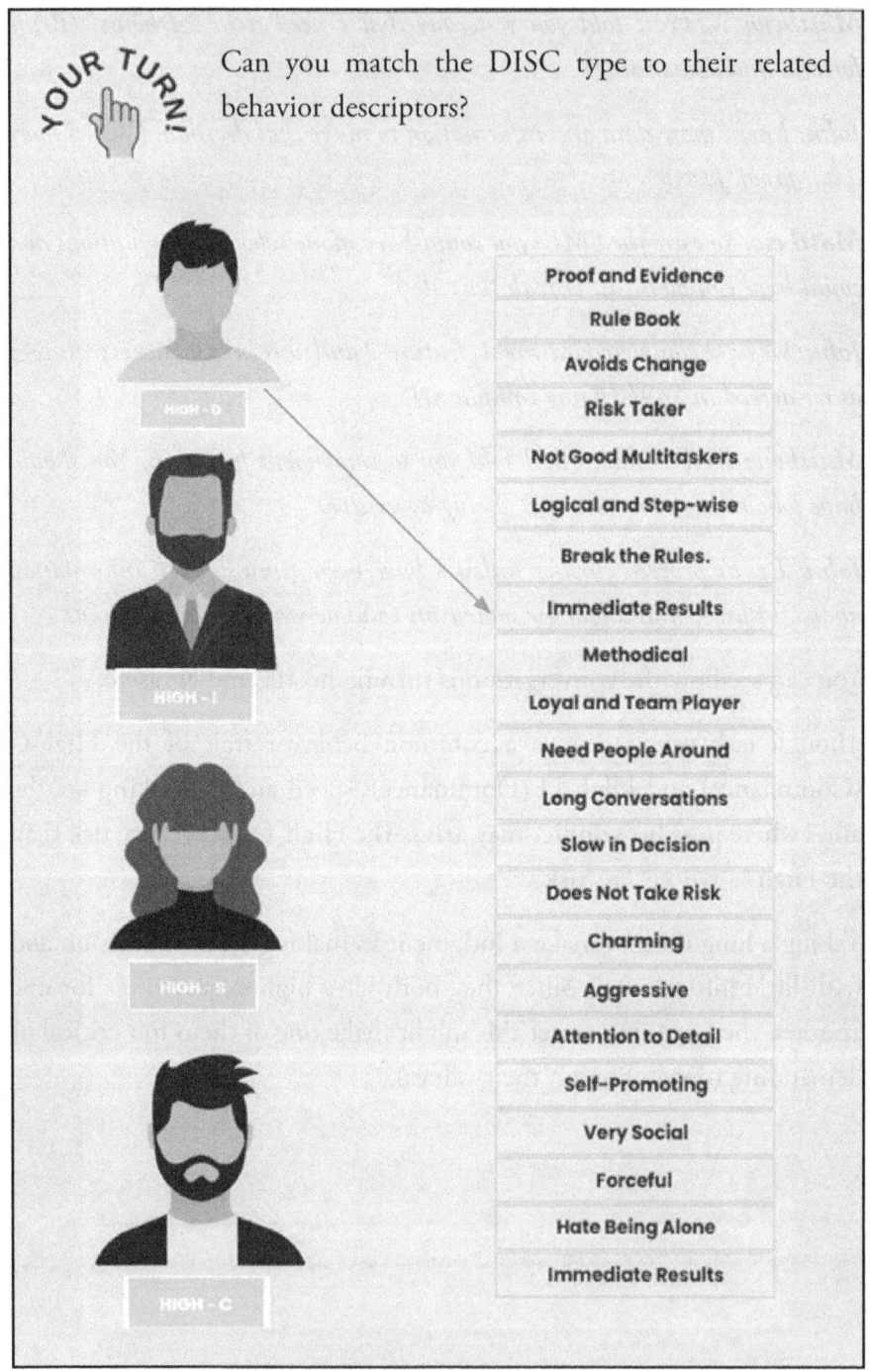

YOUR TURN! Can you match the DISC type to their related behavior descriptors?

AVOID PUTTING THE CAT AMONG THE PIGEONS

Here are some of the high DISC behaviors and how well they interact with their counterparts.

- **HIGH-C Interacting With HIGH-C**

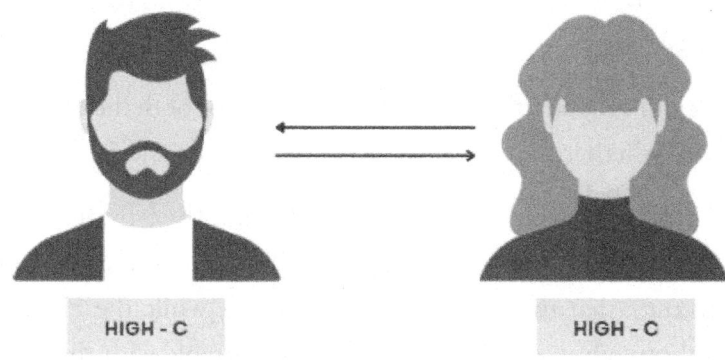

Overall, the behavioral fit is good.

Due to their shared strong inclination for requiring structure and order, the two High-Cs frequently enjoy excellent interpersonal interactions both at home and at work. Before making a decision, they must also acquire information and carefully review the available evidence and proof.

The High-Cs tend to get along quite well since they are both low-risk, deliberate decision-makers, and task-oriented. However, because of their tendency toward perfection, this one area may cause them frustration.

- **HIGH-D Interacting With HIGH-C**

Both share the same characteristic of having high expectations for one another, but this might lead to excessive criticism from the C and demand from the D.

The High-C and High-D are both task-oriented. The area of possible conflict is when there is a focus on pace and risk, the high risk of the High-D as opposed to the minimal risk of the High-C.

As opposed to quick decisions that need little information, slow decisions require a lot of information. The creation of a great team, nevertheless, might result from an understanding of their behavioral distinctions.

HIGH-S Interacting With HIGH-C

The High-S is more people-oriented, whereas the High-C is more data-focused.

A low-risk and collaborative setting are necessary for both the High-C and the High-S, whether they are at work or with friends and family.

Both often follow certain techniques and guidelines. This is the fundamental distinction between the two. The High-C will require sufficient evidence to demonstrate that the change is for the better, while the High-S will require a thorough understanding to feel comfortable with the situation while dealing with the change.

HIGH-C Interacting With HIGH-I

The High-I and High-C seem to disagree with each other point after point.

The High-C and High-I connection is the behaviorally most challenging. As you refer to the construct of the DISC, you witness the east-west difference: extrovert to introvert, optimistic to pessimistic decision-makers who are quick to make decisions. From low to high risk. The High-C needs to truly relax and start acting more like a High-I. The High-C can adjust to establish successful communication with the High- I by being more people-focused, entertaining, and joyful.

The High-C needs to ramp up the pace and use questions to guide the High-I to the desired outcome by allowing the High-I to speak along the way, and go steadily to the intended objective.

HIGH-I Interacting With HIGH-S

The High-S and High-I should get along well since their people-focused personalities make for good behavioral compatibility.

Both of these methods require verbal communication as well as empathy and conversation. To enjoy themselves more and give the High-I the chance to exhibit themselves, the High-S should unwind with the High-I.

Both styles are also deeply concerned with other people and others' responses to them. Compared to the High-I's high risk, the High-S is a comparatively modest risk-taking group. The High-S will often make decisions much more slowly than the High-I and be more analytical and systematic in their approach.

HIGH-C Interacting With HIGH-S

The High-S will require complete understanding to feel comfortable with the situation while managing change, but the High-C will need sufficient information to demonstrate that the change is for the best.

Whether with his/her family or at work or with his/her friends, the High-S and the High-C both require a low-risk, collaborative workplace. Both frequently have practices and procedures they adhere to. The S is more focused on people, whereas the C is more data-centered. This is the fundamental distinction between the High-S and the High-C.

HIGH-S Interacting With HIGH-S

The decision-making process might sometimes be excessively long or late, but a High-S with a High-S counterpart match works quite well in terms of compatibility. Two High-S individuals will get along well since their personalities are an incredible blend.

If you refer to the DISC construct, both will prioritize tasks and people highly. Both will feel a tremendous need for resolution. Their risk factor can be too low, which might prevent them from reaching their full potential.

HIGH-I Interacting With HIGH-C

The High-I will need to take things more slowly, control their emotions, and provide the High-C with the information they need. Since the High-C's private life is just that—private—personal conversation is not permitted.

The High-I and High-C won't share many behavioral traits. The High-I faces his or her most difficult behavioral match/mismatch – which is extroverted to introverted, an emotional reaction to a data-driven behavior. From high risk to low risk, direct approach to indirect approach, and trustworthy approach to untrustworthy approach.

However, this might be a fantastic partnership if both can use their behavioral advantages.

HIGH-S Interacting With HIGH-D

The High-S needs to adjust to communicate with the High-D efficiently. Picking up the speed, focusing just on the high spots, and being more direct with the High-D will be the main adaptations.

Direct people are typically much liked and respected by the High-D. The High-S must watch out for the High-D's potential to overwhelm it. For the sake of peace and harmony, the High-S will prefer to follow suit. Going along is OK as long as the High-S accepts the High-D's course of action.

All in all, it is an individual with a slower pace coping with a rapid pace. Task orientation as opposed to people-orientation and from a slow to a quick decision-maker.

HIGH-S Interacting With HIGH-I

Compared to the High-S, the High-I also has a stronger sense of urgency and a larger risk factor. To encourage the High-S to interact, the High-I is instructed to slow down.

In terms of people orientation, the High-I and High-S will undoubtedly share certain traits. Both styles have a desire for warmth and close personal contact.

Unless you are informed, you're unlikely to know what the High-S is thinking. Therefore, to establish confidence, the High-I must speak less and inquire more.

The High-I will need to tone down their approach since the High-S will perceive it as being aggressive, disingenuous, or excessively eager.

HIGH-I Interacting With HIGH-I

To avoid problems with the High-Is regarding time management, and establish firm deadlines as they are people-oriented, they tend to get into verbose mode and forget the tasks assigned to them.

High-I individuals have original, sometimes extreme views, but frequently require different approaches to help them stay focused.

Rest assured, if you are within the company of High-Is you'll have a fantastic time together. But the people orientation tends to cause individuals to lose concentration on what has been told to them to complete and there is a greater possibility of getting it undone in the given timeframe.

HIGH-I Interacting With HIGH-D

Referring to the DISC construct, both behavioral styles are outgoing and have a broad perspective, making them an excellent behavioral fit.

In their attempts to convert others to their viewpoint, High-I individuals frequently use a lot of talks and are verbose. When speaking with the High-D, the High-I must be more forthright and avoid appeasing language.

Additionally, the High-I will need to back off and let the High-D lead the dialogue while working on asking more questions rather than providing the answers.

The High-I could feel a little intimidated by the High-D's assertiveness and directness and concede when it is not appropriate to do so.

Knowing that the High-D enjoys taking risks and can put up a good fight, the High-I can hold onto their position without worrying about losing it.

HIGH-D Interacting With HIGH-D

The High-D individuals are capable of working effectively together to complete a task if a clear vision and purpose are presented. Both are high-risk takers who might need to take their time to consider the facts.

As High-Ds are aggressive, candid, and demanding, the impulse for the action of two High-Ds will be understood by one another. Both require a challenge, and both must lead could be an issue with them.

Both aren't scared of disagreement, thus the conversation between the two should be interesting. Each will need to become more cognizant of the other and mentally pause to listen before acting because they both have the propensity to be task-oriented.

HIGH-C Interacting With HIGH-D

An East-West in one being a sluggish mover and the other being a quick mover. From high to low danger/risk. There is a decision-making difference between them as one needs a little data and other has a large requirement for data. From one being quick to another being a delayed decision-maker.

The High-D must provide more details than usual while being non-personal and non-pushy around the High-C. Both the High-D and the High-C have an equal need to manage their time and surroundings.

To improve communication with the High-C, the High-D will need to modify drastically. The High-D finds it most difficult to take their time to gather information.

HIGH-D Interacting With HIGH-S

The High-S requires time to ponder things through and takes fairly little risk. While disagreeing with the High-D, the High-S may have a propensity to "go along" out of a desire for harmony.

Due to the sense of urgency and significant risk associated with the High-D, it will frequently outweigh the High-S. To allow the High-S enough time to digest the information, the High-D will need to slow down considerably.

The High-S won't display emotion since they are naturally indifferent. An agreement must not be mistaken for a lack of emotional expression. To give the High-S the confidence to voice issues, the High-D must put up a lot of effort into building a trusting connection.

HIGH-D Interacting With HIGH-I

The High-D must give the High-I time to speak and a little more time to decide before proceeding.

A sense of urgency, risk-taking, and a drive to alter their surroundings and the world—for better or worse, depending on their values—are shared traits of the High-D and High-I.

Although they are both outgoing, they approach people in different ways. The High-I will utilize linguistic skills to persuade people to accept their position, whereas the High D will be blunt and to the point.

Knowing that engagement and fun are motivating to the High-I, the High-D will need to bring a little fun to the activity and take things a little slower.

Identify a High-D, High-I, High-S, or High-C in your team or BU or a client.

Make notes of how they interact with their counterparts. Now, compare your notes with the interaction styles that you have studied.

You will see some additional traits or behavior styles than those you have studied in this section.

WHAT IS THE ENERGY LINE?

You might have observed in the previous session about High-D, High-I, High-S, and High-C.

Are you wondering what it means?

The DISC behavior of an individual can be quantitatively measured through DISC assessments which have several questions based on the different behavior styles.

Depending on your answers, a DISC signature will be arrived at which will be very unique to you.

David, Edward, and Jay have taken the assessment and you can see what their DISC graph looks like. Every graph is very unique to the individual.

In the above bar graph, if any of the behavior styles far exceeds the energy line (50), we refer to that behavior as **High**.

For example, David is a High-I as his I bar has far exceeded the energy line (50). Therefore, David has High-I as his dominant behavior style.

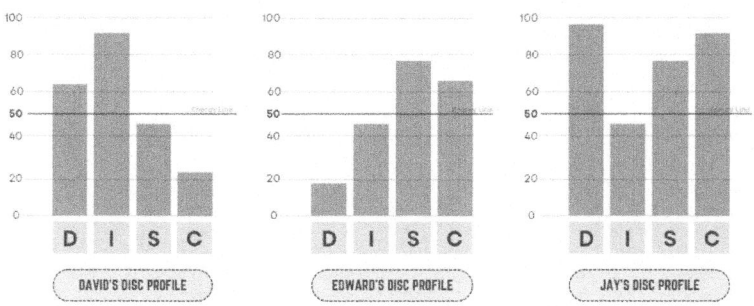

Likewise, you can figure out Edward's and Jay's graphs.

Till now, we have learned pure DISC styles and interactions between them.

However, every individual possesses all DISC parameters in different proportions or intensities. You can see that in David's, Edward's, and Jay's cases.

Therefore, every individual has different intensities of DISC styles and hence everybody behaves differently in the same situation.

Likewise, if you take the DISC assessment, you will also have all the DISC behavior styles in different intensities.

DECODING YOUR PERSONALITY STYLE

	D	I	S	C
	5	6	7	8
	25	26	27	28
	9	10	11	12
	13	14	15	16
	41	42	43	44
	21	22	23	24
	1	2	3	4
	29	30	31	32
	17	18	19	20
	37	38	39	40
	45	46	47	48
	33	34	35	36
TOTAL				

Now, transfer the scale values (1,2,3,4) you have marked for each of the questions to this DISC grid.

The pre-printed numbers on the grid are the question numbers.

E.g.: If the pre-printed number on the cell is 5, then transfer the score that you have given to question 5.

Likewise, fill all 48 cells with the relevant scores for those 48 questions.

Next, add all 4 columns of DISC.

Now, with the DISC total values, locate those values on the chart and color the bars (with a color sketch pen) in the graph to reveal your DISC signature.

Here is Kathy's DISC total and her graph for your reference.

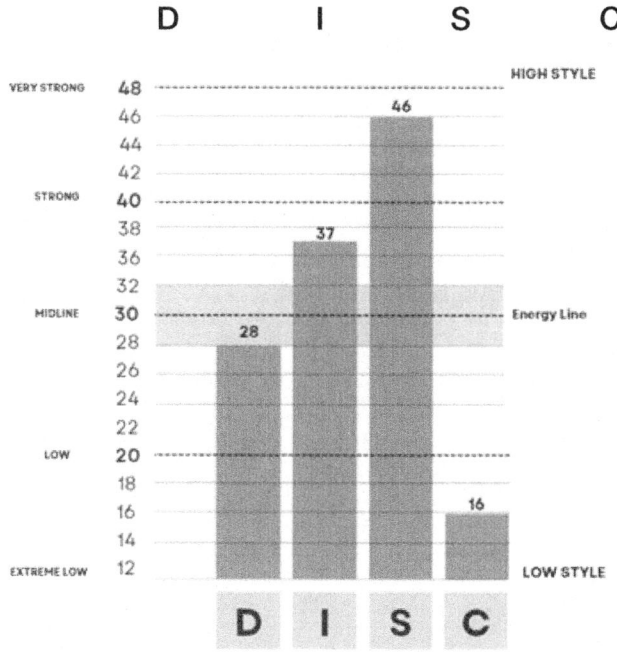

DISC INTENSITY LOW-HIGH RANGES

High Type	D	I	S	C
	Demanding	Optimistic	Non-Emotional	Careful with Details
	Ambitious	Political	Resistant to Change	Cautious
	Forceful	Warm	Patient	Systematic
	Aggressive	Convincing	Possessive	Accurate
Energy Line	Decisive	Sociable	Consistent	Open-Minded
	Calculating	Trusting	Active	Unbiased
	Undemanding	Factual	Alert	Factual
	Cautious	Logical	Impatient	Adamant
	Modest	Suspicious	Impulsive	Disorganized
	Peaceful	Pessimistic	Emotional	Careless with Details
Low Type	D	I	S	C

DISC Sequences	Personality Patterns
IS – SI	**RELATED:** Advisor/Merciful/Counselor Warm, sympathetic, understanding; good listener, stable, dependable; won't force ideas on others; criticism of his/her work a personal affront; can overuse the indirect approach; the goal is maintaining friendships; fears social rejection.
SCI – SIC	**SUPPORTER:** Advocate/Peacemaker/Agent Can be very detail-oriented; moderate, thorough, dependable; steady, sociable, independent, individualistic; tends to support underdog; the goal is acceptance from others; fears dissension, conflict.
IC – CI	**PROMOTER/ANALYZER:** Assessor/Teacher/Appraiser Outgoing, at home with strangers, develops friends easily; promotes projects of others and his/her own; seeks freedom from control; the goal is approval, popularity; fears loss of social recognition.
DS–DSC–SD	**CONDUCTOR/COORDINATOR:** Attainer/Achiever/Perseveres Objective, analytical, determined, task-oriented; independent, questioning, practical; may appear blunt and non-demonstrative; the goal is a personal accomplishment (sometimes at the expense of the group); fears those with inferior work standards.
DI	**PERSUADER:** Concluder/Doer/Gets results Forceful, direct, individualistic; can be impatient, competitive; good leadership abilities; high standards, critical when standards not met; the goal is dominance and independence; fears slowness or being seen as too jovial.
I	**PROMOTER:** Convincer/Persuader/Promoter Enthusiastic, optimistic, articulate in communication; can become careless, inconsistent, and disorganized, but tries to look good and please others; the goal is social approval and prestige; fears loss of social approval, conflict.
DC –DCS– CD	**IMPLEMENTOR/CONDUCTOR:** Designer/Administrator/Creator Sensitive to problems, creative in finding solutions; high in foresight, often quite intelligent; can overuse bluntness and criticism; bored with routine, prefers working alone, doesn't trust easily; the goal is dominance, discovering unique solutions.
D	**CONDUCTOR:** Establisher/Visionary/Developer High ego strength, high standards; approaches issues alone rather than drawing others into the process; can be manipulative, controlling; has vision of "big picture"; very direct, forceful; goal is new challenges, opportunities; fears loss of control, lack of challenge
SDC– SCD	**COORDINATOR/SUPPORTER:** Inquirer/Investigator/Consistent Patient, controlled, enjoys digging for clues and facts; easy-going and amiable; consistent, loyal, accommodating; slow to take the initiative, doesn't adapt quickly to change; holds grudges, internalizes conflict; the goal is maintaining clear systems;
C	**ANALYZER:** Logical Thinker/Analytical/Objective Practical, proper, discrete, accurate; self-evaluating, critical of self and others; enjoys detail and logic; makes decisions slowly from logic rather than emotion; can over-analyze, be hurt easily; the goal is to develop control, correctness; fears criticism, ridicule.

K.Y.C. – Do You Know Your Client Enough?

DISC Sequences	Personality Patterns
CIS- CSI- ISC-ICS	**COORDINATOR/ANALYZER:** Practitioner/Realist/Steadfast Results-oriented, verbally fluent, loyal, friendly, enthusiastic, informal, talkative; may worry too much about what others think; can intellectualize and become restless and impatient; the goal is to accomplish results through others; fears rejection
CS- SC	**COORDINATOR:** Precisionist/Traditionalist/Perfectionist Orderly, systematic, precise, attentive to detail; tactful, highly diplomatic, extremely conscientious; can become bogged down in details, dislikes sudden changes; prefers protected, secure environment; the goal is security; fears antagonism.
ID	**PERSUADER:** Prompter/Communicator/Persuader Outgoing, high interest in people, trusting; can gain respect and admiration from varied types of individuals; can be impulsive, overly enthusiastic, inattentive to the "little things"; prefers variety; the goal is authority and prestige; fears rejection, being taken advantage of.
S	**SUPPORTER:** Technician/Specialist/Steady Patient, loyal, consistent, helpful to friends; steady, calculating, reserved; not bored by routine; needs clear guidelines and rules; avoids confrontation, internalizes feelings; the goal is maintaining status quo and an environment with few changes; fears loss of security, unplanned change
All Scores Around 30	Transition/Stress pattern Lack of goal clarity; insufficient action planning, confusion, uncertainty, anxiety about expectations; behavior alternates between furious activity to slow, methodical action; can be brought on by periods of change—new job, new home, bad health, etc. Person will make quick decisions and then try to gain approval from others.

KYC: FOR YOUR STAKEHOLDERS, TEAM MEMBERS
Stakeholder Assessment

Fill in the blanks with your stakeholder's name or team member's name or family member's name.

You directly can't ask your stakeholders to take this assessment to know their DISC style. However, if you are able to observe the descriptors in each question and map your stakeholder on the scale, you will approximately get to know their DISC style and accordingly partner with them.

By now you know what your primary (highest score) and secondary (second highest score) DISC styles are. Once you get the scores of your counterparts' through this assessment, you can partner and collaborate well.

1. _____ is independent and confident in his/her abilities

    1   2   3   4

2. _____ is enthusiastic and eager, and excited by challenges

    1   2   3   4

3. _____ tries to empathize with people's emotions and listen to them.

    1   2   3   4

4. _____ maintains high standards

    1   2   3   4

5. _____ **direct and candid with everyone around him/her**

    1   2   3   4

6. _____ **gets animated and excited for small wins, gains, and news.**

    1   2   3   4

7. _____ **is agreeable and sincere and likes to help other people**

    1   2   3   4

8. **In the tasks that _____ works on, he/she makes sure it is accurate and correct**

    1   2   3   4

9. When it comes to performing the tasks, _____ is aggressive most of the time

    1   2   3   4

10. When _____ sees someone in need, he/she gets emotional

    1   2   3   4

11. _____ is accommodating and helpful to people around him/her

    1   2   3   4

12. _____ consistent in delivering his/her tasks every time and each time

    1   2   3   4

13. _____ **is forceful most of the time people**

    1   2   3   4

14. _____ **enjoys social gathering, is very lively, and enjoy people's company**

    1   2   3   4

15. **Most of the time,** _____ **is modest, and unboastful of his/her belongings and achievements**

    1   2   3   4

16. **I am very tactful and thoughtful when I am executing my daily work**

    1   2   3   4

17. _____ is bold and courageous about speaking his/her opinions

    1   2   3   4

18. _____ is very spontaneous

    1   2   3   4

19. _____ is stable in his/her thought process and emotions

    1   2   3   5

20. _____ is organized in whatever he/she does

    1   2   3   4

21. _____ is **a very daring person.**

    1   2   3   4

22. _____ **a very impulsive buyer**

    1   2   3   4

23. _____ **usually tends to be kind to others**

    1   2   3   4

24. _____ is **cautious whenever he/she speaks or executes his/her tasks**

    1   2   3   4

25. _____ likes competing

    1   2   3   4

26. _____ very expressive in his/her action, talks

    1   2   3   4

27. _____ sees himself/herself as a supportive person of others

    1   2   3   4

28. _____ tends to execute tasks correctly and precisely

    1   2   3   4

29. _____ is **very candid and blunt in his/her approach**

    1   2   3   4

30. **Everyone describes** _____ **as a cheerful, easy-going, and pleasant individual**

    1   2   3   4

31. **Loyalty is** _____ **strength**

    1   2   3   4

32. _____ **doesn't take life seriously**

    1   2   3   4

33. _____ argumentative with others when they don't agree with his/her decision or thoughts

    1   2   3   4

34. _____ is outgoing, fun-loving, and optimistic about life

    1   2   3   4

35. _____ is very patient

    1   2   3   4

36. _____ is logical in his/her thought process and work

    1   2   3   4

37. _____ **likes taking risks to experience new challenges**

    1   2   3   4

38. _____ is **talkative and conversational, and he/she has no trouble sharing his/her thoughts with people.**

    1   2   3   4

39. _____ is gentle and friendly with others; _____ is not stern or rough

    1   2   3   4

40. Before taking any decision, _____ always check facts before acting on it

    1   2   3   4

41. _____ acts tough on others when trying to get results

    1   2   3   4

42. _____ is friendly, outgoing, and warm

    1   2   3   4

43. I see _____ as a gentle person.

    1   2   3   4

44. I consider _____ a perfectionist in whatever he/she does

    1   2   3   4

45. _____ prefers to take charge and handle things because he/she becomes restless.

    1   2   3   4

46. _____ is optimistic, outgoing, and fun-loving about life

    1   2   3   4

47. _____ feels peaceful, he/she doesn't quarrel and is not easily disturbed

   1   2   3   4

48. _____ is conscientious and analyzes things carefully

   1   2   3   4

D	I	S	C
5	6	7	8
25	26	27	28
9	10	11	12
13	14	15	16
41	42	43	44
21	22	23	24
1	2	3	4
29	30	31	32
17	18	19	20
37	38	39	40
45	46	47	48
33	34	35	36

TOTAL

His/Her Name _____

His/Her High Style(s) are
(only those values above the energy line)
_____
(Should be written in descending values of the total score)

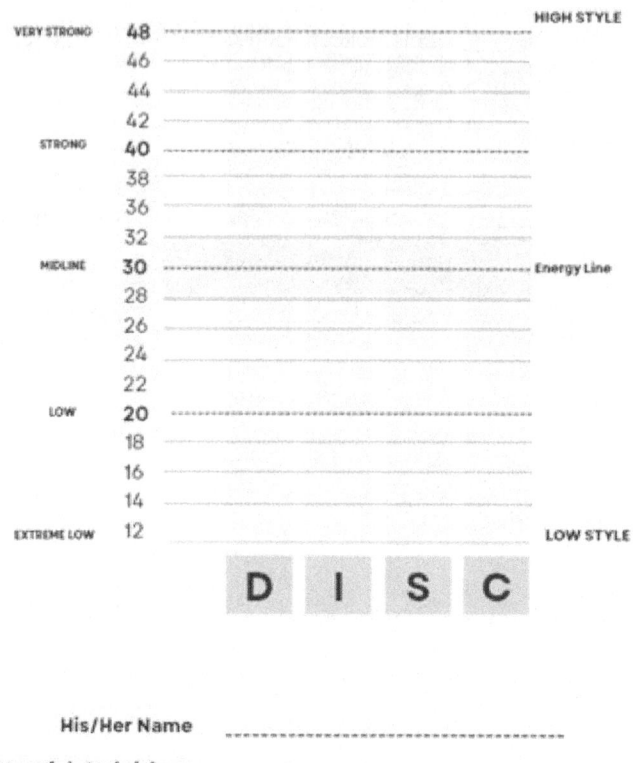

HOW DO YOU DEAL WITH A HIGH-D STAKEHOLDER?

- Avoid ranting or wasting their time.
- Avoid chit-chatting or attempting to establish personal connections; instead, focus on your work.
- Go prepared with all specifications, goals, and supporting documentation in a concise presentation.
- Logically deliver the information; effectively prepare your presentation.
- Avoid asking pointless or rhetorical inquiries. Use "what" type of questions.

- Give them options and alternatives so they may choose for themselves - don't go to them with the choice made, allow them to choose from the alternatives.
- Give statistics and data on the likelihood of success or the efficiency of your alternatives.
- You must show that you are competent in your work.
- Focus on results, RoI, the bottom line.

HOW DO YOU DEAL WITH A HIGH-I STAKEHOLDER?

- Plan interactions with them before getting to the business point
- Give them time to interact and socialize.
- Avoid being abrupt, detached, or silent.
- Discuss people and their objectives.
- Don't get into facts or data right away.
- Maintain a high level of energy.
- Instead of more pragmatic concerns, put your attention on what makes you enthusiastic about your product or service (you can get to those later if needed).
- Make it clear to them that you cherish your relationship with them personally. If they start talking about your life, be ready and eager to provide some specifics. People who are all business all the time may be tougher for i-style people to trust.

HOW DO YOU DEAL WITH A HIGH-S STAKEHOLDER?

- Break the ice, with some informal comments.
- Avoid diving into the agenda or the task too quickly.
- Move informally and casually.
- Give them time to consider your request if they must make a choice.
- Don't press for a rapid choice; instead, give options.

- Display consideration. Tell them that your concern for them goes beyond the transaction.
- S-style people are often quite accommodating, which makes it simple for you to control the conversation – don't overpower them. They will get into the shell.

HOW DO YOU DEAL WITH A HIGH-C STAKEHOLDER?

- Prepare your case well ahead of time.
- Avoid becoming disorganized or untidy—they don't like it
- Be upfront and direct when you speak with them -- avoid being casual, informal, or private.
- Avoid pressuring them to make a rapid choice or decision. They need to cross-check the facts and that takes time.
- Give specifics and follow through on your commitments.
- Create an "Action Plan" with deadlines and checkpoints.
- If you disagree, back it up with statistics, facts, or references from respectable individuals – they are data-centric.
- They ask a lot of questions and you need to support them with facts and data.
- They like to dig deeper. Give them finer details to gain confidence.

"Those who make the worse use of their time are the first to complain of its shortness."

– **Jean de la Bruyere**

10

IMPORTANT, OR NOT SO IMPORTANT?

> ## HAVE YOU BEEN IN ERIC'S SITUATION?
>
> Eric is working on one of the client-facing projects from Mexico. He has been assigned to a couple of more projects. He has a project team to manage, mentor and guide.
>
> By the end of every day, most of Eric's work is either in a partially-completed or untouched state. He is feeling stressed every day. He thinks he has been doing so much work throughout the day, sometimes skips his meals, water-cooler chats; yet, by end of the day, when he reviews his work, he discovers nothing much has been completed from the day's assigned tasks.
>
> This is impacting his health and family time as he has started to stretch his working hours to complete the tasks.
>
> If Eric's story sounds similar to your daily struggle, then this chapter will share some tools and techniques to overcome it.

FORGET ABOUT FORGETTING YOUR TASKS

You are in charge of multiple projects and find yourself missing deadlines and working beyond office hours to complete your tasks. Also, you constantly feel like you have too much to do and nothing seems to be moving. Or, do you often completely forget what your reporting manager or the client asked you to complete on a priority basis?

If yes, then it's a sign that you are not aware of the techniques mentioned in this chapter

Keep reading.

WHAT IS A WORK LIST?

A **work list** is a list of all the tasks that need to be done or completed within a frame of time (day/week/month). It lists the tasks that need to be completed, the most important first and the least important later.

Although it may seem like a small, insignificant thing to do, when people begin to utilize **work lists** effectively, they frequently experience their first productivity breakthroughs and begin to truly succeed in their jobs.

It has been proved and noted consistently that when we transfer or write down what's on our mind onto a paper/PDAs (Personal Digital Assistants)/digital planner, our brain gets de-cluttered and performs efficiently.

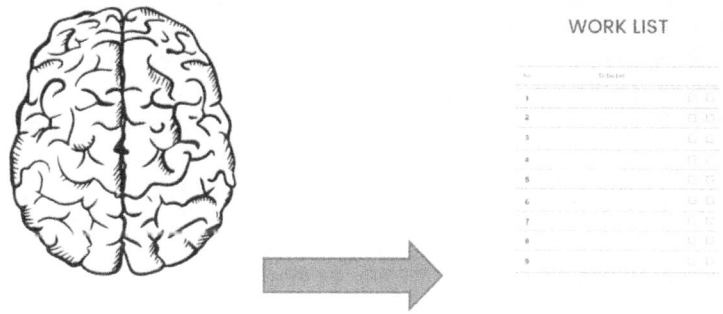

You could make sure that all of the activities you need to complete are documented in one place by maintaining a **work list**. If you do not wish to forget anything, you must do this. Additionally, prioritizing allows you to organize your workload so you can choose what tasks require your immediate attention and which ones you can put off until much, much later. This is crucial if you want to overcome job overload.

You'll come across as lightheaded, unfocused, and unpredictable to others around you if you don't utilize **work lists**. You'll be considerably more organized using **work lists**, and your individual productivity will reflect this.

You could move irrelevant tasks from one **work list** to another. Some very low-priority and trivial tasks could take a lot of time to do; hence, decreasing your productivity. If you really must worry about this, elevate their priority on your list if you are nearing a deadline for them.

Once you're comfortable with the use of **work lists**, you need to start differentiating between **urgency** and **importance**. We will study it in the next section.

 For your current project or an upcoming exam or event, can you prepare a Work List?

You can either use a digital list or a simple paper/notebook.

WORK LIST

No.	To Do List		
1		☑	☐
2		☐	☐
3		☐	☐
4		☐	☐
5		☐	☐
6		☐	☐
7		☐	☐
8		☐	☐
9		☐	☐

Once you prepare, have your Learning & Development (L&D) expert review it.

STOP PUTTING THE CART BEFORE THE HORSE

Humans often make wrong choices when we are confronted with the most **urgent** and **important tasks**, sometimes referred to as an **urgent-important syndrome**.

The research was conducted on how individuals decide what to work on when confronted with tasks that are both urgent and important.

Even though the less urgent work is lucrative and offers more benefits, it has been found that our attention is pulled to time-sensitive tasks rather than ones that are less urgent.

The **Mere-Urgency Effect** explains why humans struggle with task and time management. Regardless of their long-term benefits, people are more prone to give deadline-driven projects more priority than those without one.

Additionally, the effect is considerably more pronounced among those who report being "busy" or complain about "falling short of time" to complete the allocated tasks.

Keep reading to know how we can overcome these psychological oddities.

EISENHOWER MATRIX

Who Is Eisenhower?

He was the 34th President of the United States, **Dwight D. Eisenhower**, who was renowned for his efficiency and outcomes, and was honored with its name. It is stated that President Eisenhower set up his commitments such that only the urgent and vital issues reached his desk.

What is Eisenhower Matrix?

A simple and effective tool for assessing the long-term and short-term effects of your everyday activities and concentrating on what will make you most successful, not merely most productive, is the **Eisenhower Matrix**. It assists you in organizing all of your project activities or personal chores into an **important/urgent matrix**.

How to Apply Eisenhower Matrix?

The Work List that you created or learned to create in the previous section, make use of it to transfer your activities to the **Eisenhower matrix**.

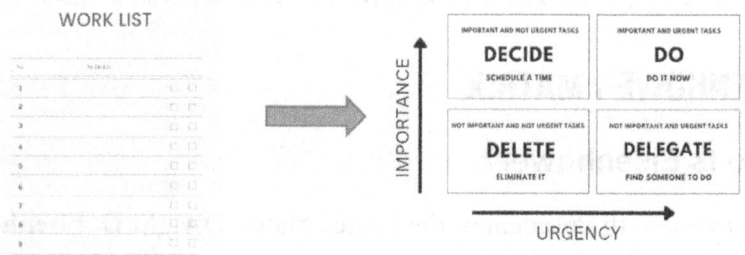

Each of these four quadrants will correspond to a specific activity or larger project you are working on today:

- **Urgent** & **Important tasks/projects** to be completed immediately to avoid negative consequences
- **Not Urgent** & **Important tasks/projects** to be scheduled on your calendar

- **Not Urgent & Unimportant tasks/projects** to be deleted
- **Urgent & Unimportant tasks/projects** to be delegated to someone else

DO Quadrant

Any jobs that are both **urgent and important** should be in the first quadrant, known as the **DO** quadrant. Transfer the items from the work list in this quadrant if it has to be done immediately, has obvious repercussions, and affects your long-term objectives.

The tasks or activities that go in this quadrant should be obvious as they are the ones that are on your mind and are probably causing you the greatest stress.

DECIDE Quadrant

The second quadrant, known as the **DECIDE** or sometimes **SCHEDULE** quadrant, is where you should place any tasks that are **important but not urgent**. You can schedule these jobs or activities or tasks for later completion since they have an impact on your long-term objectives but don't require immediate attention.

These assignments will be taken up immediately following those in quadrant one. You can complete the activities in this quadrant by using a variety of time management strategies. The **Pareto principle** and the **Pomodoro method** are two useful tactics.

DELEGATE Quadrant

The third quadrant, known as the **DELEGATE** quadrant, is where you should put any jobs/tasks/activities that are **urgent but not important**. Though urgent, these activities have little bearing on your long-term objectives.

You may assign these tasks to other team members because you don't have a personal relationship with them (tasks) and they (tasks) probably don't require your particular skill set to do. One of the best methods to manage your workload and provide your team with the chance to grow their skill set is to delegate these jobs.

DELETE Quadrant

There will be a few jobs left over after you've gone through your to-do list and added items to the first three quadrants. The things that were left undone weren't critical or urgent.

These **trivial**, **non-urgent** diversions just prevent you from achieving your objectives. Put these final tasks on your to-do list in the DELETE quadrant of the fourth quadrant.

The **Eisenhower Matrix** is also known as the **time management matrix**, the **Eisenhower Box**, and the **urgent-important matrix**.

 For the current project that you are working on, do the following:

1. Prepare the work list on paper or using a PDA (Personal Digital Assistant) or a digital planner.
2. Create an Eisenhower matrix with the proper quadrant naming conventions.
3. Transfer all the tasks or activities that you have on the work list to the appropriate quadrant of the Eisenhower matrix.
4. Try to follow the approach and you will be surprised by the enhanced productivity .

Encourage your team members to follow this technique.

INDEX

A

5-WTH (Fw-Th) technique, 12,40
80:20 Rule, 178
8-D approach, 38
Accommodating [A-2], 80
Adapt, 206
Adjourning, 245
Affinity diagram, 144
Affinity diagram, 15
Affinity mapping, 144
Arena, 227
ARMI, 92
Attractive features, 158
Autocratic I Style (A1), 123
Autocratic II Style (A2), 123
Avoiding [A-1], 79

B

Brainstorming, 26
Brainwalking, 26
Blind spot, 226

C

Cluster analysis, 144
Collaborating [C-2], 77
Combine, 205
Competing [C-1], 76
Compliance, 260
Compromising [C-3], 78
Confidence scale, 174
Conflict management, 74
Conflict resolution, 74

Conflicts, 240
Construct of Design Thinking, 5
Consultative I Style (C1), 124
Consultative II Style (C2), 124
Convergent Thinking, 7
Could-have features, 197
Credibility, 217
C-Style, 260
Customer satisfaction scale, 152

D

Decision flowchart, 46
Decision Matrix, 109,130
Decision-Making Style, 121
Define the Problem, 40
Define, 14
Dependent variable, 57
DISC Construct, 256
DISC Personality Type, 249
Discrete Response Analysis, 166
Divergent Thinking, 6
Divergent-Convergent, 8
Dominance, 257
Dot-voting, 134
Double-diamond, 5
D-Style, 257

E

Ease-Benefit matrix, 138
Eisenhower Matrix, 291
Eliminate, 209
Elimination technique, 135

Index

Empathy Interview, 11
Empathy Mapping, 18
Empathy, 9
Energy Line, 272

F

Façade, 224
Fault Tree Analysis, 64
Feature Functionality scale, 151
First Aid treatment, 44
Fishbone diagrams, 53
Five elements, 11
Forming stage, 241
Frequency analysis table, 166

G

Group II Style (G2), 124

H

High-C Stakeholder, 286
High-Compliance, 260
High-D Stakeholder, 284
High-Dominance, 257
High-I Stakeholder, 285
High-Influence, 258
High-S Stakeholder, 285
High-Steadiness, 259
Hockey stick recovery, 70
How Might We?, 23

I

ICE Scoring Model, 188
ICE scoring, 191
Ideate, 25
Impact scoring, 173
Important/urgent matrix, 292
Influence, 258
Interim Corrective Action, 44
Intimacy, 219
Ishikawa diagram, 53
I-Style, 258

J

J Curve, 70
Johari Window Construct, 222
Jo-Hari's Window, 221

K

Kano Reaction Model, 150
Kano's Response Evaluation Grid, 166
KJ analysis, 144

L

Latent Area, 224, 226

M

Mendelow Stakeholder Matrix, 87
Mere-Urgency Effect, 291
Mindmapping, 28
Modify (Magnify, Minify), 207
MoSCoW approach, 191
Multi-voting, 134
Must-have features, 155,195

N

N/3 Voting, 134
Neutral features, 161
Norming stage, 243

O

Operational decisions, 102

P

Paired comparison analysis, 102
Paired decision-making analysis, 102
Pairwise comparison method, 102
Pareto's Principle, 177
Performance features, 156
Performance-Time Chart, 70
Performing stage, 245
Permanent Corrective Action, 44
Personas, 20
PICK chart, 141

Pity, 9
Plus-Minus-Interesting (PMI), 139
Power-Interest grid, 89
Power-Interest Matrix, 87
Primary causes, 58
Prioritized action, 16
Probabilistic decision-making, 144
Problem,.35
Process Flowchart, 45
Prototype, 29
Pugh Matrix, 109
Put to Another Use, 208

R

Reverse (Rearrange, Reorder), 210
R I C E, 171
R I C E score, 176
RACI matrix, 93
Recovery curve, 70
Reliability, 218
Repair Trust, 216
Reverse feature, 162
Root Cause Analysis (RCA), 50
Rummler-Brache diagram, 48

S

Say-do ratio, 219
Scamper, 202
Secondary causes, 58
Self-orientation, 220
Should-have features, 196
Simple Decision Matrix (SDM), 127
Simple Pareto Chart, 182
Sketchstorming, 28
S-Style, 259
Steadiness, 259

Storming stage, 243
Strategic decisions, 102
Substitute, 203
Surface Area of The Arena, 226
Swimlanes, 48
Sympathy, 9
Symptoms, 36

T

Tactical decisions, 102
Team's Growth Lifecycle, 241
Testing, 30
The 5 Whys, 51
The R I C E Equation, 171
Thomas-Kilmann model, 75
Time management matrix, 294
Trust Equation, 216
Trust Equilibrium, 215
Trustworthiness, 217

U

Urgent-important matrix, 294
Urgent-important syndrome, 291

V

Vroom-Yetton-Jago Decision making Model, 122

W

Weighted Decision MATRIX (WDM), 131
Weighted Pareto Analysis, 183
Weighted score percentage, 185
DISC, 255
Won't-have features, 198
Work list, 289

Made in the USA
Monee, IL
03 May 2026